LOOKING BACKWARD

Don Banks – One TBF Turret Gunner's Story

By Stephen A. Banks, CDR, JAGC, USN (Ret.)

LOOKING BACKWARD:
Don Banks – One TBF Turret Gunner's Story

Library of Congress Control Number: 2008903489

ISBN 978-0-9817473-0-9

Printed by Signature Book Printing, www.sbpbooks.com

FOR INFORMATION CONTACT
Stephen A. Banks
CDR, JAGC, USN (Ret.)
7716 Carrleigh Parkway
Springfield, Virginia
22152

(Cover and title page photos courtesy D.A. Banks collection)

For my father and the other men of VC-66,
and for all the men and women who served
in World War II – especially those who died
before having a chance to live;

and for Ava and all grandchildren and their
grandchildren, that they may know and
appreciate.

ACKNOWLEDGMENTS

I would like to thank all those who helped me in some way with this project. There were so many of you. I am sure that I have forgotten someone, and for that I am truly sorry. In any case, I am grateful to you all. Without your help, I could not have completed what has turned out to be a real labor of love.

From the time I was six years old, I remember hearing and being fascinated by my father's Navy World War II stories – of his exploits with the great Stephens and Stoops and his other VC-66 squadron shipmates. When I was a little older, I remember playing war with my friends and wearing some of his gear from the war – like his old flight helmet. I remember watching the classic *Victory at Sea* documentary series on TV and my father occasionally saying, "I was there." I was impressed. I remember as I progressed through school, his encouraging me to look at the Navy as a possible source of education and career. I did so enthusiastically and as they say, "the rest is history."

Over the years, as I went further in my Navy career both on active duty and as a civilian, and pursued my love of military history, I came more fully to appreciate my father's World War II service. I began to encourage him to write down his experiences as best he could remember them and to collect and organize his mementoes. I am happy to say that in the mid-1990s he did so. And he did a great job of it. And that was the real beginning of this work. I decided that some day when I had the time, I would take what he had done and try to develop it into a detailed history of his wartime experiences for the benefit of our family. Two years ago I retired from my last job with the Navy – and I had the time to do the research and the writing.

Thus, first and most thanks must go to my father. If he had not taken the time to write his memoir, it is unlikely that this project would ever have gotten off the ground. His material served as the nucleus that the rest of the project was built around. And I have to say that even though he waited nearly fifty years to write things down, his memory has proven to be incredibly sharp and accurate. My approach has been to "trust" what he has said, but in every instance to attempt to "verify" it. And I am able to say that based on my research and the comments of many of his former shipmates, virtually everything he described has been substantiated.

Next, I give special thanks to Franklin T. Stephens, CAPT, USN (Ret.) – or "Ole Steve" as I know him. He calls me "Young Steve." I owe a great deal to him. First, as my father's pilot throughout the war, he brought my father home in one piece. Second, I am named after him. Finally, in an organization where officers are not encouraged to become friends with enlisted men, he in fact became a friend of my father's and maintained that friendship over the years after the war. When he heard that I was working on this project, he encouraged me from day one and provided me with many comments, notes, photos, and other extremely valuable information. He also provided me with the names of some of the other former VC-66 squadron pilots. When I started this effort, I thought that at best I might only have the memories and notes of my father and "Ole Steve" to work from, but to my pleasant surprise, I have been able to reach and communicate with almost a third of the men who served with VC-66. "Ole Steve" got me started.

I would also like to thank former VC-66 fighter pilot, DeLoach Cope, for his extensive assistance. DeLoach and I have had many telephone conversations and e-mail exchanges. He gave me a lot of good guidance and suggestions, and enthusiastically provided me with many documents and other helpful information. And having had the collateral duty of squadron photography officer, he had access to and kept several of the old official Navy photographs involving the squadron which he made available to me. These were very helpful.

I also owe special thanks to Charlie Edwards and his wife, Marnie. Charlie is another VC-66 fighter pilot. He and Marnie had me over to their beautiful home on a couple of different occasions – including having my wife, Carol, and me over for lunch. Charlie gave me many good suggestions and shared information and photographs with me. And Marnie also provided some good insights.

Thanks must also go to former VC-66 TBF pilot, Dick Krost, for his constant encouragement and willingness to help. Dick and I have exchanged many e-mails. Dick has been particularly helpful in assisting me in contacting other former VC-66 members.

Thanks also to Emidio Mardarello, a former TBF turret gunner with VC-66. He and I had some very good telephone conversations. He also wrote me a couple of very good letters and provided photographs. Emidio was particularly helpful in providing another enlisted man's perspective.

The list of men and family members from the squadron who contributed in some way to the project goes on and on. The help, support, and encouragement that I received from virtually every VC-66 veteran or family member that I was able to locate and contact was magnificent – and heart warming. I would like to thank them all for taking the time to talk with me, write to me, and share information, memories, and photos with me. This book could not have been done without their help. I have listed their names in alphabetical order at the conclusion of this ACKNOWLEDGEMENTS section.

I offer special thanks also to Joe Mussatto, former pilot with VC-66 (T-2). Joe is the historian for VC-66 (T-2) and does a great job as the editor of *The VC-66 (T-2) Newsletter*. In November 1944, after three combat deployments, my father's VC-66 was re-formed. Most of the old hands – including my father, were reassigned elsewhere in the Navy. My father's VC-66 came to be known as VC-66 (Tour 1 or T-1). Joe Mussatto was among the many new men brought in to make up the new VC-66 (T-2). In any case, Joe has been of great help, encouragement, and inspiration. Among other things, he helped me get in touch with those men who remained with VC-66 after it was re-formed.

Additionally, Sam Moore and Richard White of the USS NASSAU (CVE-16) Association and the excellent NASSAU Web Site: <http://www.ussnassaucve16.com/>, were very helpful and encouraging. And speaking of helpful Web sites, our friend, Norman Ventura, was a huge help in inviting my attention to the "people locator" site <http://www.zabasearch.com/>. Use of that site allowed me to locate several more of my father's former shipmates.

I would also like to thank the staff at the National Archives and Records Administration in College Park, Maryland for their patient assistance in helping me with my research. In particular, their helping me locate the ships' war diaries and deck logs was of immense help.

Thanks also to the staff at the Naval Historical Center in Washington, D.C. – especially Mr. Glenn Helm, Director of the Navy Department Library, who provided some excellent guidance.

I also appreciate the help of the staff at the Navy Memorial in D.C. - particularly Ms. Nan McComber of the Navy Log Department. Ms. McComber assisted my wife Carol and me in locating members of VC-66 who had registered with the Navy Log.

Several friends and family members helped. I offer thanks to my cousins, Cherie Argyle-Hardy, and Jan Banks-Doddridge, for helping me get information and photos concerning their parents – my father's sister, Joyce, and his brother, John. And I offer thanks to my aunts, Joyce Banks-Argyle, and Frances Dewey-Mowell, for providing information and encouragement. Our friend, Phyllis Ryder, found and shared some old correspondence with me that was helpful. Thank you to her.

I would also like to thank my mother for her support and encouragement – not to mention her assistance in providing information to fill gaps, helping to refresh my father's memory when necessary, and in helping to find old photos. She was a big help.

My wife, Carol, was another terrific help. Not only did she support and encourage my effort – and put up with my hiding away in our study for hour after hour, day after day, for almost two years doing the research and the writing, but she is specifically responsible for locating several of the former VC-66 men via the Navy Memorial Navy Log register.

I also want to express my thanks to the late Stephen E. Ambrose. In my opinion, Ambrose was the foremost military historian of the last fifty years. His many works, including *Band Of Brothers*, have entertained and inspired me for years. His obvious respect and admiration for the men who fought World War II provided much of the motivation for me to attempt this project.

Finally, and as mentioned above, the following members of COMPOSITE SQUADRON SIXTY-SIX (VC-66 [T-1]) and/or their family members were of immeasurable help. In various ways, they shared their memories, documents, photographs, and other information – as well as their time, support, and encouragement. Most of them also read and provided extremely useful comments concerning the draft manuscript of this book. It was an absolute pleasure working with them. Time after time, I was astonished by the vividness and accuracy of their memories concerning events that happened over sixty years ago. I am grateful to them beyond words for their willingness to share them with us all. Again, if I failed to mention or list anyone who contributed, I apologize. It was strictly an accident.

Donald A. Banks
Mrs. Jean C. Banks
  (wife)
Maurice W. "Marty" Barrett
Dean J. Birdsong
Mrs. Jean Carr
  (wife of Lawrence)

G. Berry Catterton, Jr.
  (son)
Otha J. "Bud" Clark
William E. Cook
W. DeLoach Cope
John L. "Jack" Dwight
Charles T. "Charlie" Edwards

Mrs. Marnie Edwards
   (wife)
John P. Fox
James Gander
Robert E. Holley
Russell P. Jensen
Mrs. Katy Jensen
   (wife)
Mrs. Charles R. Jones
   (wife)
Robert L. Kennon
Edward F. Keyser
Austin H. Kiplinger
Richard F. Krost
Emidio J. Mardarello

Albert J. Mayer
Mrs. Pauline Muzzy
   (wife of Robert)
William H. Piper
Mrs. Roger L. Plouffe
   (wife)
Jerome A. Rouse
Mrs. Marie Schleicher
   (wife of Raymond)
Martin J. "Lucky" Stack
Franklin T. "Steve" Stephens
Thomas A. Stoops
   (son)
Dean H. Summers
Sam Takis

Very Respectfully,
Stephen A. Banks
Springfield, Virginia
June 2008

"Any man who may be asked in this century
what he did to make his life worthwhile, I think
can respond with a good deal of pride and satisfaction,
'I served in the United States Navy.'"

President John F. Kennedy
1 August 1963
United States Naval Academy

CONTENTS

PROLOGUE

Many of the events described and discussed in this book took place nearly sixty-five years ago. Nonetheless, my goal in writing about those events was to rely as much as possible on the personal recollections of my father and his shipmates. While memories fade - as stated earlier, I was very pleasantly surprised at the detail and accuracy of the recollections of the men who lived those events – and their willingness and desire to talk about them. Moreover, time after time, they would corroborate each other's memories.

Several times, events or incidents that I at first thought might be a little exaggerated or perhaps a slightly embellished "sea story," turned out to be confirmed by one reliable source or another through my research. In an additional effort to make sure that I got things correct, I sent the draft manuscript out for review and comment by the men. I heard back from sixteen of them. Their comments were overwhelmingly positive, but where necessary, I made additions, deletions, and other corrections to the text based on their suggestions. Thus, I am reasonably confident that what is reported below is the way things happened. I tried very hard to get it right. I hope I did. If I did not, it is entirely my fault. Any errors are the result of inadequate research and I apologize in advance.

To assist the reader in knowing the basis for each of the statements and facts that I set out in the book, I have identified and cited all of the sources and references that I relied on for each in the CHAPTER NOTES AND SOURCES section at the back of the book. If the reader is interested in seeing where I got my information - or perhaps in locating a more in depth discussion of a particular event or incident that I mention, I invite his or her attention to that section. I have also included a BIBLIOGRAPHY that lists the books, magazines, newspapers, Web sites, and other works that I consulted in doing my research.

As for for matters of style and formatting, my guide was William A. Sabin's *The Gregg Reference Manual*. I relied on it often, but I am sure that this book could have been written better. Again, I did the best I could. I hope the reader is able to concentrate on the story and enjoy it without being distracted too much by errors in grammar, style, or formatting.

Working on this project has been a wonderful experience for me – better than I imagined. When I started, I had a high opinion of my father and the men he served with, but as I read their personal recollections, talked to them, and got deeper into the research, I really came to understand the enormity of what they had experienced and done. They are very special men and I am honored to have gotten to know some of them. Thank God they were available and volunteered to serve when our country needed them!

For those of you who know living World War II vets – and there are still quite a few of them around (these are tough, old warriors), I strongly encourage you to talk to them about their experiences and to record them – either orally (there are several institutions, e.g., the Library of Congress, that collect oral histories of World War II vets) or in writing. Don't wait. It really is not hard – and as author and radio personality Garrison Keillor puts it: "We need to write, otherwise nobody will know who we are."

Or in this case, who they were or what they did. In my opinion, the more people that know and appreciate what our World War II vets did the better. Accordingly, I plan to try to help a little by donating any proceeds from this book after expenses to one or more of the country's fine museums dealing with World War II history. These museums need to be supported so that future generations will have the opportunity to know.

Now, I hope you enjoy reading *Looking Backward* half as much as I enjoyed researching and writing it.

1

Joining Up

At 0810, on Sunday, 7 December 1941, the armor piercing bomb penetrated the deck of the USS ARIZONA (BB-39) and within seconds detonated in the forward ammunition magazine. There was a tremendous explosion. Many men died immediately. Many more died in the subsequent fire. Still more drowned trapped below decks as the big ship sank in nine minutes. Altogether 1,177 men died aboard the ARIZONA as she was moored on battleship row in Pearl Harbor. Only 337 of her crew survived. Another 1,213 American military personnel died on the other twenty ships that were sunk or damaged and the military airfields that were hit during the two hour, two wave, 350 plane Japanese attack on the Island of Oahu, Territory of Hawaii.

News of the surprise attack flashed across the country. The American people were shocked and outraged. President Franklin Roosevelt called it, "A date which will live in infamy." He proclaimed to Congress and the nation on 8 December 1941: "No matter how long it may take us to overcome this premeditated invasion, the American people in their righteous might will win through to absolute victory." He went on to say, "I believe I interpret the will of the Congress and of the people when I assert that we will not only defend ourselves to the uttermost but will make very certain that this form of treachery shall never endanger us again."

The United States was at war. While many if not most Americans expected the country to eventually become involved in World War II, they did not expect it to happen as quickly or as dramatically as it did.

Donald Austin "Don" Banks was born on 23 April 1923 in Buffalo, New York. He was eighteen years old and working the day shift at the new Curtiss-Wright aircraft manufacturing plant when he got word of the attack on Pearl Harbor. The plant was located on Genesee Street near the Buffalo airport in Cheektowaga – a Buffalo suburb. It made P-40 Warhawk fighter planes for the Army Air Force. P-40s were the planes made famous by the legendary "Flying Tigers" – American pilots who fought the Japanese in the sky over China. The Curtiss-Wright Corporation was very big in the Buffalo area during the war – employing upwards of forty thousand people.

In December 1941, Banks was living in South Buffalo - only a few blocks from South Park High School where he had graduated in June. South Buffalo was and still is a hard working, blue collar, mostly Irish American neighborhood. College had not been an option for Banks. He was the second of four children. His brother, John – called "Buddy" or "Buster" by the family when he was young, was five years older; his brother, David - called "Warny" by the family, was two years younger; and his sister, Joyce, was nine years younger.

Their father, John Banks senior, was a tall, handsome, athletic man – a fine semi-pro baseball player, but he was also an alcoholic who did little to help the family. Banks recalls that his father's drinking problem "had a damaging effect on the family and resulted in the loss of many jobs."

Banks remembers the time his mother, Beatrice M. "Bea" Greer-Banks, took him with her to walk from where they were living in the town of Alden into Buffalo to the lumberyard where his father was working. The family had no car. It was about a twelve mile hike one way. They were going to try to get his father's pay, but when they arrived they were told that his father had been fired. Banks believes it was because his father had been requiring customers to bribe him with bottles of whiskey. In any case, this was the last straw. Bea took the children and moved out of the Alden home back to Buffalo. Banks' father was banished from the family home. Bea would have nothing more to do with him. It was 1934 – the height of the Great Depression. Jobs were hard to come by. John was sixteen, Don was eleven, Warny was nine, and Joyce was only two years old. It was a brave, but risky thing for Bea to do.

Bea Banks is a whole other story. Born in Smethport, Pennsylvania, on 17 September 1897, she was a strong, proud, and fiercely independent woman long before those traits became more common in women. After finishing the eighth grade, Bea started work at age fourteen scrubbing floors. After taking a business course, she worked as a Buffalo lawyer's secretary for several years until she married. Her first child, John, was born when Bea was twenty.

Having to raise four children with little or no help, caused Bea to be a strong disciplinarian. Banks recalls how once when he was young his grandmother bought him a new Roadmaster bicycle. When he rode it home, Bea thought he had stolen it and had the police arrest him. Bea only believed Banks when his grandmother confirmed that she bought the bike for him. After the separation, Bea would let the kids have nothing to do with their father who did not contribute any support. Banks recalls one Christmas when their father sent presents, Bea would not let the kids open them. She sent them back to the father.

While Bea was firm with her children, she had a soft spot for her eventual nine grandchildren, thirty-two great-grandchildren, and six great-great-grandchildren. She also had a great memory. Right up until her death in 2001, she never missed sending me a birthday card – usually with a few dollars included – even when I was earning substantially more than she.

Bea worked until she was eighty. Her final and favorite job was as a cashier at the Old Faithful Lodge in Yellowstone National Park. She worked summers there for fourteen years. "Of course, I lied about my age to get the job. Took twenty years off," she would later admit in a *Whittier (California) Daily News* article by Valerie Marrs that celebrated Bea's 100th birthday. Bea's birth records had been destroyed in a fire in Pennsylvania. She loved the Yellowstone job – especially being around all of the young college students who also worked there. She wanted nothing to do with senior citizens. She said, "They act too old." She loved to read. Banks and his mother claimed to have once read all of the books in one of the Buffalo Library's neighborhood branches.

Bea lived by herself for all but the last three of her 103 years. At age 100, she was finally talked into moving in with Joyce and her husband, Clarence "Sox" Argyle. Bea was proud that she had lived on her own for so long. And she was proud that she had lived through the whole twentieth century and part of the nineteenth and twenty-first. She felt that not too many other people had done that. Above all, Bea was extremely proud that even during the Great Depression of the 1930s, by working hard at sometimes two or three menial jobs at a time, she was able to take care of herself and her children without having "to go on welfare." As to her living so long, she said, "I had to work so hard all of my life that I don't know how to quit." Her only regret was that she had outlived her sons, John and Warny. Bea died 19 July 2001.

Banks recalls that growing up in a one parent home during the Depression was tough. "We moved a lot. We went to a lot of different schools." Bea was working all of the time. Banks especially remembers her scrubbing floors at the Morgan Laundry, but she also did a lot of cashiering work at stores and theatres. John quit school to go to work at Buffalo Forge, and Banks and Warny sold magazines after school to help. One of Banks' favorite stories of those days was the Christmas when he could have only one present. Bea gave him a choice between the two things that he really wanted – an artist's easel or a set of skis. Banks chose the skis and promptly broke them on his first time down the neighborhood hill.

Banks joined the Boy Scouts (Troop 173) and enjoyed participating in their activities – particularly the camping trips. Banks remembers:

> On Friday nights, we would raid our parents' cupboards, put the food (cans and potatoes) in a sack with a blanket and a piece of canvas (formerly a sign from a store) for a tent, hop on our bikes and head out to the country. Buster (brother John) was an Assistant Scoutmaster in another troop and when he wasn't working, he went with us.

Scouting was a good influence on Banks and later in life he acknowledged it by spending many years as a Scout leader helping other boys. As a youth, he also spent time at the YMCA and had many good times with his friends – particularly his best buddy, Jim Linden, with whom Banks worked as a peanut and popcorn vendor at the old Buffalo Bison hockey games in Memorial Auditorium. He also spent a lot of time at his grandmother's house "in the country."

In high school, Banks was on the track and swimming teams. I remember him as being a good swimmer – not a bad skill to have for someone who would eventually join the Navy. It also led to a part time job at scout camp as a lifeguard. Additionally, he was on the pistol team and did well - which also would help in the Navy.

Banks made it through high school and remembers graduating in his brother, John's suit. John was about three inches taller than Banks and a bit heavier, but that was the only suit in the family.

Banks got hired at Curtiss-Wright by taking some post-graduate courses in blueprint drafting and reading - and a couple of other mechanical courses at Tech High School in Buffalo during the summer after graduation. He did well. As a result, he was accepted at Curtiss-Wright's Technical Training School to learn metalsmithing. The way things worked, if you made it through the Curtiss-Wright School, you were offered a job with Curtiss-Wright. Banks completed the school and was offered a job at the big, new airport plant.

In hindsight, it seems fitting that Banks' first job before joining the Navy was with the company founded by Glenn Curtiss – the fellow who taught the first Navy pilot, LT Theodore G. Ellyson, how to fly in 1910 - for "free." The deal was that Curtiss would teach Ellyson how to fly if the Navy agreed to buy a plane from Curtiss. It was the start of something big for both Curtiss and the Navy.

Banks was hired as a riveter, but when the plant management found out about the business courses he had taken in high school, he was placed in the stock room. After a few weeks, he was promoted to "minimum stock foreman." His job was to make sure stock supplies were adequate. If they were not, he was to order what was needed from suppliers all over the country by using a teletype machine. Banks recalls that when things were slow, time could be passed by using the teletypes to relay jokes back and forth – not unlike use of office e-mail in the twenty-first century.

The Curtiss-Wright job was a good one. It paid well and employees could literally work as many hours as they wanted. The plant operated twenty-four hours a day seven days a week. Banks recalls working ten to twelve hours a day, five to seven days a week. The P-40 was a popular plane and the Army wanted them as quickly as they could get them. As it turns out, nearly 16,000 were produced in Buffalo for both the American and British forces.

Banks remembers an accident at the plant when a P-40 was being test flown and crashed through the roof of the plant. Several employees were killed. Banks came to work after the crash, but remembers seeing finger and hand prints from burned flesh on the wings of planes waiting to be assembled.

Ironically, Banks later found out that his father was a guard at the plant at the same time Banks was working there and neither of them ever knew it.

With the news of the attack on Pearl Harbor, young men all over the country flooded the armed forces recruiting offices. They wanted to be part of the great crusade that the country was now undertaking to defend democracy from the forces of tyranny that were threatening the world. Things were in tough shape in 1941. The armies of Hitler, Mussolini, and Tojo were on the move. There was no question that they were an "axis of evil." They conquered and controlled great amounts of territory in Europe, Africa, and Asia. Many millions of people were at their mercy. They were doing horrible things all around the world. If ever a war had to be fought and won, World War II was it.

Like so many other young men on the day after the Pearl Harbor attack, Banks went down to the local Navy recruiting office in Buffalo's old Post Office building to enlist. He did so notwithstanding the fact that he could possibly have received an occupational draft deferment because he was working in an important defense plant.

He chose the Navy because as a boy he had spent a lot of time at his grandmother's house visiting her and his uncle. While there, a Sailor would occasionally visit. Banks was impressed by his "sea stories" and the list of world cities that the Sailor had visited - and had tattooed on his arm.

With the large number of men wanting to enlist, the recruiting offices were swamped – as were the recruit training centers and specialty schools where the new recruits would be trained. For example, on 8 December 1941, more men tried to enlist in the American armed forces than any other day in American history. Waiting resulted. Banks was sent home to await receipt of enlistment papers that were to be mailed to him. He was to fill them out and return with them to the recruiting office. So Banks kept his job at the Curtiss-Wright plant and waited – and waited some more to get the enlistment papers.

Even for a war that was so clearly justified, Bea like many parents was not enthusiastic about her son's volunteering for military service. And Banks' grandmother was absolutely against it. She very much disliked the military. Her feelings were so strong that when he was younger, Banks could not wear his Boy Scout uniform in her presence. There was talk in the family that she came from a Quaker background and had adopted strong pacifist beliefs.

When the enlistment papers were eventually mailed to the family home at 323 Purdey Street in Buffalo, Bea intercepted them and hid them under a rug. Banks continued to wait. He was eighteen years old – what did he know? One day when he came home from work, he found his mother washing a bedroom floor. When she threw the rug back to wash under it, Banks saw the brown envelope from the Navy. He made a grab for it, but his grandmother who was staying with them at the time, reached it first and tore it up.

Banks went back to the recruiting station, got new enlistment papers, filled them out, passed his physical, and was finally officially sworn into the United States Navy on 29 October 1942. His service number was 608 73 93. He was nineteen years and six months old. He was 5' 7'' tall and weighed 135 pounds with brown hair and brown eyes - and he was about to embark on the adventure of a life time.

After the swearing in, Banks and the other recruits were marched down Main Street from the Main Post Office to the Lehigh train station at the foot of Main Street. Bea walked along side Banks and saw him off – the first of her three sons to go to war. John and Warny would also enlist in the Navy. Joyce was too young to serve in World War II, but after graduating from high school and maturing into a very attractive young woman, she enlisted in the Air Force in the early 1950s - where she met her future husband, Sox, who was also serving. Thus, all four of Bea's "kids" – male and female - served in the military. Not many families can match that. And Bea and her "kids" were rightly proud of it.

While proud of Joyce's three "big" brothers' service during World War II, and their own service during the Cold War, Joyce and Sox Argyle are especially proud of their grandson, Army Sergeant Matt Jackson (son of their daughter Michelle and her husband Greg Jackson), who recently completed a tour of duty as an Explosive Ordnance Disposal expert in Iraq.

Because she had three sons in the military during the war, Bea qualified for and displayed a small white window flag with three blue stars – one star for each son – and a three star pin that she wore all of the time during the war.

Bea finally accepted Banks' decision to enlist – after he had the recruiter tell her that he would be drafted into the Army if he did not join the Navy. They did not bother to tell her about the possibility of a defense employee occupational deferment.

When Banks left home, Bea gave him a good watch and a USN ring with a small diamond embedded in it that had been taken from a stick pin belonging to his father. Banks wore them both. The watch made it through training and the Pacific battles, but was stolen from a barracks head (bathroom) when Banks was mustering out of the Navy in November 1945. The ring survived the war and is currently on the third finger of my right hand.

Bea Banks' four children (clockwise from top left): Donald, John, David, and Joyce. While not old enough to enlist for World War II, Joyce joined the Air Force in the early 1950s. (Photo of Donald: courtesy D. A. Banks collection. Photos of John and David: Official U.S. Navy Photographs courtesy Jan Banks-Doddridge. Photo of Joyce: courtesy Jan Banks-Doddridge.)

Beatrice M. "Bea" Banks at her 100th birthday party. Bea was born in Smethport, Pennsylvania on 17 September 1897 and died in Whittier, California on 19 July 2001. (Photo: courtesy S.A. Banks)

2

Training

When Banks and the other new enlistees boarded the train in Buffalo they were on their way to recruit training – more popularly known as Boot Camp. Enlisted men went to Boot Camp while newly recruited officers went to Officer Candidate School (OCS). For the next six weeks, the new recruits – or Boots, would undergo basic military training that would transform them from eager civilians into new Sailors ready to take their places in the Fleet.

For the men from Buffalo, recruit training took place at the brand new U.S. Naval Training Center, Sampson, New York. Sampson - as it was known, was located on the east shore of Seneca Lake – one of New York's Finger Lakes, in Seneca County. It was a beautiful area and in the heart of New York wine country. The decision to build the Center was made by President Roosevelt on 14 May 1942. It was needed in a hurry, to help handle the tremendous influx of new recruits. Construction began a few weeks later and the first recruits began training there on 17 October 1942 – only twelve days before Banks and the other Buffalo recruits arrived.

Sampson covered 2535 acres. It was divided into five training units – each to train 5000 men at a time. Each unit had its own outdoor fourteen acre parade ground and drill field as well as a drill hall with a two acre indoor drill area. Close order drill was big in Boot Camp. Each training unit also had a gym, swimming pool, administrative areas, indoor instruction areas, a mess hall, and twenty-two barracks to house two recruit companies of 228 men each. Each unit also had separate barracks for the Chief Petty Officer (CPO or Chief) instructors, two dispensaries, a recreation building, rifle range, and a storehouse. Additionally, the Training Center as a whole had a 2700 seat auditorium, a 400 seat chapel, a central administration building, post office, brig (jail), guard barracks, and separate barracks for Sailors who completed training and were waiting assignment.

In short, Sampson was no small scale operation. By the end of the war, a total of 411,429 Navy recruits had received their initial training there. And Sampson was only one of seven Navy recruit training centers during the war.

When Banks got to Sampson, like all new Boots he was assigned to a Recruit Company. A junior officer was assigned as Company Commander. In Banks' case it was an Ensign (ENS). Banks recalls, "The men liked him." Within the Company, each Boot was assigned to a Recruit Platoon with a First Class Petty Officer or Chief Petty Officer in charge. On his first day, each Boot got a haircut and his shots. He got rid of his civilian clothes – sent them home, and was issued his uniforms and other Navy gear – all of which he would stencil his name on. All of the things would then be rolled in a particular way to help it fit in his newly issued seabag. His seabag would hold virtually everything a Sailor owned as he traveled around the world – and he would guard it with his life. Each Boot was also issued a copy of *The Bluejackets' Manual* – which contained everything he would need to know about life in the Navy.

For the first couple of weeks, Banks recalls that as new Boots, "We slept in canvas hammocks before we moved to regular bunks. The Chief's room was at the end. The barracks was heated by a coal furnace."

Banks remembers Boot Camp as being "quite a change" from civilian life, but "not all that bad." His years of camping and outdoor activities with the Boy Scouts apparently eased his transition. And as a Scout, Banks excelled at knot tying. As a result, the Chief Petty Officer who was knots instructor turned the instruction over to Banks. As Banks recalls, "The Chief adjourned himself to the CPO Club."

Among other things, Boot Camp involved getting up early, physical training, much marching, learning the manual of arms with a rifle, standing watches, classroom instruction, and learning to row whale boats on Seneca Lake – in the autumn and early winter. It was cold on Seneca Lake that time of year. To keep them focused – especially when they were tired, the Boots were told to pay attention and not to fall out of the boats because the lake had no bottom. According to Banks, "It worked. Many of the guys believed the instructors." In any case, it is a deep lake and the water was cold. There was some liberty (time off) during Boot Camp, but it was pretty tame. The local towns were small. Most of the time the men would go to town to get a non-Navy meal and see a movie.

As their last big challenge before being able to graduate and become real Sailors, the Boots had to successfully pass "Hell Week" - when their weeks of instruction were put to use in a practical exercise. Banks recalls that during "Hell Week" it was very cold and as a result, "I lucked out. I was assigned to stoke the furnace in the Company barracks day and night." Notwithstanding all of the physical training, Banks does not remember many men washing out (failing to graduate).

Toward the end of Boot Camp, Banks' brother, John, drove down with the rest of the family to visit – about two hundred miles roundtrip. When John enlisted in the Navy, he also did his recruit training at Sampson. He later remarked to Banks, "If I knew what you were going through then when we visited, I would have put you in the trunk and taken you home."

After graduation from Sampson in January 1943, Banks was granted leave and went back to visit the old South Buffalo neighborhood. One of the few things that he remembers from that leave was going with Bea to the courthouse as she formally divorced his father. Banks did not see his father again until going to the funeral home for his "wake" many years later.

Because of his early Curtiss-Wright experience working with metal – his Navy service record identified his "main civilian occupation" as riveter, the Navy selected Banks to attend Class "A" School to become an Aviation Metalsmith (AM). AM would be his rating – or primary job description. The AM school was located at the Naval Air Technical Training Center (NATTC) in Norman, Oklahoma.

The Navy – and in particular Naval aviation, had a big presence in Norman during the war. In addition to the only Aviation Metalsmith School, there was an Aviation Radar Operator's School, an Aviation Machinist's Mate School, and an Aviation Ordnanceman's School, as well as a Naval Air Station, a Naval Hospital, and a Combat Aircrewman Training School.

As he had been in one of the first groups to go through Boot training at Sampson, Banks was also in one of the first few classes at NATTC. It had only been commissioned in September 1942. By late 1944, over 50,000 Sailors would graduate from the various service schools and be spread around the Fleet. It got to the point where nearly every Saturday a group graduated and on nearly every Monday a new group started. The new trainees were selected for their specialties because of their "high rating in mechanical aptitude and general classification tests."

The Aviation Metalsmith Course was twenty-one weeks long. Eighty percent of the trainee's time was spent in the metalsmith shops and the remainder in classroom and demonstration periods. Among other things, the trainees learned basic bench metal work, blueprint reading, mechanical drawing, use of hand tools, riveting, welding – both steel and aluminum, and typical squadron repair operations such as making waterproof repairs on aircraft fuselages and fabric and plastic repairing. Practical application of what was being learned was emphasized as Banks and the other trainees eventually worked on combat plane types before graduating. After graduation, most of the new AMs would be assigned to big repair shops set up around the Fleet where they would be responsible for repairing everything behind the engine on damaged planes.

In addition to learning their specialties, the NATTC trainees spent an hour each day doing physical training (PT). They made use of a large gym, a couple of obstacle courses, a couple of swimming pools, and a "natural hazard course." Everyone was taught to swim. After spending time in the general conditioning program, the trainees were then taught "combat fitness" – including boxing, wrestling, and hand-to-hand combat.

Banks recalls his five months in Norman as being "better than life at Boot Camp." There was more freedom and it was more academic. "I was in a section with thirty or forty other men. We did a lot of hands on work with much practice welding."

In addition to learning the metal work skills that he would need in the Fleet, Banks remembers some of the practical jokes that the trainees would play on each other to lighten things up – stuff like blackening somebody's welding glasses, heating a metal stool seat before a guy sat on it, and cutting welding hoses. He recalls the weekly Saturday inspections as being "murder." "We had to wear our dress blue uniforms. The red Oklahoma dust was hell on the blues requiring a weekly trip to the cleaners for each inspection."

He also remembers the "salty" old instructors teaching them simple, but useful tips such as that common kitchen variety molasses could be used to waterproof a repair patch on a float plane. And for dramatic effect in making the point that punch presses could take off one of your fingers, the instructors kept the unfortunate victims' severed fingers in jars strategically placed over the presses. Banks recalls that when female Sailors or WAVES (Women Accepted for Volunteer Emergency Service) as they were called, began attending AM school, the men were told to "clean up their act" - and the jars of fingers were hidden. But he remembers, "One woman happened to open a drawer and find them. She screamed and fainted – much to the amusement of the guys in the class."

As it turns out, those ladies did okay. On 30 July 1943, nineteen of them made up the first class of WAVES to graduate from AM School. In a later class, one WAVE – Joan

Holmes Crews, had to miss the first nine weeks of classes, yet went on to finish third highest in a class of six women and ninety-one men.

The WAVES were truly pioneers who proved their worth. During the war, not only would "Rosie the Riveter" be building the fighters and bombers as a civilian, her sister would be repairing them as a Sailor. For twenty-three years prior to August 1942, the only women that served in the Navy were a relatively small number of nurses. The large numbers of officer and enlisted women that joined during World War II had a lasting impact. And today, they not only repair the planes and ships, they fly and command them.

Banks remembers the liberty in Norman as being good. Oklahoma City was only about twenty-five miles away. NATTC had a good base Welfare and Recreation Department with special events such as trainee participation rodeos, dances, and aquacades. Moreover, Tex Beneke had joined the Navy and was stationed at Norman as the leader of the Navy band. Beneke was a famous saxophone player and singer ("Chattanooga Choo Choo") with the legendary Glenn Miller orchestra. Banks remembers Beneke driving around Norman in a sporty Cord automobile – a very rare and hot car in those days. Banks also remembers Beneke as being very popular with the ladies. It was not bad duty for Beneke who also did well after the war. As a result of Miller's being killed in the war, Beneke took over as leader of the Miller band in 1946.

One day at NATTC, Banks noticed a memo on the metal shop bulletin board requesting volunteers for aircrewman duty. The difference in position descriptions was significant. If you were selected to be an aircrewman, rather than working on planes while they were on the ground, you would be flying in them as either a gunner or radioman. Banks thought it looked like something he could do and it sounded exciting. He sent his application in to be a gunner – and it was approved. It was another life altering decision. Banks was somewhat surprised – as were others, that he was accepted into the program because the only aircrewmen he knew were either Aviation Machinist's Mates, Aviation Radiomen, or Aviation Ordnancemen. He thinks that he may have been the only Aviation Metalsmith Aircrewman in the Navy.

Banks graduated from AM school in June 1943. He did well enough – the upper half of the class – to earn a meritorious promotion in rate when he graduated. He was promoted from Seaman First Class (pay grade E-3) to Aviation Metalsmith Third Class (AM3c) (pay grade E-4 and equivalent to a Corporal in the Army and Marine Corps). A pay raise from $66 per month to $78 per month came with the promotion. But with the additional pay came additional responsibility as he was now a Petty Officer and would be expected to supervise and lead men junior to him.

Chief Petty Officer instructs a group of Boots in the proper handling of a whale boat on Seneca Lake at the U.S. Naval Training Center, Sampson, New York. (Official U.S. Navy Photograph courtesy Sampson State Park)

Boots forming on the parade ground at Sampson. (Official U.S. Navy Photograph courtesy Sampson State Park)

Aviation Metalsmith School Graduating Class 30-A-43, Naval Air Technical Training Center, Norman, Oklahoma. Banks is the third Sailor from the left in the front row. Other members of the class were: Dale Sevbin, Paul Slavey, Robert Johnson, Clarence Zickefoose, Don Van Dame, Lloyd Pontine, Frank Offenstein, Blaine Whitehead, David Richards, Gene Robbins, Robert Bussing, Jay Wong, Leo Conley, Walter Hawk Jr., Harry Cook, Sherman Nickles, Carol Worrell, and Donald Redman. (Official U.S. Navy Photograph courtesy D.A. Banks collection)

3

Learning to be a Turret Gunner

Because at the ripe old age of twenty Banks was now a Petty Officer Third Class and one of the more senior former students, when a group of about ninety of them were ordered to Seattle, Washington for aerial gunnery training, he was put in charge. In addition to being the group leader, he had to carry all of their orders in a briefcase that was handcuffed to his wrist during the train trip from Oklahoma City to Seattle via Chicago.

By the time he and his troops reached Chicago, Banks was suffering from motion sickness – not a good start for an aspiring turret gunner. He claims he never got air sick flying. In any case, the group had a couple of hours layover in Chicago so Banks took the briefcase off his wrist, put it under his head, and went to sleep on a train station bench. He woke up as the train for Seattle was pulling out. He jumped up, ran, and fortunately caught the train - but without the briefcase which was back on the bench.

Banks' was sure he would be in considerable trouble if he did not retrieve the briefcase. "Visions of many years in the brig flashed through my mind. Out of desperation, I told the conductor, 'the train must be stopped.' Somewhat amazingly the conductor had the train stopped and I ran back - and to my great relief found the briefcase."

The rest of the trip was almost as equally "exciting" as Banks tried to keep his fellow Sailors reasonably under control and on the train heading in the same direction. To say that he was happy when they finally reached Seattle is an understatement.

In Seattle, Banks reported to the Naval Air Station (NAS) at Sand Point. NAS Seattle was another busy place during the war. It was located on a peninsula in the northern part of the city that projects into Lake Washington. It had five asphalt paved runways, favorable prevailing winds - and since it was located on a peninsula, takeoffs and landings could be accomplished free of obstructions. Eight thousand military and civilian personnel worked there – and the base was home to a multitude of Navy commands, repair shops, and aviation schools.

Banks was sent there to attend a variety of courses during the next few months. The Navy believed in making sure that its airmen were trained before sending them to the Fleet. It took approximately nine months to train an aircrewman from the time of his enlistment until he reported to his squadron. In the end, all of the various training that was required probably saved a lot of lives in terms of job proficiency, fitness, and survival skills.

While Banks would attend other classes and courses, his primary reason for being at Sand Point was to attend the five week Aerial Free Gunnery Training Unit course. Free gunnery was distinguished from fixed gunnery in that the fixed gunner (pilot) aims his plane and fires along the line of flight of the enemy plane only being concerned with the target's motion while the free gunner riding in the plane must aim his machine gun and fire along the line of motion of the enemy plane while being concerned with both the target's motion and the motion of his own plane as it affects the bullet's course.

In addition to classroom work where the gunnery students learned the basic elements of sighting, deflection, range estimation, and ordnance, not surprisingly the instruction also involved a lot of shooting practice. The emphasis was placed on actual firing over classroom theory. Some of it was with .38 caliber pistols at stationary target ranges. Banks did well with the pistols and led the class. His time on the South Park High School pistol team paid off.

Some of the target practice involved trap and skeet shooting with shotguns – which was important since it taught the need to lead targets. The students each fired about four hundred rounds with shotguns during the course. The shooting was hard for some guys - causing some to wash out of school. VC-66 (T-2) TBM aircrewman, Howard Alley, also remembers gunnery training - and the pressure involved. He talks about it in the April 2008 edition of the *VC-66 (T-2) Newsletter* which is superbly edited and published by VC-66 (T-2) pilot, Joe Mussatto:

> What appeared at first to be a great sporting event with loads of fun and excitement turned out to be neither. The gunnery school soon became a nightmare of fierce competition, frustration and endless stress. Performance tests were so stringent that some people considered dropping out shortly after our exercises got underway.
>
> As the weeks passed it became increasingly difficult to attain the level of proficiency necessary to master the various categories of marksmanship. The initial phase consisted of firing 12-gauge shotguns at clay pigeons flung at random intervals from six hidden launch positions. Trap shooting it was called. This exercise usually continued for four hours each day, causing the right shoulder and upper arm to become deeply bruised and discolored from the constant battering day after day.
>
> Upon completion of this program…we were given a final test which required bursting 45 pigeons out of 50. Those who failed were dropped from the program at this point, and were reassigned to regular Navy duty.

Alley goes on to point out, "Each phase grew increasingly difficult." At the end of the course "fewer than 50% of our original class remained. And I personally felt very fortunate to be among the survivors; for on many occasions I had lain awake for hours at night fearing that I would be among the next group of washouts."

One of the trap and skeet instructors was actor Robert Stack - star of many movies and who would later play Eliott Ness in "*The Untouchables*" TV program. Stack had joined the Navy during the war. He knew what he was doing teaching skeet shooting. When he was sixteen he had been a member of the All American Skeet Rifle Team. He later became National Skeet Champion and set two world records.

Banks and the other future gunners also learned to work on and repair the .30 caliber and .50 caliber Browning Automatic Air-cooled Machine Guns (BAM guns) – including field stripping them in the dark. This was no easy task. There were times when the main spring escaped and flew across the room narrowly missing – or not – "bodies diving for cover." While Banks does not remember anyone in his section being hurt, he does recall "guys in other sections having had springs embedded in various body parts."

When the field stripping portion of the course was completed, successful students were awarded their own .50 caliber wrench – which was about one inch by six inches. Earning and being awarded the wrench was more appreciated by the Sailors than earning and being awarded their aircrewman patches – a machine gun with wings. Banks carried his wrench throughout the war and kept it afterward as one of his few war "souvenirs."

In addition to pistol and shotgun shooting, the students fired a lot of rounds – as many as sixty-five hundred, with the .30 and .50 caliber machine guns at both moving and stationary targets. Some of the training eventually involved sitting in a turret on the back of a flatbed truck shooting at targets while traveling down a rutted road at high speed. Banks was not as good at this exercise, but observes, "Who the hell was?" Alley, in the 30 April 2008 *VC-66 (T-2) Newsletter*, agrees that this portion of the training was really tough "claiming almost a third of our members as 'wash out' victims."

Banks and the other students also learned about turrets and how to operate them. Additionally, they got instruction on torpedoes, bombs, and other explosives, bombsights, radio communications, and radar - and a lot of instruction on recognition of planes and ships. Recognition training would be a constant throughout their service.

Water safety training was also part of the program. The student gunners had to jump off a thirty foot high tower into a pool. This was another must pass test. "If you didn't do it, you washed out of school." Banks recalls a fellow student who could not jump once he got to the top of the platform. He froze. An officer had to be summoned. The officer talked the student over to the edge of the platform – "just to take a look and see how close it was." Once at the edge, the student looked over. Banks recalls, "As the student looked over, the officer flicked a finger in his back and the kid went over and passed."

Another "popular" part of the training was known as the "Dilbert Dunker" – which is still being used in the twenty-first century to train Navy airmen for water crash survival. It is basically the cockpit of an aircraft that the student is strapped into and then raised to the top of a ramp above a swimming pool. The cockpit is released and it - with the student inside, plunges into the pool and sinks to the bottom – upside down. The student must get out and get to the surface of the water. It was not uncommon for instructors to have to dive into the pool to rescue confused and struggling students during their first attempts. Banks was able to "dope out" the exercise. "I discovered that the thing to do was to release your restraining harness just as you hit the water – rather than waiting until you were under water." It worked and got him through this phase of the training.

Banks also remembers being put through a lot of physical training at Sand Point. There was a daily period of PT involved swimming, hand-to-hand combat - Judo, or an obstacle course. It was as Banks recalls, "like running an obstacle course designed by the architect of Devil's Island." He recalls being amused by seeing an "old" Marine Corps Gunnery Sergeant armed with a BB gun shooting Marine Corps students – who were also training to be aircrewmen – on the helmet or on the butt if either showed above the slit trenches in which they were crawling. The inclusion of Marines ("Jarheads") and Sailors ("Squids") in the same classes led to some great competition in gunnery, field stripping machine guns, physical training, inspections, and about everything else that was going on. This traditional intra Navy Department rivalry was fueled by such things as Marine recruiters trying to "shanghai" young men interested in joining the Navy by telling them things like, "You can't join the Navy – your parents were married."

The next phase of training involved actually getting into an airplane for an introduction to flying. The first plane Banks was exposed to – he had never flown in anything before, was the Stearman Primary Trainer fondly known as the "Yellow Peril." It was a bi-plane (two wings – one on top of the other) with two cockpits – one in front of the other, and painted bright yellow.

Banks has vivid memories of "demonic" instructor pilots taking great pride in the amount of vomit that they could cause to be produced in the second cockpit where the students rode. Actually, the pilots were testing the enlisted students to see how much – if at all, flying bothered them. Banks claims to have never thrown up. This claim was seen as a challenge for the pilots – and Banks was thus exposed to a variety of interesting and stimulating aerobatic maneuvers as part of his training.

The next airplane that the students got to ride in was the North American T-6 Texan advanced trainer – or SNJ as it was known by the Navy. It was the Navy's all purpose trainer – used to train pilots and aircrews. It was a two seater monoplane with a .30 caliber machine gun mounted in the back cockpit. The machinegun shot paint tipped ammunition. The student gunner was expected to hit a thirty foot long canvas sleeve towed by another SNJ. The sleeve was towed at various speeds, altitudes, and angles. Banks remembers it as being "damn hard" to do.

When they were not flying, Banks and the other students attended ground school where they did more work with the machine guns and radio equipment, learned about ammunition handling, fuses, smoke signals, aerial photography, and basic aircraft maintenance. During all of the Gunnery School training, the students had to maintain a 3.0 average in everything they did or be washed out. Aerial gunnery was important and dangerous work. The Navy took it very seriously.

While they were doing their training flights in the Seattle area, Banks recalls looking down at a Boeing Aircraft Company facility which was blocks long and seeing something strange. "The building had an entire city landscape on its roof." What Banks had seen was Boeing's production facility where the company built the famous B-17 Flying Fortress bombers. It was a huge place – big enough for eight football fields. Thirty thousand people worked there during the war – many of them women. Because at least up until the Battle of Midway, a possible Japanese air attack was a very real concern for the west coast, the plant's roof was camouflaged. There were burlap and clapboard houses, chicken wire lawns, fake trees, and even a rooftop street sign marking the intersection of Synthetic Street and Burlap Boulevard. And when you flew over it, as Banks recalls, "It looked just like a suburban bunch of houses, lawns, trees, grass, and cars parked on it." But from the ground, it was not visible.

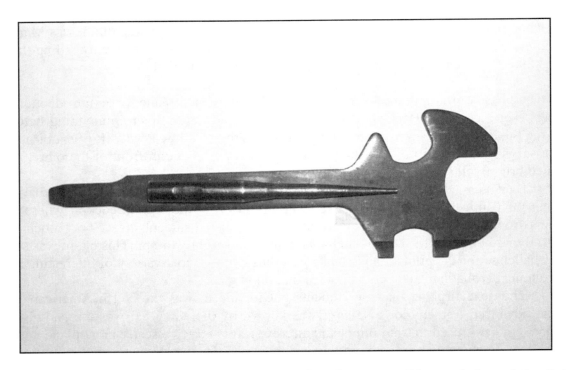

.50 caliber machine gun wrench awarded to Banks after successful completion of the field stripping portion of his turret gunner course. (Photo: courtesy S.A. Banks)

Stearman Primary Trainer – fondly known as the "Yellow Peril, on display at Naval Air Station, Jacksonville, Florida. (Photo: courtesy S.A. Banks)

4

To the Fleet

At the August 1943 graduation, the gunnery students were awarded their aircrewman silver wings and patches - a machine gun with wings, to wear on the right sleeves of their uniforms. It was a proud day and a good feeling of accomplishment - a feeling similar to that of a new Navy pilot earning his Wings of Gold. Then came the anxious scanning of bulletin boards to see the type of aircraft to which they would be assigned. It could be dive bombers, float planes, or as in Banks' case – torpedo bombers – the relatively new TBF Avengers with their three man crews.

The Navy had accepted the TBFs for incorporation into the Fleet in December 1941 – the month of the Pearl Harbor attack. Thus, the nickname: Avenger. The new gunners had no say in the type of plane assignment process. As in most Navy things, the assignment was governed by the needs of the Navy.

As it turns out, Banks was lucky with his assignment. The TBFs were hot stuff. They were the biggest single engine plane in the world at the time. They were 40 feet long, 16 feet high, and had a wingspan of 54 feet – but the wingspan could be reduced to 19 feet when the wings were folded up to ease parking on a crowded carrier deck. Their empty weight was about 10,000 pounds. Max weight was about 13,600 pounds. They were powered by one 1700 horsepower, 14 cylinder, air cooled, radial engine. Their max speed was about 270 miles per hour and their cruising speed was about 150 miles per hour. Max range was about 1200 miles and max ceiling was about 22,000 feet. They had a max bomb load of 2000 pounds or they could carry a 1900 pound torpedo. They had one fixed over the engine mounted .30 caliber machine gun that the pilot operated; one turret mounted .50 caliber machine gun that the turret gunner operated; and one low rear facing .30 caliber machine gun that the radioman operated. And the TBFs had done well since joining the Fleet a little over a year before Banks was assigned to them.

The Navy would come to like TBFs a lot. An article, "TBF TEAMWORK," in the 15 July 1944 issue of *Naval Aviation News* was full of praise:

> Acknowledged as the world's best torpedo bombers, TBF and TBM Avengers are among the most rugged and versatile combat airplanes ever built….It has left a trail of ships sunk or damaged, blasted enemy ground installations and (though its guns are primarily defensive) aircraft downed in the air and shot up on the ground….In addition to torpedo bombing, they are used for high altitude, glide and skip bombing, anti-submarine warfare and scouting, not to mention mine laying. They have flown against the Japs in all the great raids and air battles in the Pacific….Well-armed, well armored and carrying loads as big as those of many larger bombers, the Avenger has the lowest rate of loss of any plane in the forces. A workhorse of the Fleet, the Avenger is combat tested.

Banks did not have to go far to join his squadron. He was assigned to the newly formed COMPOSITE SQUADRON SIXTY-SIX (VC-66). The letter "V" is how the Navy denotes a fixed wing heavier than air squadron. The "C" indicates that the squadron was composite. "66" was the assigned squadron number.

The squadron was designated composite because it was composed of two different type aircraft: the TBF Avengers and the single seat F4F Wildcat fighters. The Wildcats were the Navy's primary fighter early in the war and the only Navy fighter to serve throughout the whole war. Small in comparison to the Avengers, the Wildcats were 29 feet long, 11 feet high, and had a wingspan of 38 feet. Their wings could also be folded. Their empty weight was about 5800 pounds. Max weight was about 8000 pounds. They were powered by one 1200 horsepower double row radial engine. Max speed was about 320 miles per hour. Cruising speed was about 190 miles per hour. Their range was about 800 miles. Maximum ceiling was about 35,000 feet. They had six fixed forward facing .50 caliber machine guns.

While considered inferior in performance in some respects to the Japanese fighters, the Wildcats were ruggedly built and with their well trained pilots had a good victory to loss ratio of almost 7 to 1.

The Navy's thinking was that the two different type aircraft would complement each other. It made sense to combine them in the same squadron where they could work together as a team. Typically there would be about nine Wildcats and twelve Avengers in each composite squadron.

As it turned out, VC-66 would become the first squadron composed exclusively of the newer model Avengers and Wildcats built by the Eastern Aircraft Division of General Motors and known as TBMs and FMs rather than the earlier TBFs and F4Fs built by Grumman Aircraft. They were generally the same aircraft except the FMs had two less machine guns. Grumman stopped building Avengers and Wildcats to concentrate on building the new F6F Hellcat fighters. Between 1940 and 1945, the two companies built a combined total of 9,839 Avengers and over 4000 Wildcats.

VC-66 had been commissioned on 21 June 1943, at NAS Sand Point, Seattle. The Commanding Officer (CO or "skipper") was Lieutenant Commander (LCDR) Herbert K. "Herb" Bragg. Bragg, a West Virginian, was a Pearl Harbor attack survivor and veteran naval aviator who had entered the Navy in 1935. He had most recently served aboard the USS ENTERPRISE (CV-6). The Executive Officer (XO) was Lieutenant (LT) Gerald O. "Gerry" Trapp. Trapp from Pomona, California, had been in the Navy since 1939. Prior to being assigned to VC-66, he was a fighter instructor at NAS Pensacola, Florida and helped train some of his future VC-66 shipmates.

In August 1943, to highlight the fact of VC-66's being the first squadron to fly exclusively GM built planes, GM sent reporters and photographers to do a story about the squadron. For security reasons, VC-66 was referred to as Squadron "X" in the company newspaper. To say that General Motors was proud of providing VC-66 with its planes would be a gross understatement. The VC-66 article appeared in the November 1943 issue of GM's *Eastern Aircraftsman*. It read in part:

> The men would deny it, of course, but there is something wonderful about
> them and their determination to give their lives, if necessary, in the

preservation of our most sacred rights. The fact that in this high endeavor they are flying on our wings is of itself a thrilling thought. But over and above even this is the fact that Squadron X is only the first to be composed entirely of Eastern Aircraft Division planes. The inference is clear: we must build and build, faster and faster, more and more until there are hundreds of Squadron X's filling the skies with the thunder of their might and the fury of their righteous cause.

For his part, in an effort to boost the morale and efforts of the folks working on the home front, VC-66 skipper, Bragg, wrote in the same article:

> To you of Eastern Aircraft who have given us our wings, we of Squadron X send you our greetings and warmest thanks. With these great fighter airplanes at our disposal we shall not fail you. We in turn are banking on you not to fail the men of the Navy who will follow us. We know how tough your schedules are and you know how tough our job is. But there's no production job and there's no fighting job that we can't lick if we give it our best and work together.

Of the original sixty-five men assigned to VC-66, fifteen – including the CO and XO – were fighter pilots, twelve were torpedo bomber pilots, one was an Air Combat Information Officer, one was an Engineering and Material Officer, and the rest were enlisted Petty Officers – including four Chief Petty Officers.

With the exception of the CO, XO, and a few veteran Chiefs, First Class Petty Officers, and Lieutenants, virtually all squadron personnel – like Banks - were new to the Navy, new to combat – and very young. One of the few enlisted men who had any Fleet experience was Aviation Radioman First Class Robert L. Kennon from Natchez, Mississippi, who – like the new squadron's skipper – had served previously on the ENTERPRISE. But most of the men were right out of the training commands.

And none – not even the CO or XO had ever served in a composite squadron before. Some were teenagers, most were in their early twenties. The oldest man in the squadron was thirty. He was called "Pop." Some were married, most were not. They came from all over the country – the pilots alone represented fifteen different states and the District of Columbia. In civilian life, they had been students, factory workers, forest rangers, semi-pro baseball players, biologists, engineers, artists, fishermen, college football players, musicians, cowboys, farmers, and reporters. Now, they were pilots, gunners, radiomen, or mechanics in a brand new squadron getting ready to go to war.

GM's *Eastern Aircraftsman* described the VC-66 fighter pilots as, "A happy-go-lucky, hell-for-leather crowd, they'd fly to the moon and back for money, marbles or chalk." As for the squadron's torpedo bomber pilots, the GM paper said, "With their crews of two men each, these 12 pilots have one of the most hazardous jobs in naval aviation – and love it." This was the team that Banks was joining.

When Banks reported to VC-66, he was assigned as ENS Ben E. "Ben" Davis' turret gunner. Davis from Danville, Illinois, and the University of Illinois, was a new TBF/TBM pilot just out of flight training. The third member of their crew was Aviation

Radioman Third Class T.F. Deeds. As time went on, Deeds had some trouble fitting in and Davis had him reassigned to a different squadron. Deeds' replacement was Aviation Radioman Third Class Thomas D. "Tom" Stoops. Stoops was from Phoenix, Arizona, and was a former college football lineman.

Banks recalls the Davis, Banks, Stoops combination as being "a good fit." He remembers:

> We liked and respected each other - and as a result, we went into training as a dedicated team. We rehearsed and drilled when others went on liberty. Our goal was to operate as a single unit. In emergencies, we wanted to know exactly what each of us would do and how we would act. We worked on our airplane with the mechanics, ordnance guys, and the plane captain – who we made sure was well taken care of with ample liberty and beer. As a result, our aircraft was kept clean and well maintained.

TBM crews had a weight limit. The big planes while powerful could only carry so much in the way of fuel, bombs, ammunition, and men. When the aircrews went for their monthly – even at sea - medical checks known as "Roscoes," Davis, Banks, and Stoops went together. Stoops as a big man was always over the crewman weight limit, but Davis and Banks were lighter and came in under the limit. Banks' relatively slim build had earned him the squadron nickname of "Dink" - which he didn't seem to mind all that much. Davis, Banks, and Stoops were able to convince the medical people to consider their combined weight. Banks recalls, "Taken together the three of us made the weight limit with a few pounds to spare."

Aside from weight requirements, the medical exam also checked nerves using a simple test. The aircrewman had to demonstrate that he could balance a clothespin on the end of a ruler. If he flunked, he was grounded until he could do it. Somebody else had to take his place in the plane. Depth perception was also important. It was tested by having the man pull strings to line up objects in a tunnel. It was simple, but effective.

TBF Avengers flying in formation. (Photo: courtesy National Archives)

Grumman F4F Wildcats. (Photo: courtesy Naval Historical Center)

LCDR Herbert K. Bragg, Commanding Officer of VC-66. (Official U.S. Navy Photograph courtesy W.D. Cope)

LT Gerald O. Trapp, Executive Officer of VC-66. (Official U.S. Navy Photograph courtesy W.D. Cope)

VC-66 standing inspection in Seattle, Washington, June 1943. (Official U.S. Navy Photograph courtesy D.A. Banks collection)

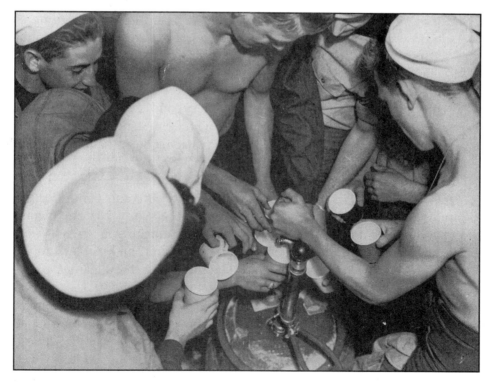

Men of VC-66 fill cups at a beer party. Banks is the Sailor with the large ring on his right hand. (Official U.S. Navy Photograph courtesy W.D. Cope)

5

Squadron Pre-Deployment Training

On 23 August 1943, VC-66 moved from the relative comfort and civilization of Seattle to the new Navy Auxiliary Air Station in Shelton, Washington. The word in the squadron was that after they completed their pre-deployment training, they would link up with their intended "parent" carrier, the brand new USS TRIPOLI (CVE-64), for combat operations.

Prior to the move to Shelton, the squadron had a big "beer bust" and an officers versus enlisted men softball game at Lake Sammamish near Seattle. The score of the game is lost to the ages, but the event concluded when the enlisted men threw all of the officers into the water.

Shelton was in a forested, rural part of Washington known as the "Gateway to the Olympic Peninsula." VC-66 was the first squadron to be based there. The men considered it "good duty." There was wildlife in abundance on and around the air station – deer, rabbits, raccoons. One of the squadron's fighter pilots, ENS Charles T. "Charlie" Edwards from Bethlehem, Pennsylvania, recalls, "After daytime flights, we would sometimes hunt deer by night." And one of the squadron's Chief Petty Officers shot and killed a bear on board the base. Since the field was subject to significant amounts of rain and fog, it was a good location for training for all weather operations.

While Shelton was "rustic" compared to NAS Sand Point, according to Banks, "The chow (food) was good as was the liberty in relatively nearby Seattle - about sixty miles away." Banks was getting to know his squadron shipmates. He considered them to be "a great bunch of guys – including the officers."

At Shelton, the squadron began work in earnest on the combat team flight training syllabus. Training included formation flying, gunnery, and tactics for the Wildcats; and formation flying, torpedo drops done out of NAS Whidbey Island, and glide bombing for the Avengers. Additionally, everyone got to participate in navigation flights and recognition training.

Recognition training for the aircrews started in their schools and continued throughout the rest of their active duty – including the combat zones. No one wanted to be responsible for shooting down a friendly aircraft or attacking a friendly ship. The aircrewmen were exposed to micro-second flashes of aircraft and ships from a projector on a screen in a black room. Hour after hour, day after day, they learned to distinguish the silhouettes of the various aircraft and ships – enemy and friendly.

Plane recognition was given the most emphasis because most free gunners would be shooting at them rather than ships. As Banks recalls, "If some poor soul fell asleep during a session, he would be rudely awakened by an instructor barking his name." It was not a kinder, gentler environment. It was serious business. To keep the attention level high, "occasionally the instructor would slip in a slide of a scantily clad young woman." Howard Alley also remembers recognition training and discusses it in the March 2008 edition of the *VC-66 (T-2) Newsletter*:

We learned to recognize and identify every aircraft in the American, British, German, Japanese, Italian, and Russian inventories, as well as their wingspan, speed, and range. As future gunners this information was vital to enable us to know what plane was approaching, and at what point to open fire, should it be a hostile aircraft. This exercise consumed hundreds of hours of intensive study, and to further sharpen our acuity we eventually were able to recognize these various aircraft as they were flashed on a screen at one twenty-fifth of a second.

For practice in their spare time, the aircrews were issued decks of cards with the various ship and aircraft silhouettes. The system worked. The end result was a group of men who could immediately recognize any ship or aircraft.

While most of the men assigned to VC-66 were either pilots or aircrewmen, not everyone was. It could be argued that the most important people in the squadron were the aircraft maintenance men. Without them, the planes could not get airborne - or stay there very long. And in charge of VC-66's mechanics was LT William H. "Bill" or "Pipe" Piper from Erie, Pennsylvania.

Piper graduated from Penn State in 1941 with a mechanical engineering degree. He had spent a couple of years in ROTC. Prior to graduation, recruiters from all of the services came to the college looking for men with technical backgrounds. As Piper recalls:

They told us that they would give us commissions as officers. I met with a young Naval aviation officer recruiter who was wearing his green uniform. The guy looked very sharp – tall and handsome. I decided to join the Navy. If I had to go to war, I might as well go with him.

Piper knew nothing about aviation. After graduation from college, the Navy sent him to the Guggenheim School of Aeronautics in New York City for three months of officer indoctrination and to learn aircraft engineering. He then got orders to go to Panama. It was September 1941. He traveled to Panama via Norfolk, Virginia, on an ammunition ship. He remembers, "sailing down the east coast of the U.S. all lit up and hoping the German U-boats saw the American flag."

He spent a year and a half in Panama at NAS Coco Solo, Canal Zone, working at a large aviation repair depot on PBYs – the kind Banks' younger brother, Warny, would later fly in. Piper recalls, "I got bored in Panama and saw an ALNAV (all Navy) message seeking an Engineering Officer volunteer to be part of a new VC squadron to be formed in Seattle. I volunteered and was assigned to VC-66 as Maintenance Officer." Piper thinks he was the first officer, if not the first person, to join VC-66.

He remembers having a Chief Petty Officer as his assistant. They worked together to make sure the planes were flyable and maintained. When they were aboard ship, his squadron mechanics worked with the men from the ship to keep the planes flying. He recalls, "My main job was talking to the pilots when they landed to see if they had any mechanical problems that needed addressing. I would watch all take offs and landings. It made for long days."

When he found out that he would be going to VC-66, Piper feels that he did something "smart." He recalls:

> I talked to an old CPO with much aircraft maintenance experience and asked him what I had to know to succeed in my new job with the squadron? The Chief told me if I ever had a sudden stoppage in an aircraft engine to make sure to put in a new engine rather than to try to repair the old one because something will certainly be wrong with it and the problem will happen again.
>
> When I got to VC-66 and we were at Shelton, a new pilot made a tough landing. He experienced an engine stoppage problem. Other mechanics said it was no big deal, repaired the engine, and said it was okay to go. But I was concerned and remembered what the old Chief in Panama had said. I did not want to turn a young pilot loose with that plane.
>
> I asked the XO, Gerry Trapp, to test the plane – to take it up quickly and see what happens. Sure enough, about seven thousand feet the engine quit. Fortunately, the XO was able to make a safe dead stick landing. I was glad the XO, an experienced pilot, was flying it and not a new pilot who might have had a serious problem. I was glad it proved the point about the need to replace the engine – and nobody got hurt.

On 21 September 1943, Banks had a liberty day coming and decided to go into Seattle for a little rest and recreation (R and R). Some of the the squadron's TBMs were practicing torpedo drops in the Strait of Juan de Fuca. Ben Davis drew torpedo spotting duty – meaning he and an aircrewman had to fly around in a Piper Cub and follow the path of the dummy (inert) torpedoes once they hit the water. Ships would then pick up the torpedoes for re-use.

Since neither Banks nor Stoops was around, Davis took another enlisted man with him. Banks recalls, "The word later was that during a lull in the training, Davis let the aircrewman fly the plane." In any case, the little plane stalled, went into a spin from which Davis could not recover, and crashed into the water. The plane sank quickly. The aircrewman was able to get out and swim to safety. Davis could not. His body was never recovered. The aircrewman was re-assigned to another squadron.

Davis was well liked. His death was a shock to the young squadron – and in particular to Banks and Stoops who were "devastated." Banks recalls:

> We wrote a letter of condolence to his parents. The squadron arranged a special TBF flight over the crash site for us. As we flew over, we drank a toast to the man who in a short period of time had not only gained our respect as a pilot, but also as a friend. In final commemoration of the good times we had with Ben, we poured a beer over the crash site.

There was little time for mourning Davis. The war in the Pacific was hot. Within little more than a month, American forces would invade Bougainville and Tarawa. Other operations were being planned. Squadron training had to stay on schedule.

On 10 October 1943, Banks and Stoops were called to the CO's office. When they arrived they were introduced to ENS Franklin T. "Steve" Stephens. Stephens had been assigned as their replacement pilot. He was twenty years old. As Banks recalls, "He was a long, lanky, drink of water." Stephens was from Topeka, Kansas, and fresh out of the pilot training pipeline. He had been thrust into a very tough spot – coming in as a new, unknown, and unproven guy to replace a very well liked fellow. As it turns out, Stephens was more than up to the challenge. As Banks tells it, "He turned out to be a great pilot, a better friend, and a truly trusted member of our team." Banks had gotten lucky again.

Stephens was born 23 October 1922. He was exactly six months older than Banks. At twenty, he would be the youngest pilot in the squadron. And with Banks and Stoops, they may have been the youngest TBM crew.

Stephens did his freshman year of college at Kansas State University. He had been in the ROTC program there. For his sophomore year, he stayed home and went to Washburn Municipal University. To pay for school, as he recalls, "I worked in the summer on the college 'paint gang' painting all of the buildings on campus. I earned 50 cents an hour – 25 cents of which went toward tuition."

While in college, Stephens joined the Civilian Pilot Training Program (CPTP). To do so, he had to agree to join either the Army Air Force or the Navy – which was okay with him – since as he advises, "I did not want to march with the Army. Everyone knew war was coming and we would be drafted."

The CPTP was started in 1938 to train civilians as pilots for the military in case war broke out. The goal was ambitious – to train 20,000 pilots a year. The goal was met and then some. Over 1100 colleges and over 1400 civilian flight schools eventually had CPT programs. From 1939 to 1944, the CPTP trained 435,000 pilots. The program was a huge success.

Stephens recalls that once the war started, "My buddy and I went to the Army Air Force enlistment office with our private pilot licenses, but the recruiter was not interested – so we went to the Navy recruiter who welcomed us. And the rest is history."

The Army's loss was a big gain for the Navy. The Navy wanted pilots – especially ones who already had some experience. They could get through the normal eighteen month training pipeline quicker and thus, to the Fleet sooner. At the start of the war, the Navy was graduating 600 pilots a month from flight training, but that was not enough. Later in the war, the number rose to 2,000 a month. It was an immense operation.

After completing pre-flight school at St. Mary's College, Moraga, California – where the new aviation cadets concentrated on physical training, learning about the Navy, and ground school subjects, Stephens did his primary flight training in Norman, Oklahoma from January to 1 March 1943. Banks' and Stephens' time in Norman overlapped some, but that was before they knew each other. Primary training was usually the first time a cadet got in a plane so there was a lot to learn. But because of his prior civilian flying experience, Stephens' primary training was condensed from four months to two and his required flying hours from sixty to twenty.

The next stop was Corpus Christi, Texas for intermediate training which included instrument, formation, air tactics, and night flying instruction and practice – much of which was done in SNJs. In ground school, significant time was devoted to survival training – including how to ditch a plane, getting out of cockpits underwater, and using life rafts and other survival equipment. After completion of intermediate training in June 1943, Stephens was commissioned an Ensign and awarded his Wings of Gold.

After getting his wings, Stephens was allowed to submit his preference card ("dream sheet") for the aircraft type that he would like to fly. On advice from an instructor, he made his first choice multi-engine planes – which Stephens soon felt was a "mistake." He got his choice, but after thinking about it, he changed his mind and swapped with a fellow who had been assigned to TBFs, but wanted multi-engine. Stephens now had the TBF assignment and was off to advanced TBF operational training at NAS Jacksonville, Florida to learn how to fly the Avenger.

Naval Aviation News in a 15 July 1944 article entitled "In Operational Training Pilots Learn Fleet Teamwork Tactics," described the job of a TBF pilot:

> First of all, the pilot of a torpedo bomber must be able to fly his plane. But he must be able to do much more. His primary job is to complete his mission. After that he must get back to his carrier. As the skipper of an expensive and valuable unit of the U.S. Navy, he has heavy responsibilities to the Fleet. He also has heavy responsibilities to his aircrewmen. The Avenger, pilots will tell you, is an honest plane with no tricks, but it is big and rugged and takes flying. And the pilot must not only be able to fly, he must be able to fly so that he plants his bombs and torpedoes where they aren't wasted. He must be an expert flying artilleryman. This requires skill, timing and a cool and calculating eye.

In TBF operational training ground school, Stephens and the other student pilots covered a whole lot - including: air combat, communications, bombing, radar, navigation, instruments, engineering, gunnery, recognition of planes and ships, and fleet operations. They also practiced instrument flying in the Link trainer. Their instructors were combat experienced Fleet pilots.

During training flights, the student pilots became familiar with the plane, practiced field carrier landings – the deck of a carrier simulated on a runway, practiced formation flying, and practiced day and night navigation with or without instruments. They also practiced ordnance delivery – torpedo attacks; high altitude, glide, and skip bombing; and gunnery runs. It was an intense and ambitious program. Stephens completed it in early October 1943, and was assigned to VC-66. But before reporting to the squadron, he had to demonstrate that he could actually take off and land on an aircraft carrier at sea – the final test for a new Navy pilot. He was sent to a somewhat unusual place – Lake Michigan near Chicago, to do his carrier qualification aboard a somewhat unique ship - the USS WOLVERINE (IX-64).

The WOLVERINE was a vintage 1913 side paddle wheel, coal burning carrier. It had been a Great Lakes excursion steamer before the Navy acquired it in its desperation to find ships when the war started. She was fitted with a 550 foot flight deck and converted into a training carrier. She was commissioned in Buffalo in August 1942 – shortly before Banks enlisted. It is likely that if he had gone down to the Buffalo waterfront at the time, he would have seen this unusual ship. But the old ship did her new job well. From 1943 to 1945, approximately 15,000 new carrier pilots qualified aboard WOLVERINE and her sister converted side wheeler, SABLE.

After Stephens completed his carrier qualification, he set out to join VC-66 on the West Coast. He got on a train in Chicago heading to San Diego. It took four days to get there. In San Diego, he got on another train heading to Seattle. It took three days to get there. When he finally arrived in Seattle, Stephens boarded a bus to join the squadron in Shelton. He recalls, "I felt like I had been traveling forever by the time I got to VC-66!"

Stephens got his relationship with Banks and Stoops off on the right foot by inviting them to meet him off base at a bar "to get to know each other and to discuss their new alliance." According to Banks, "Stephens wanted to know what we had done with Davis – the whole bit – procedures and peculiarities. He was amused at the coordinated weigh-ins and assured us that he would remain thin to keep the team together. He told us what he expected from his aircrewmen and we told him what we expected from our pilot." They discussed their backgrounds – previous training and experiences. They all agreed that the goal was to be an "efficient, knowledgeable, and number one flight crew." Banks and Stoops felt comfortable with Stephens. In short and in Navy terms, they liked "the cut of his jib."

In practice, Stephens was an excellent flight crew leader. He was a stickler for detail – making Banks and Stoops learn every part of the aircraft. They quizzed each other. You never knew what you would have to do in an emergency situation. It paid to be prepared. Stephens kept his crew informed – which they appreciated. He instructed them on his role and they felt they always knew as much about a mission as he did.

On 31 October 1943, the squadron detached from NAAS Shelton and started to work its way down the California coast. They were sent next to NAAS, Holtville, California for operational training - including night flying, gunnery, navigation, instrument flying, and skip bombing. Squadron personnel and gear were moved by train and the planes by ferry. Stephens recalls having to take the train from Shelton to Holtville. It was another three day train ride. He was feeling like he was spending more time on trains than he was flying.

Holtville, California was a big change from Shelton, Washington. Holtville is in the Imperial Valley, 115 miles east of San Diego on the border with Mexico. Instead of the damp, lush, and green of the Pacific Northwest, the men of VC-66 were now refining their flying and combat skills in the dry, barren, and brown of the California desert where summer temperatures averaged over one hundred degrees. But in spite of the heat, the flying weather was outstanding – 360 days a year of clear skies. It doesn't get much better. The squadrons training at Holtville were able to make good use of the two 4,500 by 200 feet runways. The desolate area around the base provided good space for gunnery and bombing practice, and skip bombing could be practiced in the Salton Sea - which was also good for practicing night flying. Charlie Edwards recalls, "Night flying over the Salton Sea turned day into night for us. Again, at dawn we would hunt doves and duck."

In addition to the serious training that was accomplished in southern California, Banks remembers some lighter times – such as flying over Catalina Island and watching the goats scatter. He also recalls going to the USO's Hollywood Canteen in Los Angeles and seeing movie stars - including two time Academy Award winner Bette Davis. Davis was thirty five years old at the time and the Julia Roberts of her day.

The civilians treated the Sailors well on liberty. The Navy enlisted men were easy to identify since they always had to be in uniform. One kind lady who lived in Hollywood, Alice Ignoff, used her spare time and spending money "to take pictures of the boys of all branches" of the services. She would gather them in small groups as she found them on liberty in Hollywood and take their photo. She would then send a copy of the photo to their "loving folks back home." As of March 1944, she had sent photos to approximately three thousand families in all forty-eight states and several countries.

Banks remembers one particular restaurant owner in Los Angeles. "He allowed Sailors to sleep in his booths after the place closed for the night." Banks thinks the fellow's son was a Sailor. Banks recalls, "We would sometimes get to L.A. and back by loading into a TBF and flying. The TBFs were big planes and several men could be put in the plane's belly for the trip." It was some good additional flight time for the pilots and a good morale boost for everyone involved. VC-66 Avenger pilot, ENS Otha J. "Bud" Clark, from Albuquerque, New Mexico advises, however, that you had to be careful how many men you tried to get into one of the planes. Cramming too many in could cause a problem in getting it off the ground. He recalls:

> Once while we were at Holtville, I took a cross-country flight from there to Albuquerque. Several crewmen wanted to go. I took off with 3 or 4 men in the belly, 1 in the turret, and 1 or 2 in the space between the turret and the pilot. The plane was extremely tail-heavy on take off and I sweated it out. I decided I wouldn't repeat that mistake.

On the other hand, Joe Mussatto, in the April 2008 edition of his *VC-66 (T-2) Newsletter*, tells of the time that fellow VC-66 (T-2) pilot, Wellington Smith, crowded "17 pilots in his TBM's crew area" for a short flight from Holtville to El Centro. And they made it. That may be a record for the number of men that could be squeezed into a TBM. Of note is the fact that according to Joe, "Only two of the original group flew back with him (Smith)." The others no doubt found a somewhat less crowded means to get back to Holtville.

As to the airborne liberty trips to L.A., Banks notes, "A valuable discovery was made on one of the return trips. If you sucked in oxygen from the plane's oxygen masks, it helped with hangovers. After that, it was not unusual for the planes to land with little oxygen left. In each plane, one of the pilots would be picked as the 'designated pilot' for the trip back to the base."

On 21 November, after finishing their training at Holtville, the squadron reported to NAAS Brown Field, Otay Mesa, California for completion of the training syllabus and for making final preparations to go to sea.

Otay Mesa is near Chula Vista approximately sixteen miles southeast of San Diego. It is five miles from the coast and thus, has less ocean fog and as a result, fewer reduced flying hours than other San Diego air fields. The station had only been in commission since March 1943, but with its three runways ranging from 3500 to 6000 feet it was already a key composite squadron training facility. Among other things, the squadron practiced attacks on ships at sea, catapult launches, and arrested landings. And by the time VC-66 had arrived, two Link instrument flight simulator trainers and an aircraft recognition training building had been added to the training facilities. Again, the importance of recognition training was stressed.

During the time at Brown Field, Banks was advanced in rate to Aviation Metalsmith Second Class (AM2c) (pay grade E-5 and equivalent to a Sergeant in the Army and Marine Corps). In addition to a little additional seniority, he appreciated the pay raise from $78 per month to $96 per month. He was also drawing monthly flight pay equal to fifty percent of his monthly base pay.

Advancement for enlisted men was based not only on time in service, but also performance evaluations, supervisor's recommendation, and passing an exam. In Banks' case, the exam was for the Aviation Metalsmith rating, not gunner – which made it tougher since he was not working as a metalsmith. As their immediate supervisor, Stephens was appointed to administer Banks' and Stoops' advancement exams. Banks remembers, "Stephens was tough. He knew our strengths and weaknesses - and he made sure we knew our stuff." Banks recalls one time asking Stephens for some assistance interpreting a question, but "Stephens would not budge."

By now, as a result of progressing through the rigors of the training regimen, some pretty strong bonding was taking place among the men of VC-66. Banks became close friends and spent a lot of liberty time with Aviation Ordnanceman Second Class Russell P. "Russ" Jensen from Medford, Oregon, and Aviation Machinist's Mate Third Class Robert L. "Bob" Keough. Keough was from Colville, Washington, and was newly married. He had washed out of pilot training because of his height. He was too short. His feet fell out of the plane's pedal loops when it was upside down.

The three shipmates spent all of their spare time together. Stoops had his own buddies with whom he spent his liberty time - as did Stephens. In fact, the Navy discouraged officers and enlisted men from "fraternizing" on liberty.

Banks recalls a fellow they called "Pop" – the oldest enlisted man in the squadron. He was a thirty year old southerner who used to infuriate the younger guys by being very neat and "squared away." As a result of his age and the fact that he was used by the Chiefs as an example for the younger Sailors – which they did not appreciate, "Pop" became somewhat of a loner. Banks remembers that one time when Pop was off on liberty, "We glued his bunk sheets. He never said a word."

In early December 1943, after successfully completing their training syllabus, the squadron detached from NAAS Brown Field and reported to NAS, San Diego, California for further assignment.

NAS San Diego was located on Coronado between San Diego Bay and the Pacific Ocean. It was one of the Navy's biggest and busiest air stations. When VC-66 was there, the training command was in full operation. With the world's largest paved landing area, the station logged an average of 1400 – 1800 takeoffs and landings per day. On any given day, it was home to an average of 1200 aircraft. It also had large piers where the aircraft carriers could tie up. During the war, an estimated 4,000 pilots and 16,000 enlisted gunners trained there. Bud Clark remembers training in San Diego, "NAS San Diego, called North Island, had a circular landing area. With many planes landing it was sometimes a little hairy making sure that we were on parallel paths." VC-66, however, was not to remain in San Diego for very long.

VC-66 TBF/TBM pilots, August 1943. Front row from left: William A. Bennett (died while serving with VC-66), Ben E. Davis (died while serving with VC-66), Guy B. Catterton, Austin H. Kiplinger, and Robert A. Weaver. Back row from left: Joe P. Klaus, Otha J. Clark, Joseph S. Trichel, Francis J.M. McCabe (died while serving with VC-66), Raymond H. Traynor, James O. Mayo, and Joseph N. Polski. (Official U.S. Navy Photograph courtesy D.A. Banks collection)

VC-66's William H. Piper (on left) and Albert J. Mayer (on right). (Official U.S. Navy Photograph courtesy W.D. Cope)

VC-66's Franklin T. Stephens in TBF cockpit. (Official U.S. Navy Photograph courtesy D.A. Banks collection)

6

To the Carriers

On 8 December 1943, the squadron went to sea for the first time as they embarked aboard the USS MANILA BAY (CVE-61) in San Diego for carrier qualifications. When the pilots were qualifying, the aircrewmen would not be in the planes, but instead, according to Banks, "We would be lined up on the carrier's catwalks rooting – and praying for our pilots – sometimes placing a bet on which of the three landing wires he would hook with the plane's tailhook." And Bud Clark recalls:

> After our VC-66 TBM pilots had completed our carrier landing qualifications we went to the carrier catwalk to watch a group of Marine pilots qualify in F4U Corsairs. It was quite a show, with many wave-offs. The F4U had a long nose with limited forward visibility on approach. Forward visibility in the TBM was very good on approach.

The time aboard MANILLA BAY demonstrated the danger involved in carrier landings as a plane from another squadron went over the side of the ship.

MANILLA BAY was the first of several escort or so-called "jeep" carriers that VC-66 would operate from during the next year. Escort carriers were designated by the letters "CVE." Not one of them existed before the war, but during it American industry was able to turn out eighty-six. Several of the early ones used converted merchant ship hulls to speed construction. Thus, on the average, two CVEs were built every month of the war. It was an amazing accomplishment. And the effort was worth it. The little carriers proved to be very versatile. Their original intended purpose was to act as anti-submarine platforms and to escort convoys, but as the war progressed they took on additional roles and did them well – as when they were organized into Task Groups to provide air support for amphibious invasions.

The CVEs won Fleet Admiral Nimitz's respect and gratitude. In a 24 September 1945 post-war letter to their crews, he wrote:

> …the escort carriers of the Pacific Fleet bore a heavy responsibility for the safety of our beachheads and the air support of our forces ashore during the critical days after the landings. To the officers and men who made such success possible, I send a hearty "Well done."

It was a nice "atta boy" from the big boss.

Compared to twenty-first century aircraft carriers, the CVEs were small. The typical CVE was about 500 feet long with a flight deck of about 450 feet in length and about 80 feet wide. They had one aircraft launching catapult. With a full load, they displaced about 10,000 tons. They had an 860 man crew and carried one 60 man squadron with its approximately 25 aircraft. CVEs burned oil and were steam propelled. Their top speed was about 20 knots. Their main armament was one or two 5 inch guns and approximately thirty 40mm and 20mm guns.

By comparison, the late twentieth century carrier named after Fleet Admiral Nimitz - the nuclear powered USS NIMITZ (CVN-68) - and her modern sister carriers are 1,092 feet long with a flight deck width of 252 feet and four catapults. With a full load, NIMITZ class carriers displace about 97,000 tons. They have crews of 3,200 (men and women) with an additional 2,480 people when an air wing is on board with its 85 aircraft. Top speed is 30 plus knots (34.5 plus miles per hour). Main armament is two or three missile launchers and three 20mm Phalanx close in weapons systems. In short, the CVNs are big, fast ships with large crews. The CVEs were small ships with relatively small crews who had a big job which they did magnificently.

While the CVEs had one straight, short deck on which to launch and land aircraft, the carriers of the early twenty-first century are not only twice as long and twice as wide as a CVE, but also have a side angled flight deck. This angled deck allows landing aircraft that miss the arresting cables to go to full power and take off again – hence the nickname "bolters." If a landing plane's tailhook missed the arresting cable on a CVE, there was no place to go but straight ahead into the emergency wire barriers that were set up on the flight deck to protect the other aircraft likely to be parked there. It was a dangerous – and not uncommon occurrence even for good pilots.

To put a 450 feet by 80 feet CVE flight deck in perspective, the shortest runway at Washington's Dulles International Airport is 10,000 feet long and 150 feet wide, and the shortest runway at Reagan National Airport at the time it was built in 1941 for propeller aircraft, was 4100 feet long. Today, it is 4911 feet. 450 feet by 80 feet was not a lot of room to operate - particularly when there were other planes on the deck. There was little to no margin for error.

Among papers that Banks kept from his war experience, are four pages (23-26) that were removed from what looks to have been an official Navy manual circa 1943. The manual apparently was meant to provide an introduction to life aboard an aircraft carrier for Sailors who would be spending time on one. Page 26 contains a description of how the arresting gear and emergency crash barrier were set up on the flight deck:

> Running across the deck, at spaced intervals, is a series of wire cables. This is the arresting gear. Its crew stands in the catwalks and, by means of levers, raises the gear on "yielding elements," little pieces of pipe that come out of the deck and elevate the arresting wires approximately 6 to 9 inches to catch the plane's hook. Collapsible stanchions, 5 feet high, emerge from the side of the deck forward. Between the stanchions, across the width of the deck, run two heavy cables, which are held into position above the deck by means of short, small cables running from the top of the stanchions and attached to the heavier cables by clamps and shear pins. These are the barriers. They are resilient and stretch gradually enough to stop a plane in full flight with comparatively little damage.

"Little damage" – easy for the authors of the manual to say. Even with an outstanding pilot like Stephens, Banks recalls always being nervous before landing on a carrier. Fear of the tailhook missing the arresting cable and the plane then hitting the barrier was one thing – Stephens recalls doing it once and the plane tipping forward and "the air boss being upset" - but wave offs by the Landing Signal Officer (LSO) were also hard because "you didn't know if the plane had enough power to get airborne again." As to LSOs, Bud Clark observes:

> The LSO was a key man. He not only could judge if a pilot on landing approach was too high or too low, or too fast or too slow, but also whether the pitch of the deck would be timed to facilitate a safe landing. Pilots appreciated a good, experienced LSO.

In the article, "Hold-Off Barrier Crashes" in the 1 October 1945 issue of *Naval Aviation News*, tips on avoiding barrier crashes are presented, but the piece goes on to say, "Admittedly, it takes some pretty fancy piloting, coupled with keen depth perception, to fly down to the deck without diving, and to get and hold the tail down without floating."

Landing on a carrier at night was even more difficult. In those days, they did not have all of the sophisticated lighting and homing gear now used by the Navy. Banks describes it as "sheer terror!" Stephens describes it as being "very hard." Radio silence was often required. There was a coded homing beacon, but it had a "real range of about five miles vice the twenty that it was supposed to have." Stephens recalls the joke of the pilots being, "If you could not find the carrier, look under the nearest rain storm."

Thus, landing on a CVE was a challenge – especially after returning from a three or four hour mission during which people were trying to kill you, you were tired, your plane might be shot up, visibility was poor, and the short flight deck was pitching and rolling because of the sea and winds. And each CVE had its own peculiarities. Some rolled more than others – especially those that were built on merchant ship hulls. And some of the planes had their own peculiarities. The FM-2s had a tailhook that moved or flopped around after it was extended for landing. The movement made "hooking" the arresting cable even more of a challenge.

VC-66 TBM pilot, ENS Edward F. "Kay" Keyser from Philadelphia, Pennsylvania, also remembers the challenge of landing on CVEs:

> Regarding the numerous landing mishaps – the pilots adapted to dealing with a no wind and reduced ship's speed of 17 knots. However, the problem involving tailhooks was another matter. To extend or retract the hook, the pilot turned on a switch. A light on the instrument panel would remain lit while the hook was traveling to the down or up position. It would then turn off. For whatever reason, probably corrosion from exposure to the salt water, the hook failed to locate in the correct locked position even though the light turned off. If the hook caught an arresting wire in this unlocked position, it would pull out. If it missed and eventually bounced into proper position it could engage a wire further up the deck. In either case, the aircraft would end up hitting the barrier or going over it. Some of our senior pilots were caught up in this dilemma until we resolved it.

Given all of the above, it is no wonder that barrier crashes were not uncommon. VC-66 radioman, Bob Kennon, recalls being in three of them. The real wonder is that more pilots, aircrewmen, and flight deck personnel were not killed or seriously injured – which is not to say that there were not plenty of bad crashes. In one of them, another VC-66 radioman, Aviation Radioman Second Class Charles R. "Chaz" Jones from Granite City, Illinois, split his head open. According to Jones' wife, "The medical personnel treating him were short of supplies and had to give him 'torpedo juice' (grade A alcohol drained from torpedoes) to quell the pain." Jones died in 1999 from severe Parkinson's disease. His wife advises, "The Doctors think it may have been in some way brought about by the injury he suffered while landing on the carrier."

While landing always had the potential for disaster, taking off from the short deck of a CVE was also stressful and potentially hazardous. VC-66 turret gunner Aviation Machinist's Mate Second Class James Gander from Soldier's Grove, Wisconsin, recalls that when a TBM was fully loaded, "We had to be catapulted off the flight deck. We could not do a fly away. The catapult was only forty-five long. We would come off the catapult at ninety knots – barely flying speed. We would dip down when we left the deck until we got our flight speed up."

And VC-66 fighter pilot, ENS W. DeLoach "Bubbles" Cope (Cope advises his nickname, "Bubbles," came from his fondness for champagne while on liberty) from Hollandale, Mississippi, recalls:

> When the sea was calm and no wind, the Captain of the ship had a choice to make – use the catapult – or take chances that we could fly off. When he thought a sub might be close by we flew off. He did not want to stay on course for a long period of time to use the catapult. This was always dangerous for the pilots who flew off first. With full power and flaps when you left the deck you still were at stalling speed – so you had to let the plane settle and just a few feet above the water the air was a little heavier and you begin to pick up speed – you rolled the wheels up as fast as you could and left on the flaps until you could get enough speed to start a climb – after sufficient air speed you would raise the flaps and climb out. You could look back and see the wake in the water left by the wind from the propeller.

Cope adds that if a pilot did not understand this calm day, no catapult take off procedure and pulled the stick back too soon, he could flip over and be run over by the ship. Fellow FM pilot, Charlie Edwards, also remembers the experience of the planes "dropping" after launch – especially when there was not much head wind.

Taking off at night was worse. In a well written biographical article by Don Moore in the 8 April 2007 *Charlotte (Florida) Sun*, former VC-92 (a squadron that Banks and Stephens would serve with briefly late in the war) fighter pilot Harley Cox described one of his night launches from the USS TULAGI (CVE-72):

One of the worst experiences I had was being catapulted in the dark in the rain at 3 a.m. It was all timing. You can't see anything and neither can the guy in front of you who just flew into the night. The guy in front flies away from the carrier for so many minutes and then turns left. Then you follow him. That was scary.

Banks concurs with the scariness of night launches. "Joining up on the flight leader was quite a sweating out experience. We had to look for the exhaust stacks on the engine or after they put arresters on the stacks, we had to watch for blotting out the stars in sections of the sky." It was not easy.

Moore's article describes another "scary" launch experience Cox had during the invasion of the Philippines. As soon as he was catapulted from the TULAGI, the engine of his Wildcat died. The plane fell into the ocean right in front of the carrier. "When I went into the sea in front of the carrier, the captain turned the carrier away from me. The wake of the ship pushed me away. My plane quickly went to the bottom, and I floated around in my life raft until I was picked up a few minutes later by a DE (Destroyer Escort) that trailed the carrier for this purpose." The men who flew from the CVEs had to have nerves of steel and know what they were doing.

After finishing carrier qualifications, VC-66 detached from the MANILLA BAY on 14 December and went directly to the USS TRIPOLI – which had been commissioned just six weeks before - for a ten day shakedown cruise. The squadron thought they were joining what would be their "own" carrier. On the 16th, the squadron CO made the first ever landing aboard the TRIPOLI.

The shakedown cruise proved costly. On 23 December, there was a mid-air collision between two of the squadron's Wildcats as they were joining up. One of the pilots was able to bail out safely and was picked up by a destroyer, but the other - ENS E.B. "Deg" Degankolp, who was relatively new to VC-66, was killed. The squadron had already lost two men and they had not yet been in a combat zone. Banks realized that this flying was not just a big adventure – it was serious, dangerous business.

Its training complete, the squadron detached from the TRIPOLI on Christmas Eve 1943 and returned to NAS San Diego to spend Christmas. While happy to be off the ship for Christmas, the men of VC-66 were disappointed when they learned that the TRIPOLI was not to be their assigned carrier. Instead she was to be diverted for use as a carrier qualification ship. But VC-66 did not have to wait long for new orders. On 29 December, they detached from NAS San Diego and embarked aboard USS WHITE PLAINS (CVE-66) for transportation to the then Territory of Hawaii and the Pacific Theatre of Operations (PTO).

They were going to "America's War" as James Bradley referred to the war in the Pacific in his outstanding book about the battle of Iwo Jima - *Flags of Our Fathers* (2000). Bradley reasons that in the war in Europe, Americans had a lot of help fighting the Germans. There was a great alliance with the British, French, Canadians, Russians, and other countries that had been fighting the Germans before we ever became involved. And in fact, the Russians inflicted the most casualties on the Germans during the war while losing many millions of troops and civilians themselves. But in the Pacific, it was really America's show – and the Navy played a big role.

The only thing the squadron knew when they left San Diego was that they were going west to join an as yet unidentified carrier for a two month deployment to somewhere. There was no flying while they were aboard the WHITE PLAINS. A regiment of Marines with whom they were sharing the ship had their combat gear all over the deck and strapped down. The men of the squadron passed the time by standing security watches, resting, and trading "scuttlebutt" (gossip) about where they would go and what they would be doing during their upcoming deployment. In any case, all of the training of the last six months would now be put to good use during the new year of 1944. The squadron looked forward to it.

USS NASSAU (CVE-16) – one of several escort or so-called "jeep" carriers that VC-66 flew from – and the first that they operated from during a combat deployment. When Banks sent the photo home, he wrote a cryptic note on the back to get by the censors: "This is our ship, the one we did what we did on out here! U.S.S. Nassau. Show this to Mom, (I'll send her's soon as I can). Save this for me please." (Official U.S. Navy Photograph courtesy D.A. Banks collection)

Rear of TBM on display at NAS Jacksonville, Florida. Shows the tailhook used to catch one of the arresting cables on a carrier's flight deck during landing. VC-66 TBM pilot, Martin J. "Lucky" Stack, was instrumental in obtaining the TBM for display when he was Commanding Officer of NAS Jacksonville. (Photo: courtesy S.A. Banks)

Photo of barrier cables designed to stop an aircraft that is unsuccessful in hooking one of the arresting cables when landing. (Official U.S. Navy Photograph courtesy W.D. Cope)

VC-66 TBM on deck of USS ALTAMAHA (CVE-18) after a barrier crash. (Official U.S. Navy Photograph courtesy D.A. Banks collection)

VC-66 TBM tipped forward on deck of USS ALTAMAHA (CVE-18) after a barrier crash. (Official U.S. Navy Photograph courtesy D.A. Banks collection)

7

The Marshalls

After six days at sea, on 4 January 1944, VC-66 arrived at NAS Ford Island, Pearl Harbor, Oahu, Hawaii. The squadron detached from the WHITE PLAINS and reported aboard USS NASSAU (CVE-16) for their first combat deployment – and their first lengthy period at sea.

NASSAU had recently returned from the Gilbert Islands where she had participated in the bloody, but successful invasion of Tarawa Atoll. She was one of the early CVEs that were originally meant to be merchant ships – the so-called BOGUE class which was named after the USS BOGUE (CVE-9); but when the war started, their hulls were obtained by the Navy and converted to escort carriers.

When VC-66 reported aboard NASSAU, the squadron was composed of 31 officers (16 Wildcat pilots, 13 Avenger pilots, an Air Intelligence Officer, and an Aircraft Maintenance Officer) and 38 enlisted men (26 aircrewmen and 12 support personnel – mostly aviation maintenance checkers). LCDR Herb Bragg was still CO and LT Gerry Trapp was still XO. VC-66 was the only squadron on board NASSAU - which was normal for a CVE. Because of their small size, they could generally only accommodate one squadron.

Banks remembers life aboard ship as being, "not bad" for the squadron's enlisted men. They were berthed in "officers' country" in their own bunkroom where they had more space and bigger bunks than the enlisted men in the ship's crew. And because they were often away from the ship at unusual hours flying and were thus precluded from eating many regular meals on the mess decks with the ship's crew, they were assigned their own mess attendant. As was common in those days, he was a black Sailor.

Mess Attendant was one of the few jobs or ratings that the Navy allowed black men to hold during the war – even after one of them, Ship's Cook Third Class Doris "Dorie" Miller, was awarded a Navy Cross – second only to the Medal of Honor - for his bravery during the attack on Pearl Harbor.

At the time of the attack, Miller was assigned to the USS WEST VIRGINIA (BB-48). He was up early collecting laundry when the general quarters alarm sounded. His normal battle station had been wrecked by a torpedo, so after helping wounded shipmates to safety Miller manned a .50 caliber machine gun shooting at Japanese planes until he was ordered to abandon the sinking ship.

Miller was personally presented the Navy Cross by Admiral Nimitz who said about him, "This marks the first time in this conflict that such a high tribute has been made in the Pacific Fleet to a member of his race and I'm sure that the future will see others similarly honored for brave acts."

Miller was killed on 24 November 1943 while serving aboard the USS LISCOME BAY (CVE-56) when it was torpedoed and sunk. In 1973, the Navy named a frigate after him.

In any case, VC-66's mess attendant took good care of them – including providing "huge" sandwiches and good coffee at all hours – and the men appreciated it. The enlisted men in the ship's company did not get this kind of treatment and as a result, they were somewhat jealous of – as they called them - their "Airdale" or "Feather Merchant" passengers whom they considered to be pampered.

Banks' fellow turret gunner, James Gander, was also reasonably satisfied with life aboard ship. He does remember the flight crews' berthing compartment being in the bow of the ship right under the catapult – which made things noisy at times, but all in all, Gander states, "I can't complain."

Gander was a young guy. He enlisted when he was seventeen. He went through Boot Camp at Great Lakes, Illinois, and Machinist's Mate "A" school in Memphis, Tennessee. As he recalls, "I volunteered to fly because I was too dumb to realize it was risky." He went to gunnery school in Jacksonville, Florida and joined VC-66 when it was formed in Washington.

Life aboard ship was not bad for the squadron's pilots either. While they did not have single or even double staterooms in "officers' country" like many of the ship's officers, they did live in a junior officers' bunkroom. It served as both their sleeping and recreation area. Word has it that many a "casual" card game took place there – sometimes late into the evening. Their XO described it as, "A combination gymnasium, card room, country club, and boulevard for aimless traffic....and the scene of the squadron's greatest evenings."

If they desired, the VC-66 pilots could eat in the wardroom with the rest of the officers from ship's company. The wardroom was a more formal setting with sit down meals at designated times with food that was generally better than that served on the mess decks for the enlisted men – but not always. The difference was that the officers had to pay for their food. The enlisted men did not. A slot machine in NASSAU's wardroom helped keep the officers' mess bill down.

Charlie Edwards recalls life aboard the carrier:

> I enjoyed being aboard. Morale was good. There was little bickering or jealousy. Food was pretty good considering. Bunks were clean and poker games filled many quiet times. Some of the poker games were "high stakes." It was nice to have our flight pay. The constant presence of danger was always there and was palpable in combat conditions.

Banks remembers an incident involving the bunks in the enlisted men's bunkroom. Evidently, the leading petty officer in charge of the compartment was regularly on the guys to change their mattress covers – which were like a large white envelope or sack that fit over the bunk mattress. At one point, Stoops and his buddy Aviation Radioman Second Class Leo P. Chamberlin from Delta, Ohio, got tired of the reminders and basically said, "The hell with it." According to Banks, "They decided to sleep on the bare mattress which was mighty scratchy. They got ribbed often and much." How long this uncomfortable protest went on is not known.

One aspect of life at sea that Banks did not care for was the salt water showers. Because fresh water is limited at sea, the opportunity to take a fresh water shower was a rare luxury. And when you could take one, it had to be a "Navy shower." You turn the water on briefly to wet down. Turn it off. Wash yourself with soap. Turn the water back on to rinse off quickly. Turn it off. The shower is over. There were no long fresh water showers – known as "Hollywood showers," at sea. In place of fresh water, showers had to be with salt water - which was plentiful. As to the salt water showers, Banks recalls, "When you finished, you felt dirtier coming out than going in."

With rare exception, alcoholic beverages other than for medicinal purposes are not authorized on U.S. Navy ships – then or now. Many other Navies of the world allowed them and still do, but not the U.S. Navy.

Nonetheless, Banks recalls that on one occasion it came to the attention of the squadron's enlisted men that some of the squadron's pilots had smuggled a few bottles of beer aboard. The contraband beer was kept in a champagne bucket in the middle of the officers' bunkroom. The enlisted men's sleeping compartment was right below the officers'. Envy being what it is, one night the thirsty enlisted men decided to raid the officers' beer cache. A raiding party was formed and sent out. The raiders crawled along the deck to within about five feet of the coveted beer when suddenly they heard a series of "clicks" and the compartment lights went on. The raiders looked around. The pilots were lying in their bunks with their .38 caliber service pistols pointed at the champagne bucket. The enlisted men beat a hasty retreat.

Weapons were apparently treated a little more "casually" aboard ship during the war. There is a squadron photo that pictures the VC-66 men – many in their flight gear, grouped in four rows on the NASSAU's flight deck. Several of the men are wearing their service revolvers. And one fellow sitting in the front row on the far right has his finger stuck in the barrel of his buddy's pistol that is pointed his way.

Bob Kennon recalls another incident when some thirsty VC-66 enlisted men went to great lengths to try to obtain some alcohol aboard ship. According to Kennnon:

> We were berthed on the second deck below the hangar deck (we being the aircrewmen) and had time on our hands so we built a "still" out of a hot-plate, a bucket of water, some copper tubing and distilled "Mennon After Shave Lotion." We made about a quarter of a cup total. LT Polski (a VC-66 pilot) came down into our quarters and let us know that some of the people attending the movies on the hangar deck were becoming ill from the sweet smell. We stopped operations.

As it turns out, the VC-66 officers smuggled more than just "a few bottles of beer aboard." DeLoach Cope recalls an occasion that a number of his shipmates remember:

> We used to hide our beer in a standard Navy locker in our compartment. When we were finished with a can of beer, we could not just throw it away in a trash can to be picked up with the regular trash. Someone would see it and put us on report. We would put the empty cans in a sack and put it back in the locker until it was full. When we had a full sack of beer cans,

we would wait until late at night when lights were out on the ship and then take the sack and throw it overboard into the ocean. One time shortly after we had thrown a few sacks of cans overboard, the ship sounded the General Quarters alarm and everyone had to man his battle station. It seems that the ship's radar had picked up our sacks of cans floating behind the ship. The ship's CO thought it might be a Japanese submarine! Fortunately for us, they never did accurately identify the "contact."

When they were not flying, Banks remembers that athletic contests were a popular way to pass time at sea. Sometimes the squadron enlisted men competed against the pilots and sometimes against the ship's crew. The games were spirited.

Volleyball games were held in the flight deck elevator – which would be positioned halfway between the hanger deck and flight deck so that the ball would not go into the sea.

Touch football was played on the hanger deck. After a while, Stoops – the former college lineman - was banned from the games because of too many injuries to the pilots.

Shooting their .38 or .45 caliber pistols from the carrier's fantail was also popular - the targets being condoms that were inflated and thrown into the ocean. Banks maintains that he was quite good at this event which earned him some additional income.

Almost every night, movies would be shown on the hangar deck for the crew and in the wardroom for the officers. A good movie was a valuable commodity at sea. Ships would trade movies when they got the chance – sometimes extra incentives had to be added to the deal such as containers of ice cream – also a valuable commodity.

Banks recalls that the guys used to get a good laugh out of Hollywood war movies. "We were never allowed to 'chit chat' on the plane's intercom on flights. The Hollywood flyboys were laughed at when doing this in films. Clark Gable (of *Gone With The Wind* fame) drew real guffaws as an aircrewman gunner – and he was a captain in the movie!"

Banks and the guys may have been watching Gable in MGM's *Hell Divers* or *Test Pilot* – or they may have been watching *Combat America* – the movie Gable produced at the request of the Commanding General of the Army Air Force, Henry H. "Hap" Arnold. *Combat America* dealt with the life of an Army aerial gunner. Arnold wanted the movie made to hopefully encourage men to choose to be gunners on his bombers

To Gable's credit, he had actually enlisted in the Army in August 1942 at the age of forty-one. He entered as a private, but after completing Officer Candidate School he was commissioned as a second lieutenant. He also completed Gunnery School and then as a first lieutenant, joined the Eighth Air Force in England where he flew bombing missions over Europe as a gunner in B-17s. Some of those missions he filmed for use in *Combat America.* The Germans knew he was there and offered a bounty to their pilots if they could shoot the plane he was flying in down. When he left the Army, Gable had reached the rank of major.

Some feel that after the war, Gable's film career never got back to the heights that it was at before the war. It is interesting to note that actor John Wayne, who has come to be perceived by many as a "super-patriot," and who was six years younger than Gable, chose not to serve in the military during the war. In fact, when the Selective Service tried to classify Wayne as 1-A – which would have made him eligible for the draft, his studio – Republic, appealed and got Wayne deferred. Wayne continued to make movies during the war and his career blossomed.

Banks remembers growing a goatee when he went to sea. He thought it made him look more mature and "salty," but the CO thought otherwise and directed him to shave it off. The CO's reasoning was that the goatee would interfere with the fit of Banks' oxygen mask. Evidently Banks then made some comment about "TBMs not flying high enough to ever need their oxygen masks." The skipper was not impressed. After he shaved the goatee, Banks then attended to washing several TBMs with kerosene as the CO suggested. That concluded the goatee "discussion."

The squadron spent the 5th through the 7th of January 1944 training and doing carrier qualifications aboard NASSAU.

Early on the morning of the 5th, there was some excitement when a plane reported that an unidentified submarine crash dived eight miles dead ahead of NASSAU. The plane acting as anti-submarine patrol dropped a smoke flare where the submarine went down and dove toward the flare which was now only four thousand yards directly ahead of the carrier. NASSAU changed course to avoid the possible enemy submarine. A couple of minutes later, the submarine was reported as friendly, and NASSAU and her escorts got back to training.

The carrier test fired her guns while a TBM towed a sleeve as a target. Acting as a target tow plane was not without its hazards. Banks' younger brother, Warny, was an Aviation Electrician's Mate who sometimes flew as an aircrewman in PBY Catalina flying boats in and around Puerto Rico and Central and South America. One of their jobs was to tow target sleeves for ships doing gunnery exercises. One time a ship missed the sleeve and hit Warny's plane. The plane crashed. Fortunately the crew got out and was rescued, but for some reason Warny had his seabag on board and it went down with the PBY. As per direction from his mother, Banks obtained and sent new uniforms to Warny. Apparently Warny was stationed in a remote area where uniforms were hard to come by.

The three Banks brothers – all now in the Navy - had come up with a way to beat the military censors who would not let the troops tell where their units were located in their letters. The Banks boys devised a scheme in which they divided the world into numbered areas. They each had maps showing the areas as did Bea. In their letters, they would discretely and cleverly find a way to use the number of the area where they were at the time in an otherwise innocent context. Thus, they could let Bea and each other know where they were or had been. As far as Banks knows, neither the Navy censors nor the Japanese ever cracked the "Banks Code."

When the pre-deployment training was finished, NASSAU returned to Pearl Harbor and moored at NAS Ford Island where she and the squadron remained from 7 through 12 January. While at Ford Island, the men could watch as salvage crews blew up the hull of the USS UTAH (BB-31). The UTAH had been badly damaged during the attack on Pearl

Harbor. On the 11th, the squadron's aircraft for the deployment - fourteen FM-1s, four TBM-1s, and five TBM-1Cs - were loaded aboard.

The squadron got underway again aboard NASSAU on 13 January for more pre-deployment training. This time it was for a multi-day exercise with the ships of Task Group 52.9. The exercise involved practicing surface ship shore bombardment, amphibious landings at the Maui and Koohoolawe, Hawaii training ranges, air support, and anti-submarine patrols.

Squadron aircraft flew a lot during the exercise. In addition to flying combat air patrol (CAP), and anti-submarine patrol (ASP) missions, they practiced making dummy bombing runs and strafing runs ahead of the landing troops. The TBMs also practiced making live bomb drops while the FMs practiced strafing with live ammunition. The planes also made simulated attacks on the ships of the Task Group.

The exercise served as a good dress rehearsal for the invasions of the Japanese held islands yet to come. And while this time it was only practice, there was always danger involved. On the 14th, while two of the FMs were attempting to land on NASSAU, their tailhooks missed the arresting cables, and the planes crashed into the emergency barrier. The propellers and tail wheels of both planes were damaged, but there were no injuries to the pilots or ship's personnel.

Banks recalls a particularly unpleasant experience that almost ended his Navy service. It also reinforced for him the danger that is present on a carrier's flight deck. The plane captains – senior enlisted men who were responsible for each plane - were all in their planes warming them up for the pilots. Banks came walking out of the carrier's island and was making his way down the flight deck to his TBM for the start of a flight when he suddenly got caught up in the combined propeller wash of the planes being warmed up. As he tells it, "I went flying down the deck – feet moving quickly - out of control - being pulled toward the propellers. Luckily, I quickly thought to throw myself on the deck. By doing that, I escaped the prop wash and serious injury."

On 18 January, Task Group 52.9 concluded its training exercise and returned to Pearl Harbor. NASSAU moored at NAS Ford Island where she and the squadron remained for the next several days loading supplies and making final preparations to deploy.

At 1156, on 23 January 1944, as the Commander Naval Air Force, U.S. Pacific Fleet Band played "Aloha Oi," NASSAU with VC-66 on board got underway from Pearl Harbor heading southwest for combat operations in conjunction with the invasion of the Marshall Islands – code named "Operation Flintlock."

The Marshall Islands are approximately 2200 miles southwest from Pearl Harbor. They formed the eastern rim of the Japanese Pacific empire and were the next objective in the American Central Pacific "Island Hopping" strategy designed to secure forward operating bases in the Pacific while pushing the Japanese back - and bringing the war closer to Japan. This was the so-called "Road to Tokyo."

The Gilbert Islands had been successfully invaded a couple of months earlier in November 1943, but only after fierce and bloody fighting – especially involving Tarawa Atoll. The Marine Corps' 2nd Division took Tarawa, but at a cost of almost 3000 casualties. Out of the 4700 Japanese defenders, only 17 surrendered. The rest died fighting. It was hoped that the Americans had learned some things and that the invasion of the Marshalls would not be as hard or as costly – otherwise it was going to be a long war.

The invasion of the Marshall Islands would be the biggest American amphibious operation to date. It was under the overall command of Vice Admiral (VADM) Raymond A. Spruance, Commander Central Pacific Force – Task Force 50. NASSAU was part of the Majuro Atoll Attack Group - designated as Task Group 51.2 commanded by Rear Admiral (RADM) Harry W. Hill. Also in that Task Group were the attack transport USS CAMBRIA (APA-36); the cruiser USS PORTLAND (CA-33); the escort carrier USS NATOMA BAY (CVE-62); the destroyers USS BULLARD (DD-660), USS KIDD (DD-661), USS BLACK (DD-666), USS CHAUNCEY (DD-667), and USS KANE (DD-235); the mine sweepers USS CHANDLER (DMS-9), USS SAGE (AM-111), and USS ORACLE (AM-103); and a Landing Ship Tank (LST-482). The Task Group also carried an infantry battalion and reconnaissance company – together about 1600 troops.

En route from 23 January until 30 January, the squadron flew CAP, ASP, and training sorties for the Task Group. Training consisted of practice group attacks, bombing, strafing, and carrier launches and landings. The anti-submarine patrol missions were generally considered boring with many uneventful hours flown over the water. But again, danger was always present. On 28 January, the Task Group entered the combat zone.

On 30 January, one of the squadron's TBMs flown by ENS William A. "Ernie" Bennett from Los Angeles, California, was waved off while attempting to land on NASSAU. After the wave off, the plane turned to the left, but could not gain altitude and suddenly dived into the sea. Two destroyers raced to the scene, but the TBM and its crew went under. In addition to Bennett, turret gunner Aviation Machinist's Mate Third Class Edward J. "Ed" Hebert, and radio operator Aviation Radioman Third Class Martin T. "Lav" Lavin were lost. James Gander was good friends with Hebert. Gander recalls, "Some of my other friends in the squadron told me that the plane that crashed had a damaged rudder." Whatever the reason, it was a tough loss. The three shipmates would be missed.

31 January 1944 was D-Day for the invasion of the Marshall Islands – including Majuro Atoll. VC-66's assigned mission was to provide anti-submarine patrols in the Majuro lagoon area, fly combat air patrols, and fly strikes against targets as directed by the Commander Support Aircraft. During D-Day, the squadron flew 31 ASP and CAP sorties - 17 by the TBMs and 24 by the FMs.

Majuro Atoll was captured quickly without a lot of combat action for most of the squadron – "to our disappointment," as Banks remembers. But getting Majuro and its big lagoon - which within a couple of days would provide a fine anchorage for a big proportion of the ships of the new Pacific Fleet – carriers, battleships, cruisers, and destroyers, and smaller craft, was a major accomplishment. VC-66 felt that Majuro was the atoll that they played a big part in helping to capture and they were proud of it. Coincidentally, one of the infantry units involved at Majuro was a battalion of the 106th Infantry Regiment of the Army's 27th Infantry Division. The 27th was the federalized

New York State National Guard Division. Banks' future father-in-law, Elmer Dewey, had fought in France during World War I as a corporal in the 27th.

Also on 31 January, TBM pilots LT Guy B. "Cat" Catterton from Oakland, California, and LT Joe P. "Santa" Klaus from Duncan, Nebraska, and their aircrewmen - Aviation Ordnanceman First Class Ira W. Whitlock from Weslaco, Texas; Aviation Radioman Second Class Chamberlin; Aviation Machinist's Mate Second Class Thomas F. Yagodzinski; and Aviation Radioman Second Class Melvin E. Hawbaker from Rush City, Minnesota, gained the "distinction" of becoming the first VC-66 men to encounter Japanese anti-aircraft fire. They had been assigned to fly an air patrol to the Jaluit and Mille atolls – 300 miles round trip. They were flying at about 1500 feet approaching Jaluit minding their own business when all of a sudden they ran into heavy anti-aircraft fire. They made it back to the carrier okay, but from that point on VC-66 knew they were in a war.

Petty Officer Whitlock's being from the small southeastern Texas town of Weslaco – population of about 5,300 in 1940, means that he was likely a Weslaco High School classmate of Corporal Harlon Block, USMC. In just over a year, Block would become famous as one of the six American flagraisers on Mount Suribachi, Iwo Jima. A few days after the flag raising, Block would be killed on Iwo Jima.

While Majuro had been captured relatively easily and quickly, the fighting would continue on, over, and around the other atolls and islands in the Marshalls for days – including Kwajalein, Eniwetok, Wotje, Maloelap, Jaluit, Mili, Roi, Namur, and Arno. VC-66 would get its share of the action in support of the attacking 4th Marine Division and the Army's 7th Infantry Division. Both units were under the command of famed Marine Corps Major General Holland M. "Howlin Mad" Smith.

Before the war, Smith had worked hard to develop the concept of amphibious warfare for the Marine Corps and was now putting the concept to good use. He had led the Marines during the invasion of the Gilberts, was now leading them during the invasion of the Marshalls, and would lead them in the subsequent invasions of the Marianas, and Iwo Jima. James Bradley refers to Smith as the "the Patton of the Pacific" and says that "by early 1945 he had put together an unbroken string of victories over thousands of miles that even Patton would envy."

During the period 1 through 21 February, the squadron would fly CAP, ASP, and strike missions - as well as photographic reconnaissance, and spotting missions for the invasion forces.

Banks remembers his first combat mission well. The ordnance handlers had fused the bombs and loaded them into the plane's bomb bay using a small trailer. General purpose bombs had nose and tail fuses and became armed shortly after being dropped by the aircraft. As always, the squadron mechanics had checked the plane before the flight. But the aircrew always walked around it double checking things. It was in their best interest to do so.

Banks was responsible for checking the life raft, his parachute – and his machine gun. The .50 caliber machine gun was belt fed, had a muzzle velocity of 2800 feet per second, and a rate of fire of 700 to 850 rounds per minute. Its bullets weighed three times as much as a .30 caliber round. The .50 caliber ammunition came in cans with 400 rounds per can. For weight reasons, each TBM was only supposed to carry one can, but one can did not last all that long in a fast firing gun. And running out of ammo was not a good thing. Accordingly, Banks had acquired several extra boxes of .50 caliber ammunition - not wanting to take any chances. As he says, "I ran a "hot" gun." He also made sure that he could charge and load it – and once in the air on the way to the objective, the crew would test fire the guns.

He recalls launching from the carrier at dawn. The TBM was loaded with bombs. He recalls flying over and seeing the troops in their landing craft heading for the beach. But then since Majuro fell so quickly, after all of the build up, the day was not particularly "exciting" for the aircrews. But things would get more "exciting."

The few pages that Banks saved from the "introduction to life aboard a carrier" manual give a good description of what went on just before and during launching a dawn combat mission. Here is part of the description:

> Planes have long since been spotted in take-off sequence, like a crazy quilt-work, at the far end of the deck. The palisades are down and the long runway stretches out 400 feet into the wind. Over the huge bull horn comes the order: "Man your planes."
>
> The air whistle blasts once to wind up the starters, then twice to start engines. The squadron leader, first on the line, is "ready." Above him, in the "bird cage" on the island, the Air Control Officer hangs out the white flag, the signal to launch. In front of him stands the plane director, who signals the chockmen to pull chocks, then turns over the launching to the Flight Deck Officer.
>
> With his left hand upraised, the Flight Deck Officer instructs the pilot to "rev engines." Then estimating the roll or pitch of the deck with an experienced eye, he motions downward with a checkered pennant.
>
> The plane roars down the deck, gathering speed quickly, and disappears into the faint streaks of dawn. Rapidly now, the plane directors motion the other aircraft to the line. The Flight Deck Officer carefully controls the number of seconds between take-offs to allow the slip stream to dissipate. As each plane takes off, it turns slightly to the right to avoid the slip stream of a previous take off.
>
> So the attack is on! Deck crews relax briefly, move chocks up to the bow and prepare arresting gear and barriers for the planes' return. Gunners on the catwalk man the antiaircraft batteries, peering intently into the lightening sky. Fighters drone thousands of feet above, an umbrella of protection.
>
> It is quiet, unbelievably tense. Minutes, then an hour pass, and the first returning planes flash suddenly out of the clouds over the carrier, rendezvous, and then prepare to come aboard the tiny floating airfield, silhouetted like a thin splinter against the vastness of the blue ocean.

Flying everyday from 1 to 4 February, VC-66 had a total of 93 ASP and CAP sorties - 35 by the Avengers and 58 by the Wildcats. On 3 February, ENS William E. "Cookie"

Cook from Tupelo, Mississippi, made the 2000th landing aboard NASSAU. He had no idea of what he had done until the ship's CO called him to the bridge to congratulate him. On 5 February, NASSAU was anchored – along with most of the new post-Pearl Harbor Pacific fleet: carriers, battleships, cruisers, destroyers, and various other ships and boats, in the newly captured Majuro lagoon. There were no flight operations.

On 6 February, the squadron was given the word that in conjunction with the impending invasion of Eniwetok Atoll on 17 February – code named "Operation Catchpole," they were to work with a squadron from the NATOMA BAY to neutralize Japanese forces and airfields on two of the other atolls still under Japanese control. Those atolls were Wotje - with its airfield on Wotje Island, and Maloelap - with its airfield on Taroa Island.

Eniwetok is 375 miles northwest of Kwajalein. Its capture was important because it would provide the Americans with another good anchorage to work from on the push west. Operation Catchpole was under the command of RADM Hill.

On the 6th, the squadron flew 34 ASP, CAP, and air support sorties - 10 by the TBMs and 24 by the FMs. Squadron planes acted as spotters for cruiser gunfire support. They also strafed Japanese planes, buildings, a boat, and the source of anti-aircraft fire coming from Taroa Island. Taroa was a major Japanese airbase. It had two runways – with a third being built, two hangars, a service apron, fuel farms, power stations, a pier for large ships, several ammunition bunkers, a large barracks area, and over three hundred buildings. It also had two radar stations and two squadrons of planes assigned.

In order to confuse the Japanese radar operators, VC-66 became one of the first squadrons to use chaff – small strips of aluminum that were thrown out the side door of the TBMs as they were approaching a target. Banks remembers, "We called it 'windows.' It was about a six foot long box with stacks of aluminum foil stapled together at one end; and when thrown out of the plane, it became a fan. We would toss it out the side door." And as far as he could tell, "it seemed to work." It would show up on radar as multiple contacts that would be confused as incoming aircraft. The Japanese would not know how many aircraft were approaching or from what direction.

Notwithstanding the Japanese radar, aircraft, and the many coastal defense and anti-aircraft guns surrounding the island, Taroa was to be hit hard and often. In addition to the pounding it took from the air and sea, all of its supply lines were cut off. Of the approximately 3000 Japanese troops on the island, about 1000 survived. Many starved to death.

During air operations on 7 February, VC-66 flew 31 ASP, CAP, and air support sorties - 11 by the TBMs and 20 by the FMs. This time Wotje Island was one of the targets. The TBMs dropped 350 pound bombs there. Wotje Atoll is made up of seventy-two small islands with Wotje Island being the largest – a thousand yards wide and three thousand yards long. Like Taroa Island, Wotje Island was a major airbase for the Japanese. And while like Taroa it would not be invaded, Wotje was to be bombed, strafed, and shelled regularly. The Wotje airfield had two runways, two hangars, a service apron, seaplane ramp, large pier, and hundreds of wooden buildings. Wotje was defended by coastal defense batteries, some ninety anti-aircraft guns, a radar unit, and up to two squadrons of aircraft. About 3300 Japanese troops were stationed on Wotje – and as on Taroa, only about a third of them would survive the fighting and lack of food.

Squadron planes also went back to Taroa on the 7th. They dropped seventeen 500 pound bombs on runways and buildings; four 1000 pound bombs on a runway; and thirty-two 100 pound bombs on runways, anti-aircraft positions, and barracks areas. They also strafed buildings serving as the source of anti-aircraft fire coming from both Wotje and Taroa. A radio shack and other buildings were also strafed. In addition to the bombs dropped, 11,200 rounds of .50 caliber ammunition were expended. The squadron reported considerable damage to its targets.

While inflicting considerable damage on the 7th, the squadron suffered some damage of its own. A couple of planes were hit by anti-aircraft fire, but were able to make it back to the carrier. ENS John "Andy" McNeeland from Bridgewater, Massachusetts, had a hole in the propeller of his Wildcat when he landed; while ENS Austin H. "Kip" Kiplinger from Bethesda, Maryland, with his aircrewmen Aviation Machinist's Mate Second Class Joe Fernandez from Sunnyvale, California, and Aviation Radioman Second Class Donald R. "Don" Swenson from St. Paul, Minnesota, brought back an Avenger that had taken a hit in the left wing and another in the bomb bay.

ENS Sam Takis from St. Louis, Missouri, was not as "lucky." His FM was hit in the engine over Taroa while he was attacking an anti-aircraft battery. But Takis was able to crash land in the lagoon a mile or two off shore. While dazed, he was able to get out of the plane, inflate his life jacket, and pull his dye marker. Fellow squadron FM pilot LT John P. "J.P." Fox recalls the situation, "We radioed the Task Force which was about one hundred miles away and the cruiser Salt Lake City (CA-25) sent a seaplane to pick him up." Fox remembers the anti-aircraft fire "as particularly heavy that morning." Thanks to what was called "a highly creditable performance" by the pilot of the float plane, Takis was rescued and in the cruiser's sick bay after spending about an hour and a half in the water. VC-66 planes flew cover while the rescue was being accomplished. As to Takis' condition, Fox remembers, "His face hit the gun sight and he was pretty well banged up. We got him back about six weeks later."

J.P. Fox was the squadron Flight Officer and like the XO, Gerry Trapp, had been a flight instructor since the start of the war at NAS Jacksonville, Florida and NAS Grosse Ile, Michigan before joining VC-66. He had earned his wings in November 1941.

Like Banks, Fox was a native of Buffalo. He lived on the Westside and went to Lafayette High School. During high school, he recalls working in a gas station weekends and summers and earning fifteen cents an hour.

After VC-66, Fox would be assigned to a unit training to fly night fighters, but the war ended before they were assigned to a carrier. After the war, he stayed in the Navy and among other things: served as Assistant Naval Attache to the American Embassy in Spain, CO of VF-123, Instructor at the Naval War College, CO of USS FORT SNELLING (LSD-32), and CO of USS INDEPENDENCE (CVA-62). He retired from active duty as a Captain (CAPT) (0-6) in 1972.

In 1996, Fox was retired and living in Florida. One day while in Pensacola, who should he accidentally bump into but old VC-66 shipmate - Sam Takis. Fox had not seen Takis since their VC-66 days. They quickly renewed their friendship and have been playing golf together weekly since. Fox recalls that Takis "had gotten out of the Navy after the war to help his father in the restaurant business in St. Louis. When the Korean

War broke out he was recalled and then stayed in the Navy as an active duty reserve pilot." After the Navy, Takis had a career in real estate in California. He now lives about twenty miles from Fox in Florida.

DeLoach Cope remembers the rescue of Takis as being "impressive – and Takis still has the scar from it."

VC-66 on the deck of USS NASSAU (CVE-16) on the way to the invasion of the Marshall Islands. Note the number of service revolvers being worn or displayed. Buddies Banks and Jensen are in the middle of the very last row wearing their flight helmets. (Official U.S. Navy Photograph courtesy D.A. Banks collection)

Part of the Marshall Islands invasion Task Force. (Photo: courtesy National Archives)

Some men work on bombs while others watch a movie on a carrier's hanger deck. (Photo: courtesy National Archives)

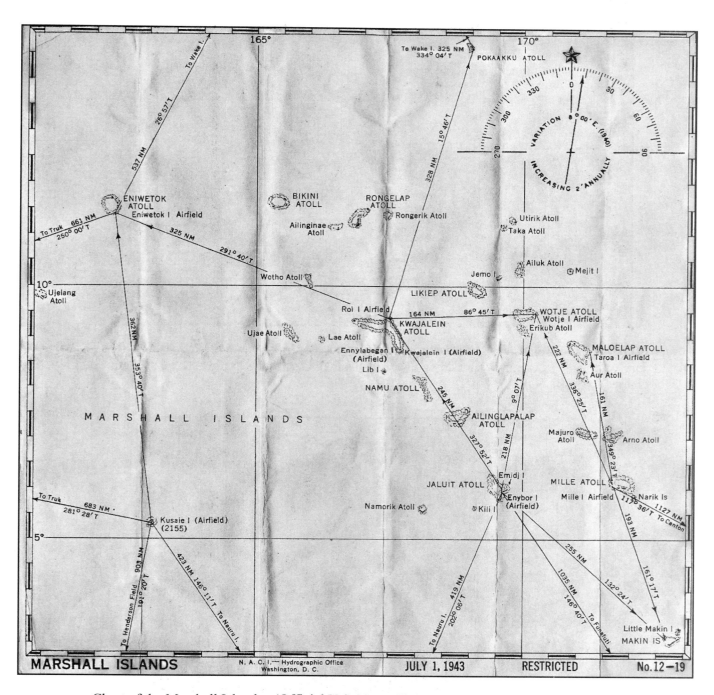

Chart of the Marshall Islands. (Official U.S. Navy Chart courtesy D.A. Banks collection)

PBY Catalina on display at NAS Jacksonville, Florida. Banks' younger brother, "Warny," survived being accidentally shot down in a Catalina that was towing a target sleeve. (Photo: courtesy S.A. Banks)

.50 caliber machine gun rounds on display at the Mighty Eighth Air Force Museum, Pooler, Georgia. (Photo: courtesy S.A. Banks)

TBMs on carrier flight deck preparing to launch for a mission. (Photo: courtesy National Archives)

8

Trouble over Wotje

During the 8th and 9th of February 1944, the squadron flew 41 ASP and CAP sorties - 25 by the TBMs and 16 by the FMs.

On 10 February, only the torpedo bombers flew. They flew 11 sorties and dropped thirteen 325 pound bombs on targets of the pilots' choice on Taroa and Wotje. Targets picked were mainly runways. The goal was to keep the enemy aircraft from using them. They also spotted targets for cruiser shore bombardment of Taroa.

Stephens, Banks, and Stoops had a memorable flight early in the morning on the 10th. They were sent to Wotje on a low level bombing and photographic reconnaissance mission. As Banks remembers it:

> We were flying at 1000 feet down one side of Wotje to get to our picture taking and bombing run start when our port (left) wing suddenly exploded after being hit by an anti-aircraft shell. It left a two foot hole in the wing. With the wing on fire and .50 caliber ammunition from the wing gun cooking off and sending tracers by the cockpit and turret, I thought we were going down.

Stephens recalls that at that moment, "I was a young pilot scared out of my wits." He was twenty-one years old. Dealing with his fear, he stayed cool. "I flew to keep the plane in the air." Being too low to bail out, and notwithstanding waves that were too high for a "safe" water landing, he had Banks and Stoops prepare for a possible ditching while he pointed the plane away from Wotje and toward an unoccupied atoll twenty miles away. His goal was "to try to get there to land on the beach and hopefully survive." Banks was thankful that they had talked about and practiced ditching many times. Stephens had made them practice dry runs on the carrier deck in case they had to ditch at sea.

Now, the twenty year old Banks began carrying out the ditching plan:

> I released the emergency turret door – which was the whole side of the turret – reached around the side of the turret and released two thumb screws on the life raft compartment cover which was slightly below and forward of the turret. I released the screws now to save time because we thought in case of a water crash Stephens would likely hit the instrument panel and be knocked unconscious. Even though the pilots were strapped in, they tended to hit the instrument panel during a crash. I would have to make my way from the turret to check on Stephens and help him out of the cockpit if necessary. Stoops would have to get out of the plane through the bottom door which was a job in itself – and make his way up to help me get Stephens in the raft. On my way to get Stephens, I was to yank the life raft out of its compartment to make sure it was out and ready for use.

Not wasting any time in getting out of the plane once it hit the water was all important because TBMs were known to sink quickly.

Stephens, Banks, and Stoops remembered what had happened to their shipmates – Bennett, Hebert, and Lavin just eleven days ago. In any event, with the raft compartment cover screws unloosened, the raft started to come out of its compartment. This was a potentially dangerous development. If it came out, it could very well fly back and hit the plane's tail doing serious damage. Banks then noticed that the raft compartment cover had already come off and wrapped around the tail restricting some side to side movement.

In the meantime, while all of this was going on, Stephens was able to regain control of the plane and the flames went out, so he turned it back toward Wotje to complete the mission. Banks recalls Stephens saying something about going back to "show those bastards they didn't knock us down." Banks further recalls that he and Stoops were not overly enthusiastic about the return to Wotje under the current conditions, but Stephens was the boss so they went back and strafed and bombed until their ammunition ran out. Stephens remembers going back. "We dropped our bombs from a reasonable altitude. I did not want to get shot again."

The raft situation, however, was not getting any better. It was a large multi-man raft filled with all kinds of survival gear which was now about half out of its compartment. Stephens directed Banks to make a line that could be used to loop over the raft and hold it braced in its compartment. Banks and Stoops commenced tearing off their oxygen mask straps and any other cords - such as those holding their parachutes in place inside the plane, and their belts to make the line. They knotted it all together and Banks went out the left side of the turret into the prop wash to try to get the makeshift line over the raft. It didn't reach.

Plan B was then implemented. Banks decided, "The only way I could keep the raft from coming completely out of its compartment was to hold onto it bracing it against its compartment wall." Thus, he hung out the side of the turret from his waist up holding onto the raft with both hands with the prop wash hitting him in the face while Stoops stood holding on to Banks' leg so that he would not be blown out. They stayed like this for the two hour flight back to the carrier. It worked. They were successful in preventing the life raft from breaking free and damaging the plane's tail.

Stephens managed to get the disabled TBM back to the NASSAU, but when they arrived and he started to make his landing approach, "I discovered that we had no hydraulic fluid. No hydraulic fluid meant landing with no flaps." Not to be deterred, Stephens made a difficult no flaps landing "on the second go round after going around once to get situated and oriented. It was something I had not practiced and something that probably was a first for the squadron." Banks got back in the turret just before the plane touched the deck.

It had been a mission to remember. Banks' view is that Stephens did a "great job in getting back to the carrier." As for Stephens, he calls Banks "the best damn gunner in the Fleet – hung out of the plane for two and a half hours holding on to the raft line." Banks recalls that when they landed, the medical officer met them and offered each a shot of medicinal brandy. The CO had given the order to "splice the main-brace" - which was one of those rare exceptions when alcohol could be consumed on Navy ships.

Banks recalls not taking the drink and "just wanting to go somewhere quiet for a while." Banks' friend and fellow turret gunner, Russ Jensen, came up to greet him right after the crippled TBM landed. It was common practice for men to be standing by waiting for their shipmates to return to the carrier after a mission – particularly if there had been a "problem." Jensen recalls, "Banks asked me if I had any smokes? I said, 'why – you don't smoke.' Banks said, 'I do now.'" And Banks continued to smoke until the mid-1950s when he suddenly quit.

Sometime after the Wotje incident, Stephens was given an Air Medal. An Air Medal could be awarded to someone who "distinguishes himself by heroic/meritorious achievement while participating in an aerial flight."

Banks – thanks to a letter sent to *The Buffalo Evening News* by fellow VC-66 "Buffalonian," J.P. Fox – was written up in an article in his hometown newspaper. The 22 March 1945 *News* article entitled "Gallantry Disclosed" described the incident in detail and mentioned "Petty Officer Banks' unusual display of gallantry." It said his ambition now was, "To walk down the main street in Tokyo."

As for news articles, Banks remembers posing one time aboard ship with another gunner for a photographer representing a now forgotten publication. The photographer had them wear their flight gear and stand by a TBM. He also had each of them drape .50 caliber ammunition belts over their shoulders. They looked very warrior like and ready for battle. Banks recalls that the rest of the guys in the squadron were quite amused by the photo shoot and saw it as an opportunity to have a little fun. As the photographer was taking the picture, the squadron guys stood behind the photographer doing all sorts of crazy things trying to make Banks smile broadly to show his missing two front teeth. He had lost them in a hard landing.

Looking back, Stephens thinks that what hit them over Wotje was something like a 40 millimeter shell that "definitely exploded on the wing – not shrapnel." He remembers seeing the tracers from anti-aircraft fire coming at them. The Japanese had opened up as the TBM began its low level run. As Stephens recalls, "We had been assigned to take pictures. We didn't expect any flak. There was not supposed to be any." So much for the accuracy of intelligence reports. Stephens also observes, "We were supposed to have one fighter escort with us, but it was not around when we got hit."

Stephens, Banks, and Stoops over the Pacific in a TBM. (Official U.S. Navy Photograph courtesy D.A. Banks collection)

Banks and a VC-66 shipmate next to a TBM. (Official U.S. Navy Photograph printed in a lost and forgotten publication: courtesy D.A. Banks collection)

9

Continuing to Pound the Marshalls

During the 11th and 12th of February, VC-66 flew 36 ASP, CAP, and air support sorties - 20 by the TBMs and 16 by the FMs. They spotted for surface ship shore bombardment of Wotje. They also dropped twelve 325 pound bombs on Taroa, and six 325 pound bombs on Wotje – mainly on runways which were the primary targets and anti-aircraft positions which were the secondary targets.

The squadron suffered additional damage from anti-aircraft fire. Charlie Edwards recalls, "I took a hit through my propeller blade and one through my right wing." He made it back to the NASSAU.

DeLoach Cope recalls a mission when a flight of VC-66 FMs flew cover for some Army B-24 Liberator bombers:

> The B-24s flew at about 21 – 22,000 feet while we could not go higher than 16 – 18,000 feet. I was flying wing for Carr and Birdsong was flying wing for Trapp. The anti-aircraft fire would explode low near us. It never made it to the B-24s. We ended up drawing fire for the Army planes. The B-24 guys got Air Medals for the mission and we never got mentioned. After the B-24s dropped their bombs, we went in and bombed and strafed. We were told to pull out at a "safe" altitude to avoid the bomb blasts – 1000 to 1500 feet or so, but I was pursuing and shooting at a target at full throttle and did not pull out until I realized I was at treetop level! It was the first time I saw Japanese troops on the ground and they were running every which way.

Given the Stephens, Banks, Stoops experience of 10 February over Wotje, Banks recalls that on their next bombing mission, things were done a little differently. "We did the bomb run, dropped the bombs, and Stephens pulled the plane up sharply." As old Navy attack pilots say, "Speed is life" and "There are old pilots and bold pilots, but no old, bold pilots."

Banks sitting in his gun turret facing backward was able to see the results of the bomb runs as the plane pulled up. He recalls admiring the fireworks on the ground caused by the bombs - but not the streaks of light of the tracer shells coming up in long arches from the anti-aircraft guns. As he tells it, "They seemed to be coming right at me. The worst part was that there was nothing I could do about it except to sit and watch them come." He admits that the first time it happened, "I was very scared." He admits that he quickly lost his "swagger" and attitude of, "I am a white scarf wearing, hot shot, gung ho, aircrew gunner." He realized there were people down there trying to kill him and his buddies – and there was not a hell of a lot that he could do about it. It was a sobering, maturing experience.

There was some sense of protection in sitting on the "hard homo" (homogenized steel) seat in the turret. The turret gunners were told it was bulletproof. Banks believed it until later when one of his shipmates was killed by an anti-aircraft round that came up through the bomb bay and entered the turret through the "hard homo" allegedly bulletproof seat.

In addition to having to watch the anti-aircraft shells come at you as you were leaving a target, Banks also did not enjoy facing backward as they made their carrier approaches and landings. It was tough to tell where they were and what was going on. "You had to have great faith in your pilot." And Banks is grateful that Stephens was one of the best.

The TBF/TBM had been the first plane to have an electric powered turret rather than a mechanical or hydraulically operated one. The turret may have been easier to operate, but it was not a very comfortable place to spend four or five hours. As Banks describes it:

> You sat on the hard homo seat. In front of your face was a two inch thick plexiglass screen that was also supposed to be bulletproof. The .50 caliber machine gun was offset to the left - next to your left ear. The controls for the gun were in a pistol grip in front of you. Occasionally, you also had a camera – a big baby, hard to get up into the turret. Sometimes you could let your legs hang down to straighten them out, but then your feet would be only inches from the radioman's head who was sitting below on his bench. The turret was a small, crowded space. A big man would not do well there.

Flying looking backward also presented a minor challenge in trying to use the traditional face of the clock system for pointing things out to the rest of the crew. The nose of the plane is the 12 o'clock position. So, for example, if something was to the plane's right and slightly behind, you would say it was at about the 5 o'clock position and high or low if it was above or below the plane. But since the turret gunner was looking backward, the clock was reversed for him. He had to do some quick mental corrections before he tried to point something out - or he could really confuse things. And confusion is not good in a combat situation.

While Banks and the other turret gunners had their challenges and "issues," Stoops and his fellow radiomen did not have an easy time of it. Former TBF/TBM pilot and retired Commander Warren Omark described the TBF radioman position in a 1 May 2006 *Navy Times* article by Robert F. Dorr:

> The radioman sat in the lower rear of the aircraft. He was on a narrow bench most of the time. It was dark, loud, and cramped down there. His job was to keep the radio in commission – though the radio was operated by the pilot – and he had a .30 caliber machine gun with a limited field of fire below and behind the aircraft.

Before he got to the Fleet, an Aviation Radioman had been to Boot Camp, Radio School, and Gunnery School. Like the pilots and turret gunners, they were all volunteers and they were well trained. Their schooling included significant training in use of the Morse code. They had to be able to receive sixteen to eighteen words a minute. They learned naval message form and phraseology. They studied electronics. They learned radio operation and maintenance and practiced it. And before graduating, they had to demonstrate that they could also communicate by semaphore flag, blinker light, and ship signal flags.

In Banks' view, "The radioman in a TBF/TBM was mainly a backup or utility position. While the pilot normally did most of the communicating, the radioman had the same radio gear as the pilot and could use it if necessary. He could also tell if the bombs were released and could man the .30 caliber rear facing machine gun." And having been trained as gunner, if something happened to the turret gunner, he could assume that position. In addition to the noise, smell, and close quarters, the radioman's tunnel area had very little armor protection. In short, it was neither a comfortable nor a safe place to be. Thus, later in the war as Japanese fighters became less of a threat, TBMs started eliminating the radioman position and flew with only a pilot and turret gunner. If necessary, the turret gunner could slide down into the tunnel and do what was needed.

The turret gunner and radioman were completely dependent on their pilot. If anything happened to their pilot or he screwed up, they were in big trouble. The enlisted aircrewmen were not trained to fly the plane. They had no access to the cockpit because of an armor plate behind the pilot's seat – although they could crawl up the "greenhouse" between the turret and cockpit and reach in and tap the pilot on the shoulder - which they did for "fun" sometimes on a long, boring flight. According to Banks, "It would startle the pilot. Payback would usually involve the pilot having some 'fun' of his own by putting the plane into a dive or doing a few dips or a wingover as the aircrewman tried to crawl back to his position." Banks also claims that on one or two occasions, "Stephens rolled the plane causing the stuff that had collected on and under the deck – solid and liquid – to come falling down."

Another aircrew "prank" that Banks recalls hearing about involved one of the aircrewman plugging the pilot's "relief" tube. There was no bathroom on a TBM. This act of sabotage may have been "fun" for the aircrewman, but not so much "fun" for the pilot. But it did relieve the boredom. As for the turret gunners and radiomen "relieving" themselves during a long flight, Banks advises that the guys got creative and "various guys used bottles, cans, and bags." He claims he was known as, "Iron Kidneys Banks" - who would go straight to the head as soon as they landed.

Banks remembers a practical joke that Stoops played on him. Their monthly flight physical was coming up and Stephens directed Banks to try to get Stoops to eat less and lose a few pounds. Again, Stoops was a big man. Banks decided to get the rest of the enlisted men in the squadron to help. As he tells it:

> We all stared at Stoops while he was eating. Stoops decided to retaliate. As my feet were hanging down in front of him during our next flight, Stoops tied the laces on my boots together making it difficult for me to get out of the plane once we got back to the carrier. Before I could get out, the plane captain started moving the plane to the side to make room on the flight deck for the next plane. He opened the turret door to check the turret and as he did so I yelled. It scared hell out of the plane captain.

If the crew had to bail out of a TBM, it was no easy thing – especially for the turret gunner. While the pilot and radioman wore their parachutes – the pilot could use it as a seat cushion, the turret gunner could not. It would not fit in the turret. In an emergency, the turret gunner would have to climb down through the bottom of the turret and cross over the plane's "belly" to get to his parachute which was hooked over the right rear door. He would have to unhook it and attach it to his harness. Once he had the chute on, he would then have to push the side door open against the prop wash and jump out. And during this time, the aircraft was not likely to be flying "straight and level."

Banks does not remember hearing about any turret gunner ever successfully bailing out of a TBF or TBM – including former President George H.W. Bush's turret gunner. Lieutenant Junior Grade (LTJG) Bush's TBM was shot down on 2 September 1944, during an attack on Chi Chi Jima. Bush was able to successfully bail out and was picked up by the submarine USS FINBACK (SS-230), but neither his gunner nor his radioman made it. Judith S. Gillies, in a 4 May 2008 piece in *The Washington Post* entitled "A Presidential Portrait," advises that while Bush was on the FINBACK, "he agonized over the fate of his gunner and radioman…" She goes on to quote Bush over sixty years later: "It still plagues me if I gave those guys enough time to get out… I think about those guys all the time.

The turret gunner's chances were better if the plane ditched in the water. It was relatively "easy" for him to get out of the turret and get into the raft that hopefully he had released. But then as seen from the Stephens, Banks, Stoops experience over Wotje on 10 February 1944, the concern had to be for the pilot. Again, the crew could not waste any time in getting out as the planes were notorious for sinking quickly.

Once they did get out and into their raft, the aircrews relied on their survival packs. They included food, knives, candy, medical items, dye markers, and a scarf with a map of the area printed on it. And not having anything similar to twenty-first century plastic ziplock bags to keep small items waterproof, they got creative and used condoms.

Banks recalls every combat mission being a source of stress and anxiety. "We were just happy to make it back to the carrier." He remembers that after a bombing and/or strafing mission, "There was no celebration, no back slapping, laughing, or joking, but rather we would seek out some solitary spot like the bow or fantail to reflect on what had happened." And it was worse when shipmates were lost. "There were empty bunks and lockers to be cleaned out with personal belongings to be packed up and sent home to families."

To take his mind off things, Banks began to spend some of his spare time drawing cartoons of the day's happenings and hanging them in the squadron ready room. After he put them up, "I made myself scarce since some were slightly 'irreverent.'" Even though he would "sign" each with what would become his future personnel logo – a script variation of his initials "dAb" - it took some time before anyone figured out the identity of the VC-66 phantom cartoonist. He also remembers spending some quiet time sitting on the forward part of the flight deck watching dolphins leaping in the carrier's bow wave.

There were no flight operations on 13 February as NASSAU was anchored in Majuro lagoon. The ship and squadron got underway again on 14 February. During flight ops on the 14th and 15th, 40 ASP, CAP, and air support sorties were flown - 28 by the TBMs and 12 by the FMs. Squadron planes spotted for cruiser shore bombardment of Wotje. They also dropped twenty-two 500 pound bombs on Wotje runways; fourteen 500 pound bombs on Taroa runways; and twelve 100 pound bombs on Taroa runways, a hanger, and apron area.

On 16 February, the squadron flew 26 ASP, CAP, and air support sorties - 11 by the TBMs and 15 by the FMs. Seven 500 pound bombs were dropped on Wotje and Taroa runways; three 1000 pound bombs on Taroa runways; eight 100 pound bombs and eight incendiary clusters on anti-aircraft positions and buildings on Taroa; and thirteen 100 pound bombs on gun positions, buildings, and an ammunition dump on Wotje – which blew up. 6,800 rounds of .50 caliber ammunition were used to shoot up enemy gun positions and installations on Taroa lagoon. Two Japanese boats were also strafed and seriously damaged.

From the 17th through the 19th, 58 ASP, CAP, air support, and gunnery practice sorties were flown - 38 by the TBMs and 20 by the FMs. 2850 rounds of .50 caliber ammunition were expended strafing a Japanese ship in Wotje lagoon and a large boat that had beached at Ollot Island, Maloelap Atoll.

20 and 21 February 1944 were the squadron's last two days of combat operations in conjunction with the invasion of the Marshalls. They again flew ASP, CAP, and air support sorties – 10 by the TBMs and 17 by the FMs. They spotted for a battleship shore bombardment of Taroa; shot up gun positions and buildings on Taroa; strafed targets on Ethel Island, Maloelap Atoll; and dropped incendiary clusters on building areas on Wotje and Taroa with the desired result of starting fires. They also dropped seven 100 pound bombs on Wotje gun positions and ammunition dumps and eight 100 pound bombs on a Taroa ammunition dump. In addition to the bombs, 11,060 rounds of .50 caliber ammunition were fired in the strafing runs.

During the Marshalls campaign, the men of VC-66 flew a total of twenty-three days of combat missions as they supported the invasion of Majuro and Arno atolls; protected the fleet anchorage in Majuro lagoon; attacked and neutralized Japanese airfields on Wotje and Taroa islands in conjunction with the invasions of Kwajalein and Eniwetok atolls; and conducted long range patrols to Jaluit and Mili atolls spotting enemy installations for shore bombardment by surface ships. The squadron was commended several times for its work. During this period, VC-66 flew 1478 combat hours during 487 combat flights.

The invasion of the Marshall Islands was a success. While several hundred Marines and Army troops died in sharp fighting during the various landings, overall there were fewer American casualties than were suffered during the earlier invasion of the Gilberts. As a result of the Marshalls campaign, the Americans demonstrated that they had learned valuable lessons in amphibious tactics, firepower, and mobility; Japanese bases and forces in the area were battered; the Japanese perimeter had been pushed back hundreds of miles closer to Japan; and the American Navy now had use of the Marshalls for advance bases to push further west.

U.S. 7th Division troops attack a Japanese block house during the Marshall Islands invasion. (Photo: courtesy National Archives)

A Marine returns to a ship for a break "after two days and nights of Hell on the beach of Eniwetok in the Marshall Islands." (Photo: courtesy National Archives)

A Japanese plane goes down in flames while attacking the U.S. Marshall Islands invasion Task Force. (Photo: courtesy National Archives)

Kwajalein, Marshall Islands after its capture. (Photo: courtesy National Archives)

10

Back to Pearl Harbor

On 22 February, there were no flight operations as NASSAU was at anchor in Majuro Lagoon. And on 23 February, Eniwetok Atoll now under American control was declared secured. Also on the 23rd, all VC-66 aircraft that were still operational – only six TBMs and ten FMs - were transferred from the NASSAU to the NATOMA BAY for use by another squadron. Damaged planes were retained aboard NASSAU for return to Pearl Harbor.

Before getting underway, seventeen Japanese prisoners of war were brought aboard NASSAU to be taken to Hawaii. This was a somewhat unusual event. Given the ferocity of the fighting in the Pacific war, there were relatively few POWs taken by either side. The Japanese considered it dishonorable to surrender and if they did so, it was likely that even their families would not forgive them.

Stephen Ambrose - probably America's leading military historian and my personal favorite, points out the difference between the war in Europe and the war in the Pacific in his excellent book *To America – Personal Reflections of an Historian* (2002): "When they ran out of ammunition, German squads would surrender. Not the Japanese. They fought with hand grenades, bayonets, even their teeth, to the end. Their aim was to kill ten Americans before they were killed themselves." And: "If the Japanese ever managed to capture a live Marine – which almost never happened – they tortured him to death."

Ambrose considered the war in the Pacific, "The worst war that ever was. World War II in Europe involved more people and land area, but it was a different war. It did not have the ferocity and rage that defined the war in the Pacific."

Likewise, James Bradley in *Flags of Our Fathers* talks about the difference in the way the war was fought in the two theatres. "Combat was fierce, casualties were heavy, and passion ran high when fighting the Germans. But rules were followed, and a sense of restraint existed in Europe that was absent in the Pacific."

In short, the Japanese did not like the Americans. They thought them weak and inferior – unwilling to fight to the death. And the Americans did not care for the Japanese – some would say they hated them. The sneak attack on Pearl Harbor was bad enough, but then there was the awful treatment of the American Army troops in the Philippines – and other atrocities committed against captured Americans in the Pacific battles. And there was the brutal treatment of civilians by the Japanese as most graphically evidenced by the slaughter of an estimated 350,000 Chinese civilians when the city of Nanking was captured.

Nonetheless, the Japanese POWs aboard NASSAU were treated humanely. They were fed, given clothes to wear from the ship's "lucky bag" – the place where any lost or confiscated crew clothing ended up, and allowed to exercise. As it turns out, Stoops had one of his shirts confiscated by the ship's Master at Arms (known as the ship's "sheriff") because it had been drying on a planes' radio antenna. This method of drying laundry was frowned on by the NASSAU's CO. The enlisted men of the squadron resorted to it because being away from the ship so much on missions meant that they often had to wash their own clothes and the radio antennas were good for speedy air drying. In any case, Stoops' shirt went to the "lucky bag" and before Stoops could reclaim it by working off his penalty by painting, swabbing decks, chipping paint, or the really disliked washing down the planes with kerosene or something similar - which he was neither excited nor in a hurry to do, the shirt was given to a Japanese prisoner.

The matter came to Stoops' attention when he and Banks were on the flight deck enjoying some "steel beach liberty" - sunning themselves during the trip back to Hawaii. The flight deck elevator that usually carried planes between the hanger deck and the flight deck started to come up, but stopped half way between the two decks – as it did for some athletic contests. Banks and Stoops noticed Marine guards standing around the elevator so they walked over to check it out. They looked down onto the elevator and saw the Japanese POWs exercising. Stoops noticed that one prisoner was wearing a shirt with "T. Stoops" stenciled on the back. Stoops – normally a mild mannered guy - went "berserk." According to Banks, he demonstrated a remarkably creative and colorful vocabulary and even tried to get down to the elevator to "rip the shirt off the prisoner's back." Banks and the Marines had to restrain him – not an easy thing to do since Stoops was over two hundred pounds.

VC-66 left the Marshall Islands aboard NASSAU for the return trip to Hawaii on 25 February 1944. The trip back to Oahu was unremarkable. Banks and the other aircrewmen got an opportunity to stand some watches on the carrier. It gave them a little taste of what shipboard life was like for the Sailors of ship's company. Moreover, the aircrewmen made good lookouts because of all of their ship and aircraft recognition training.

During a particularly uneventful mid-watch – midnight to four in the morning – Banks got the idea to write a letter to the good looking girl who had once lived next door to him in South Buffalo. Her name was Jean Dewey. The Banks family had lived at 101 Imson Street and the Deweys at 99 Imson. That was several years ago. Now, in 1944, the Deweys currently lived next door to Banks' grandmother.

Jean Camilla Dewey was born on 1 April 1925, in Buffalo. Like Banks, she was the second of four children. Her brother, Dan, was four years older; her sister, Frances, was seven years younger; and her sister, Ann, was fourteen years younger.

Jean was sixteen at the time of the attack on Pearl Harbor and recalls hearing about it as she was going to the movies at the Shea's Buffalo Theatre with her cousins, Rita and Eugene "Sonny" Beeny, and a friend. After hearing of the attack, she remembers that they still went to the show.

Jean graduated from Our Lady of Victory High School in 1942 when she was 17. While in high school, she sang with the choir and enjoyed performing during Mass at the beautiful Our Lady of Victory Basilica. After graduation, she immediately went to work as a secretary for the Army Corps of Engineers in Buffalo. College had not been an option for her either. While the Deweys were better off than the Banks' – Jean's father had a relatively good job as a dispatcher for the Corps of Engineers, there still was not a lot of money. And she was a woman. In the early 1940s, it was still fairly uncommon for women to attend college.

Jean does not remember talking or reading much about the war while in high school or later at work. She does remember virtually all of the young men she knew –

her brother, Dan, her several cousins, and friends going off to war. One cousin, Elmer Shriver, became a POW when his B-24 was shot down over the Ploesti oil fields.

She recalls having to use rationing stamps for buying things like sugar, butter, coffee, gas, and meat – things also needed by the military. But the family was never really short of anything because her mother did a good job of managing household supplies. There was not a lot of complaining or whining in those days. The country's motto was: "We are all in this together."

Banks had never written to Jean before - and in fact, they had rarely spoken. It is fair to say that Jean had not been much impressed with any of the Banks boys when they were younger. "We used to call them the Banks brats when they lived next door on Imson Street." Banks did not even know her current house number only her street – since it was the same street his grandmother, Harriet Zelt, lived on. But Banks felt that it was a slow mid-watch and there was time to kill so why not take a chance and see what happens? As it turns out, a lot happened.

Much to Banks' amazement, Jean not only received, but answered the letter - and a long distance courtship began. Little did she know at the time, but by answering Banks, Jean was destined to be surrounded by military men for many years. Her father and brother were Army men, while her future husband and future son were Navy men. She would find it best to stay neutral during Army - Navy football games.

Distance was not the only challenge to Banks and Jean's young relationship. Time was also a problem. There was no e-mail or cell phones in those days. It sometimes took weeks for mail to catch up with the men in the squadrons and on the ships as they moved around the Pacific. Additionally, there was the annoyance of "censorship." Mail leaving the squadrons and ships was reviewed and censored as necessary. The saying was "loose lips sink ships." Thus, some stranger was going to be reading your mail.

Banks recalls that on one occasion, the squadron's censoring officer gratuitously added an inappropriate comment in one of his letters to Jean. Banks was not happy when Jean told him about it. He reported the matter to the squadron CO who was not happy either. The offending censoring officer was made to apologize to Banks. Worse, when Stephens found out about it, he invited the censoring officer for a TBM ride in which the censoring officer took Banks' place in the gun turret. Apparently Stephens decided to practice a wide range of aerobatics that did not sit well with the censoring officer's stomach. As a result, the censoring officer spent a significant amount of time after they landed cleaning up the turret.

The NASSAU arrived at Pearl Harbor on the 3rd of March and after mooring at NAS Ford Island, unloaded the damaged aircraft and prisoners. The men of VC-66 could now proudly consider themselves "Fleet Sailors" as they had completed their first shipboard deployment.

The general feeling in the squadron was that NASSAU had been a good ship to ride. They liked her Air Officer, Commander (CDR) Born, and they liked her skipper, CAPT Michael. They felt that the squadron and ship had worked together as a good combat team. Bill Piper summed it up well, "The NASSAU was a great ship. She had a super crew and a great Captain. They really impressed me."

Facing enemy fire and the rigors of a combat tempo of operations for the first time, VC-66 had performed well and made a significant contribution to the success of operations Flintlock and Catchpole. They were rightly proud of what they had done.

VC-66 enlisted men on a carrier deck. Russ Jensen is second from left and Banks third from left in the front row. Bob Keough is fifth from the right in the second row, and Tom Stoops fifth from the right in the third row. (Official U.S. Navy Photograph courtesy D.A. Banks collection)

VC-66 officers and enlisted men on a carrier deck. (Official U.S. Navy Photograph courtesy D.A. Banks collection)

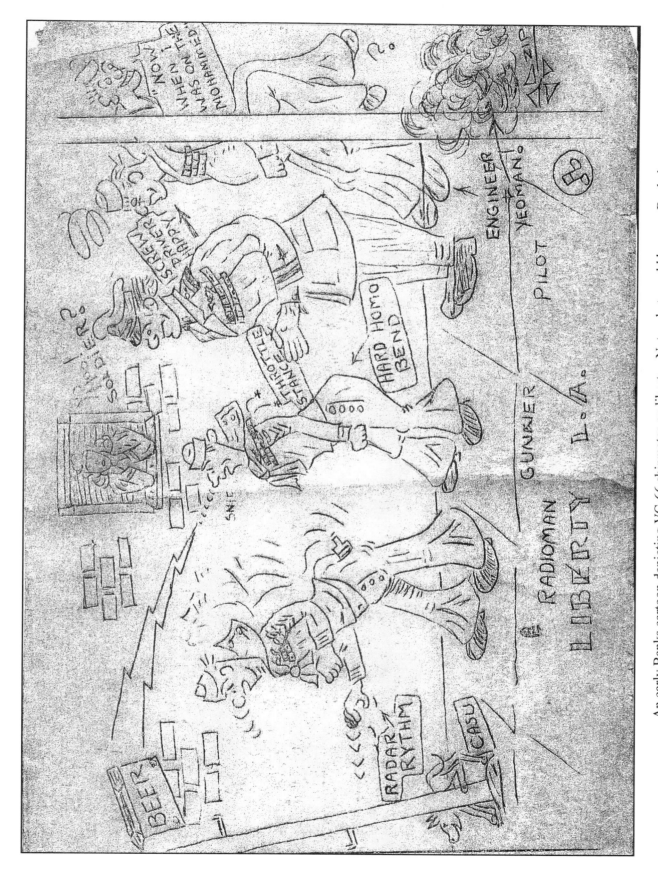

An early Banks cartoon depicting VC-66 shipmates on liberty. Note what would become Banks' lifelong artistic signature "dAb" in lower right hand corner. (Cartoon: courtesy D.A. Banks collection)

The first of two Banks VC-66 cartoons depicting an unsuccessful attack on a Japanese submarine. The cartoons were posted anonymously in the squadron ready room. (Cartoon: courtesy D.A. Banks collection)

The second of the two Banks VC-66 cartoons depicting an unsuccessful attack on a Japanese submarine. (Cartoon: courtesy D.A. Banks collection)

11

Rest and Recreation – and Training in Hawaii

On 5 March, squadron personnel disembarked from NASSAU for transfer to the Naval Air Facility (NAF), Barking Sands, Kauai, Hawaii for some well earned rest and recreation after what had been an intense two months aboard the carrier. It was also to be a time for the fighter pilots to get used to their new FM-2s with their more powerful engines. As J.P. Fox recalls, "They were slightly faster and could climb faster." And another of the VC-66 fighter pilots, ENS Dean J. "Bird" Birdsong from Marquette, Kansas, remembers that the FM-2s were "better and more powerful. Only real difference was the FM-2 had a Wright Lycoming engine and swung a more powerful prop. Made all the difference in the world."

Banks and many of the men made the trip to Kauai via the SWAN – a 110 foot long utility craft that was a far cry from the NASSAU. As soon as the SWAN was on the open ocean, the men knew they were at sea because of the extreme pitching and rolling. As for the carriers - at least according to any destroyer Sailor, they were so big and rode so smooth that - "The only time carrier guys know their ship is underway is when the word is passed over the 1MC (ship's public address system)." And thus, "The only real Sailors are destroyer Sailors."

As the junior officer in the squadron, Stephens also had to ride to Kauai on the SWAN. He recalls, "As the junior guy (officer), I got some 'unusual' assignments." The junior officer in a Navy command is generally known as the "SLJO" (shitty little jobs officer). The name says it all. As to the trip to Kauai aboard the SWAN, Stephens remembers:

> It was supposed to be a one day in the daylight trip, but the SWAN had engine problems causing us to get to Kauai after dark. Regulations would not allow us to enter port after dark so we had to cruise back and forth on the ocean during the night killing time while waiting for sunrise. I stayed in a cabin, but most of the men stayed on deck all night. And squadron rumor has it that somehow alcoholic beverages showed up and considerable drinking took place during the night. There was speculation that it came from some officer's seabag.

Kauai is the farthest west of the major Hawaiian Islands - about one hundred miles west of Oahu. Banks remembers the men of VC-66 having some good times at Barking Sands. While the base was pretty rustic, for a while at least, VC-66 was the only squadron stationed there and they had the whole place to themselves. The Kauai beaches were great and they could load up a TBM with several guys and fly to Honolulu on Oahu for liberty. Banks recalls as an aircrewman being bought drinks by grateful Marines and ships' company Sailors in the bars. He also recalls the occasional "good natured" bar fight between Sailors and Marines.

And Banks knows a native Hawaiian that had some "good natured" fun at the expense of some of the squadron's Sailors. Once while on Kauai, Banks and a group of the VC-66 men went down to the beach. There was a native Hawaiian fellow there so they decided to ask him how the place got the name Barking Sands? He told them, "Sometimes the wind picks up the sand and blows it against the cliffs and it sounds like barking." He also told them, "If you throw sand against the beach cliffs you can sometimes get the barks." The Hawaiian left and the Sailors decided to give it a try. An hour or so later after much throwing of sand and no barking heard, Banks and his buddies decided that they might have gotten some bad information. They figured that the Hawaiian would be having a good laugh with his friends that evening at their expense.

The VC-66 officers also enjoyed Kauai. In addition to visiting the beaches and the relatively spartan officers' club, fishing, and hunting goats, they would frequently be invited to dinner and drinks by various local island families.

As it turns out, one of them, DeLoach Cope, later married the daughter of one of the ladies who enjoyed hosting the pilots for dinner at her home on Kauai. Her husband was the chief engineer of a sugar mill. Cope met the daughter again after the war when she was going to school in San Francisco. They married and settled in Mississippi. Cope began an eighteen year career in public service with the state government. Afterward, the Copes would raise cotton, corn, and rice on their farm. They also bought an airplane and "flew all over" as they enjoyed it. DeLoach and Allegra have been married sixty-one years. As Cope tells it, "I have had a very good life."

On 15 March, the squadron's TBM pilots and aircrewmen detached from NAF Barking Sands and were sent to NAS Kaneohe Bay on Oahu for two weeks of anti-submarine warfare (ASW) training and training in use of the relatively new and super secret Norden bombsight.

Banks recalls, "The Norden sight was so secret that each one was guarded by an armed Marine." Banks was sent to the bombardier course in case anything ever happened to Stoops, he would be able to fill in. Banks remembers the Norden sight as, "being a very complex instrument that required a lot of concentrated attention." He also recalls suggesting to the instructors that he was wasting his time in the class because in his opinion, "The new sight was more suited to high level bombing like that done by the army's big bombers rather than the low level stuff that the TBMs were doing." He stopped short of using the old Navy expression, "They didn't know shit from Shinola." But he does remember telling them that, "Heck – sometimes the TBMs flew so low on their bombing runs that they came back with their bomb bay doors wet!" The instructors listened, disagreed – and Banks remained in the class.

On 24 March, while the TBM crews were still in ASW training, the squadron's fighter pilots went to Honolulu for 5 days of R and R.

VC-66 TBMs taxiing on a runway. (Official U.S. Navy Photograph courtesy D.A. Banks collection)

Banks with a Hawaiian statue. The photo is stamped on the back, "Passed by Naval Censor." (Official U.S. Navy Photograph courtesy D.A. Banks collection)

VC-66 officers wait to bat during a softball game against the enlisted men. Left to right: Joseph S. Trichel, William E. Cook, James O. Mayo, Fay W. Hamilton, Robert A. Weaver, William H. Piper, Herbert K. Bragg (the Skipper), and Dean J. Birdsong. (Official U.S. Navy Photograph courtesy W.D. Cope)

12

Anti-Submarine Warfare

As soon as the ASW training was completed and with little prior notice, on 30 March 1944, the squadron was directed to report for duty aboard the USS ALTAMAHA (CVE-18). There they would put the recent training to good use. By the time squadron personnel reported aboard – including several new replacements, their aircraft: eleven TBM-1Cs, one TBF-1, and fourteen FM-2s, had already been loaded on the ship while she was moored at Ford Island. Banks recalls that when they flew in new planes, they would occasionally find notes hidden in them from the factory workers wishing the airmen good luck. It was a nice touch.

The TBMs were now fitted with four rocket rails mounted under each wing. The rails were seventy inches long and caused more drag on the plane while it was flying. Stephens recalls, "The rails had the effect of making landings more challenging because more power had to be used."

By late afternoon on the 30th, ALTAMAHA was ready and got underway for what was described as an "emergency anti-submarine hunter–killer mission." The assigned operating area was 300 miles east of the Marshall Islands. William T. Y'Blood in his detailed and thorough book, *The Little Giants – U.S. Escort Carriers Against Japan* (1987), indicates that the mission may have resulted from an Operation Magic intercept and decoding of Japanese radio traffic.

The hastily put together hunter-killer group's objective was to find and destroy Japanese submarines that had been operating against the Pearl Harbor – Marshall Islands supply lines. While hunter-killer operations were relatively common in the Atlantic, they were relatively new in the Pacific.

Accompanying ALTAMAHA were the destroyer escorts WILEMAN (DE-22), H.C. THOMAS (DE-21), ELDEN (DE-264), and CABANA (DE-260). They were designated Task Group 11.1 with ALTAMAHA's CO, CAPT A.C. Olney, serving as Task Group Commander. This would be the first time these ships would operate together as a dedicated ASW force. That they would do as well as they did with as little training as they had was pretty remarkable.

ALTAMAHA had been built in Tacoma, Washington and commissioned in September 1942. Like NASSAU, she was one of the BOGUE class CVEs – built on a merchant ship hull. Since her commissioning, she had steamed many thousands of miles ferrying planes all over the Pacific. It was not exciting work, but it was important.

30 March through 2 April 1944 was spent en route to the assigned operating area. Time was passed by doing carrier refresher landings and gunnery practice – as well as first time practice for the TBMs firing their new Mark 7 rockets. Concerning the gunnery practice, Banks recalls:

> Once in a while, the squadron CO would request that a target raft or sled
> be launched and towed behind the ship. The CO of the carrier would

grudgingly agree because the new pilots and gunner aircrewmen would sometimes shoot at the raft or sled from the 12 or 6 o'clock position relative to the ship – which meant the aircraft would fly over the ship from bow to stern with guns blazing (the ship's crew would be noticeably absent from topside areas); or from the stern to the bow. In either situation, if the shooting plane led the target too much – well, use your imagination. The guilty parties (pilots and aircrewman gunners) would join the "report to the Captain on the bridge after landing" line – or worse yet, the carrier's Chief Boatswain's Mate who was responsible for upkeep of the ship's topside spaces.

The Task Group arrived at the operating area on 3 April 1944. VC-66 began flying combat anti-submarine patrol sorties in addition to doing more carrier refresher landing practice. During landing practice, the squadron's lone TBF crashed into the port side of ALTAMAHA's bridge. There were no personnel injuries, but the port side wing of the bridge was smashed in, a signal searchlight was damaged, and various signal halyards and radio antennas were cut loose and insulators broken. The TBF was damaged beyond repair. It was probably the last TBF to be flown by VC-66.

Stephens remembers a typical TBF/TBM weapon load for an anti-submarine patrol being a homing torpedo, two depth charges, and four rockets on each wing. The rockets did not have an explosive head, but rather a metal head to penetrate the submarine's hull.

According to fighter pilot Dean Birdsong, "The TBMs had it tough. The TBMs often landed with the anti-submarine torpedoes still onboard. The anti-submarine ordnance was too expensive to drop before landing. It made landing tough – and there was often little wind to land into." Birdsong was right. The dangers involved with landing a TBM while still carrying depth charges and other ordnance would be vividly experienced by a VC-66 TBM pilot and his aircrew within the next couple of weeks.

On 4 April, the squadron flew more ASP sorties. In general, Banks recalls the anti-submarine patrols as being "the worse job - very boring - over water hour after hour – flying around looking at the sea."

But not all ASP missions were boring. At 1408 on the 4th, TBM pilot LTJG Joseph N. "Jobbo" Polski from Minneapolis, Minnesota, reported a Japanese submarine on the surface 108 miles west of ALTAMAHA. The submarine had been seen first by Charlie Edwards who was flying fighter escort for the TBM. As Edwards recalls:

I spotted the sub which was totally on the surface. It was probably recharging its batteries. There was no one in the conning tower or on deck. Polski and I had just turned left onto to a new leg of our triangular search pattern. My job was to strafe the sub with armor piercing .50 caliber rounds to keep people off the sub's deck and not able to shoot at us while the TBM attacked and sank the sub.

Polski and his aircrew - turret gunner James Gander and radioman Aviation Radioman Second Class David R. Irvin from Greggton, Texas, in their Avenger (which

Polski had named "Stasha" – the one I love) immediately began an attack on the sub. The attack is described in ALTAMAHA's official *War Diary* entry of 4 April 1944:

> Being in excellent position, Lt. (jg) J.N. POLSKIE (sic) immediately nosed over into a 20 degree dive, increased speed to 190 knots IAS. At slant range 1200 yards, altitude 1000 feet, he fired three pairs of rockets in succession. The submarine was still proceeding fully surfaced. The rockets entered the water athwart the conning tower, short by an estimated 75, 50 and 25 feet successively. The fourth set of rockets failed to discharge when the master rocket electric switch snapped off. Following the rocket discharges the submarine slowed noticeably and started to submerge.

Then the TBM crew went to their depth bombs:

> Lt. (jg) J.N. POLSKIE (sic) continued in his dive and at 400 feet altitude, released both depth bombs in train with intervalometer setting of 70 feet. At time of release, the submarine's deck was completely above water. Two explosions straddled the conning tower, throwing water 30 feet higher than the plane.

Then Edwards in his fighter joined in:

> Immediately after the bombs exploded, the fighter dived down diagonally across the submarine from the starboard quarter, concentrating his attack on the base of the conning tower. The after deck was still above water, the submarine making way very slowly, its wake partially obscured by oil spreading over the surface.

When the TBM recovered from its first dive, it winged over and made another attack run with its last pair of rockets. The rockets entered the water 40 feet short. They were aimed just ahead of the sub's conning tower which still could be seen amidst the oil and foam. Edwards also made another strafing run. From ALTAMAHA's *War Diary*:

> Three minutes after the submarine's submergence, 20 feet of the bow rose out of the water at a 45 degree angle and remained up for four minutes. The keel could be seen clearly. Ens. C.T. EDWARDS made four strafing runs on the upended bow; the flash of his bullets striking the hull could be seen by the TBM crew. After four minutes the bow sank and the conning tower could be seen under water. The entire submarine settled straight down with no forward motion whatever. There was no propellor (sic) wash, wake or swirl. Two minutes later a bubble of air, about 20 feet in diameter, boiled to the surface. The submarine was not seen again.

Turret gunner Gander has a good memory of the attack on the submarine. He recalls that in the excitement of the action their radioman forgot to take the lens cap off his camera as he was shooting pictures. As a result, the only photos of the incident came from the camera mounted on Gander's .50 caliber machine gun as he strafed the sub – and they were "grainy."

Edwards feels that he put "many rounds into the sub's conning tower. No one ever came out on deck." He has always been upset that his gun camera did not work during the attack. His film was also very "grainy." He believes, "I would have some good photos to look at." Edwards recalls the attack on the sub as an exciting time for him. For his role in it, he was awarded an Air Medal and his photograph was published in his hometown, Bethlehem, Pennsylvania, newspaper making him and his wife, Marnie, both "famous" there.

Just a few minutes after the attack on the first Japanese sub, at 1420, TBM pilot LTJG John L. "Jack" Dwight from Upper Darby, Pennsylvania, and his aircrew - Aviation Machinist's Mate Third Class James A. "Jim" Rathbun from Cincinnati, Ohio, and Aviation Radioman Second Class Rex A. Tappan from Santa Monica, California, patrolling in a different area, reported another Japanese submarine cruising on the surface. J.P Fox was flying fighter escort for the TBM. Fox recalls, "I was with LTJG Dwight when I spotted the Jap sub. His radio was not working so I motioned to him and started the first of my two strafing attacks." The ALTAMAHA *War Diary* describes the action:

> The fighter, piloted by Lieut. J.P. FOX, Jr., A-V (N) USNR, VC-66, nosed over from 5,000 feet and made a steep diving attack on the submarine from the port quarter. He opened fire at 2000 feet with all four guns, aiming at the base of the conning tower and continued firing down to 500 feet. The submarine was fully surfaced throughout the attack and seemed to be maintaining normal speed. Lieut. J.P. Fox saw his bullets strike the water just short of the waterline, then walk up the deck to the conning tower where he got in a long burst.

A few seconds after Fox completed his attacking run, Dwight and his TBM crew began one from 2500 feet, but ran into some mechanical problems. The *War Diary*:

> At slant range of 700 yards, he (Dwight) fired his first pair of rockets, saw them enter the water 100 feet short headed straight for the conning tower. His second pair of rockets failed to fire. (He discovered later that overload of the circuit had turned the master rocket arming switch off). At 500 feet altitude he pressed his bomb release button, but the bombs failed to drop.

By now, the TBM was down to 200 feet above the water where it leveled off and began to climb for another attack. Fox meanwhile was back up at 2000 feet and began another strafing run. The *War Diary*:

> He (Fox) opened fire at 1,500 foot altitude and continued firing down below the normal safe altitude for pull out, managing to level off ten or twenty feet above the waves.

Fox got some long bursts off and watched his bullets enter the conning tower and the deck in front and behind it. The TBM was now making its second attack run, but again its bombs failed to release. Upon investigation back at the carrier, it was discovered that the bombs did not release because they had not been armed. After Dwight's second attack, the sub submerged completely. But as it went down, it left a large oil slick thought to be probably caused by fuel tanks punctured by Fox's .50 caliber bullets. The sub was not seen again.

After sorting out some communications and radar navigation problems, all planes returned to ALTAMAHA safely at 1800, but some had only a few gallons of fuel remaining - if that. ENS Richard F. "Dick" Krost from Mankato, Minnesota, recalls the situation: "Polski, his gunner, and his radioman had spent almost five hours in the air. When they landed, the TBM's engine quit. It was out of gas." It was a close call. VC-66 was credited with sinking one submarine and damaging the other. It was a good day's work.

From 5 through 9 April, the squadron continued patrolling the operating area. Several multiple plane submarine search missions were flown daily with search launches usually at or about 0700, 1130, and 1530. Each TBM launched had a fighter escort.

On 6 April, while attempting to land, one of the TBMs crashed through the barrier on the flight deck and hit the carrier's bridge. The plane's tailhook had missed the arresting gear wires on the deck. The TBM's motor, propeller, and right wing were damaged. The pilot suffered general body bruises, a mild concussion, and possible fractured neck. The turret gunner suffered a mild concussion, and general body bruises. The radioman suffered general body bruises.

Again, barrier crashes were a very real occupational hazard of landing on CVEs. Banks remembers one time when his turret gunner buddy, Russ Jensen, was involved in a bad one. Jensen's TBM missed the arresting cable, went through the barrier, hit the carrier's island, shaved off a wing, and landed on its nose. As Banks recalls:

Jensen was high in the air in his turret. The deck crew threw him a line to fix on the plane so that they could pull it down. Jensen, a cowboy before the war, was more than happy to tie up the plane for the deck guys – but before doing so, he made the line into a lasso and put on a little twirling show. After the initial excitement was over, it was observed by Jensen's buddies that his cowboy skills were truly impressive and had come in handy. To honor the occasion, they painted a lasso on the side of his turret.

Jensen was also known for being a little sentimental. At sea, he liked to play a record (records were like large CDs) on a windup phonograph and listen to a song about a girl with "pretty blue eyes." And according to Banks, "Every time Russ heard it, the tough, cowboy, gunner would cry. When we were bored, we used to like to play the record and hide to watch our buddy cry. But it was not good when Russ discovered one or more of us laughing."

There were no flight operations on 10 April. VC-66 found itself back at Majuro Atoll Lagoon in the Marshall Islands as ALTAMAHA and the Task Group anchored there to allow the destroyer escorts to refuel.

The ships got underway again on the 11th to return to the anti-submarine operating area east of the Marshalls. On the way, the squadron flew strafing, rocket, and depth charge practice runs. In the afternoon, one of the TBMs while attempting to land failed to hook the arresting gear wires and crashed through the barrier into two other TBMs. All three planes were damaged, but there were no personnel injuries.

Banks recalls that after a particular mission the squadron CO was supposed to make the 1000th landing on the carrier. There would be a small celebration afterward with cake and photos. But before the skipper could land, Jobbo Polski radioed that he had an "emergency" and needed to land right away. The ship gave him priority clearance to land and he did. It was the 1000th landing. The CO was not pleased. Afterward, the mechanics checked Polski's plane and did not find any problems. The CO was suspicious, but the enlisted men loved it.

The Task Group reached the operating area on 12 April and resumed its hunter-killer mission. The squadron began flying multiple plane anti-submarine patrol sorties again. Late in the morning on the 12th, a landing TBM missed the arresting cables and crashed through both barriers into two other TBMs. Once again, while all three planes suffered damage, there were no injuries to the aircrews or ship's personnel. It was proving to be a hard cruise on the planes.

From the 13th through the 18th of April, ALTAMAHA and Task Group 11.1 were steaming as before in the anti-submarine operating area with the squadron continuing to fly multiple ASP sorties.

While the daily routine was roughly the same, there was significant excitement on 15 April. At 1844 in the evening, while ALTAMAHA was zig zagging as required to make tracking her difficult for a submarine, two definite torpedo wakes and probably four were sighted 4000 yards southwest of the carrier. The torpedoes were broaching indicating that they were probably fired from extreme range. The torpedoes passed 400 yards forward of the destroyer escort ELDEN's bow headed toward ALTAMAHA. The carrier turned to starboard (right) with full rudder and went to flank speed (as fast as it could go) to avoid the torpedoes and comb their tracks. At 1845, two torpedo tracks were sighted about 200 yards off ALTAMAHA's port beam and parallel to her course.

All of the torpedoes had missed. ALTAMAHA began radical maneuvering to avoid other possible attacks. None occurred. The destroyer escorts picked up what they thought was a submarine contact and made a depth charge attack, but without any definite results.

Aviation Ordnanceman Second Class Emidio J. Mardarello from Hoboken, New Jersey, remembers the torpedo attack on the ALTAMAHA well. He had just joined VC-66 in March 1944, as a replacement turret gunner. He was nineteen years old – and as he puts it, "I was the baby of the squadron." Everything was new to him and he was "impressed" with it all. While his training had led him to believe that he would be assigned as a gunner on land based patrol bombers, the needs of the Navy prevailed and he found himself with VC-66 aboard ALTAMAHA.

Mardarello has a good memory concerning his somewhat unusual and unsuspected route to VC-66:

On completion (of Gunnery School), I was given a 30 day leave and then reported to San Francisco. From there I served as an SP (Shore Patrol – similar to the Army's MPs) for 2 weeks before being ordered to report to a tanker loaded with aviation gasoline. We left (for Hawaii) unescorted, but we did have the armed guard (Navy personnel) on guns both fore and aft. I stayed over 2 months in Kaneohe, Oahu. A bulletin was posted looking for gunners to volunteer to go south. In March 44, I volunteered. To my surprise, the vessel I was to report to was the CVE Altamaha. It was converted from a tanker vessel. On arrival, 9 of us were questioned by the enlisted men if we were the new "CA" (combat aircrewmen) to replace the lost men? It was a surprise to us because I was trained as a turret gunner on a land based PV or Patrol Bomber by Ventura.

But that was all okay with Mardarello. As he recalls, "It was not that difficult to adjust to the TBF turret. Of course had I been trained on a TBF, it would have been much easier." More important, he was a young guy – only seventeen when he enlisted in January 1943 – looking for adventure. After Boot Camp, his first choice for duty was submarines, then aviation, and then PT boats. As he observes today, "Those were not the choices of a mature man." He had joined the Navy only after unsuccessfully trying to get a buddy to enlist in the Marines with him. The buddy said no to the Marines, but said he would join the Navy. So they went down to the Navy recruiting station and enlisted together. Mardarello never saw his friend again after he was sworn in. The friend was killed in the Pacific while serving as a member of the Navy armed guard assigned to man the gun mounts on U.S. merchant ships – similar to the tanker Mardarello rode on to get to Hawaii. The armed guard was not a particularly favored job of the Navy men.

On the evening of 15 April 1944, when ALTAMAHA was attacked by the submarine, Mardarello remembers going back to the fantail for a smoke and to relax with some of the guys. He recalls, "We saw the torpedo wakes in the water and thought they were fish or dolphins playing near the ship. It was dusk. We didn't realize what was going on until we heard the general quarters alarm!"

To the amusement of the Americans, the matter of ALTAMAHA's encounter with the Japanese submarine was concluded when Radio Tokyo's female propagandist, "Tokyo Rose" (American born Iva Toguri), announced that ALTAHAMA had been sunk. Apparently the Japanese submarine skipper did not hang around to check the results of his attack. In any case, while this was the first time that a ship the squadron was riding was attacked by a submarine, it would not be the last.

There was more excitement on the morning of 17 April. At 1000, while a TBM was landing, its tailhook gave way after catching one of the arresting gear wires. The plane continued down the flight deck, jumped the barrier and went over ALTAMAHA's starboard bow into the sea. A minute after the crash, the ship felt a severe impact, but there was no apparent disturbance in the water. The thinking was that a depth charge probably fell off the TBM's bomb rack when it went into the water and exploded somewhere below the ship. Fortunately, there was no damage to the ship.

In the meantime, the Avenger's crew: pilot Dick Krost; turret gunner Aviation Machinist's Mate Third Class Vincent T. Ruthman from the Bronx, New York; and radioman Aviation Radioman Second Class Charles S. Riffle from Newport, Rhode Island, were all rescued uninjured from the water thanks to some quick work on their part - and by destroyer escort CABANA charging in and picking them up. Living up to its reputationn as being a quick sinker, the TBM had remained afloat for only four minutes before it went under.

Krost remembers the accident as happening quickly and being "very scary." He recalls, "It was a good thing we got out of the plane and into the life raft quickly since the depth charge went off and the plane sank quickly. We might have been killed." Fortunately, like Stephens, Banks, and Stoops; Krost, Ruthman, and Riffle had talked about and practiced escapes. Krost relates, "When we went into the water, our reactions to escape the plane were automatic. The radioman pulled the three man raft out and we got in it just in time."

Fellow TBM pilot, Bud Clark, also recalls the crash:

> From the starboard catwalk we watched Dick Krost and his crewmen get out of their plane and inflate and get into their rubber boat. It was a textbook operation. They were in the boat and away before the plane sank. Later we watched as they were transferred back to the carrier from the DE on the highline. As Dick said, it was scary.

As for the number of barrier crashes, Krost remembers the ALTAMAHA as being harder to land on because it was built on the rounded oiler hull which caused the ship to act like a "cork in the water." The ship rolled and pitched more than a "real" CVE. He adds, "We called ALTAMAHA 'Tippy Canoe.'"

After their crash and rescue by the CABANA, Krost, Ruthman, and Riffle had to be transferred back to the ALTAMAHA while the two ships were still at sea and underway. This process is always exciting and somewhat risky – particularly for the transferees.

To accomplish the underway transfer, the two ships must steam side by side about 150 feet apart and match course and speed. Doing this on the ocean is not as easy as it might sound. The maneuver requires good seamanship – especially for the smaller destroyer. It pitches and rolls more and has to battle the rough seas caused by the coming together of the two ships' bow waves. Once the ships are close enough and have matched course and speed, a line is literally shot from one ship to the other, and the cargo or personnel are then "highlined" - via a basket that hangs slightly above the water - from the one ship to the other. Once the highlining has begun, it is critical for the two ships to maintain position. A couple of degrees difference in course could quickly result in either a collision or an emergency "breakaway." Neither event is good for the person being highlined at the time. Krost describes the highline experience as also being "very scary."

Again, almost everything involved with landing on a CVE was frightening – especially for the aircrewmen who were always part of the action, but could do nothing about it.

Emidio Mardarello recalls that when he first joined VC-66 as a replacement gunner, he was assigned to fly with an Ensign who was a new replacement pilot.

According to Mardarello, each new pilot was required to qualify for flight ops by successfully completing three take offs and landings from ALTAMAHA's flight deck. Mardarello recalls watching from the ship as his Ensign's first attempted landing resulted in a crash into the carrier's bridge. Mardarello had to wonder what he had gotten himself into. He was then assigned to fly with one of the squadron's other pilots until his Ensign qualified.

Mardarello also remembers a couple of other landing incidents that caused him some stress and anxiety at the time. One demonstrates again the advantages - or not - of the turret gunner's backward looking position:

> We landed correctly and passed over the lowered barrier. The next TBF hit the deck so hard that they jumped over the barrier. As the turret gunner, I was the only one of the crew that was aware of what was about to happen. The TBF that jumped the barrier came behind our plane and was chewing away our tail section. The pilot of our plane was not aware of this and our poor radioman (Aviation Radioman Second Class Dean H. Summers from Englewood, Colorado) didn't know what happened until he could see the sky (where the tail was supposed to be) from his position.

Mardarello's pilot, Ed Keyser, also recalls what he describes as that "hairy" incident:

> (I) was being being directed to a parking spot where several aircraft were already in place. Suddenly the taxi man's eyes looked like two silver dollars. His hand signaling stopped as he and the deck crew abandoned me and ran to the catwalks. Looking over my right shoulder I could see another TBM that was airborne. The siren was blasting away. I switched off the engine and dropped my seat hoping the armor plate would protect me. The TBM hit us and our plane lurched forward. It looked like we would be ending up in the water or crashed into the parked aircraft. The tail section was being chewed to pieces. I am practically standing on the brakes while the control stick is thrashing wildly against my legs. It would have been a complete disaster had not my folded wings positioned against the other TBM's wing roots stopped further destruction. Over night the maintenance crew removed the engine from the wrecked TBM and installed it on the errant TBM. It was back on the flight schedule.

Mardarello recalls another incident that demonstrates the hazards of landing at night and the general dependence of the TBF/TBM aircrewmen on the skills of their pilots and the carrier's crew:

> Our plane was the last TBF in the group to return to the carrier. We got a wave off and by this time it was getting dark and our fuel was low. We got two other wave offs and we were instructed to cool off our engine. We circled the carrier and for the only time aboard ship, they lit up the carrier deck (normally where there may be enemy submarines, the ship is

kept dark).   On our next approach we landed.   Talk about shaking somewhat.

And forget about take offs and landings, just being around the flight deck could be hazardous. Keyser remembers one of his flight deck experiences:

I was standing in the catwalk observing aircraft recovery. A TBM landed and the tail wheel broke loose; hurtling across the flight deck directly toward me. I ducked! It missed striking my head by inches, slamming into a 20 mm gun mount. It so happened to be my 21st birthday. It could well have been my last.

Dick Krost is aware of a very close call experienced by J.P. Fox. It was quite similar to one of the landing incidents that Mardarello and Keyser recalled.   Fox remembers his as "one terrific crash." He elaborates, "I had landed and taxied up to the bow where the deck crew folded my wings. At the same time I heard the crash sirens sound and saw the deck crew who had just parked me start to scatter." Another FM had just landed. "It bounced over the barrier and came steaming up the deck. His right wing knocked off my rudder and passed right over my head." Fortunately Fox was still in his cockpit. The crashing fighter's spinning propeller chewed up Fox's folded left wing. Several of the carrier's deck crew were injured – a couple were pinned under the oncoming plane, but neither Fox nor the other pilot was hurt.

The incident is evidence of why some say that the men who work on carrier flight decks have one of the most dangerous jobs in the Navy.

As for Fox, he was lucky that he was not climbing out of his cockpit at the time the other fighter's wing passed over it. And Krost showing his pilot's coolness says of Fox's near decapitation, "I thought it was an interesting episode that is just part of carrier landing under adverse conditions."

Dick Krost had joined VC-66 on 30 March 1944 as it was embarking on ALTAMAHA. He joined as a replacement pilot along with three others to make up for losses during the Marshalls campaign. He had been in college before the war. While in college, like Stephens, he had joined the Civilian Pilot Training Program and obtained his private pilot's license.

Krost recalls that when the war broke out, "pilots were in demand and I had no problem getting into the Navy. TBFs were the hot new plane and were my first choice. They were to replace the TBD Devastators which were beaten up at Midway." Beaten up is right. Only four of the forty-one TBDs that were used in the crucial Battle of Midway made it back to their carriers. And none of them scored a hit on a Japanese ship. The Devastators were old and slow. The Navy needed a newer, tougher torpedo bomber – enter the Avenger.

Krost has no regrets about flying TBFs/TBMs. "They were a good stable airplane – a good carrier airplane." He also observes, "Life on carriers was good in my opinion. We lived in a junior officer bunk room. No one had a single room. I enjoyed the comradeship of the squadron. It was like a big family. It was a good experience. The Navy treated me well."

Krost has particular respect and fondness for Guy Catterton who was his TBM division leader, "I flew wing on him whenever we were launched. I always appreciated the advice and help he offered me, and respected him as a person, as well as a leader and mentor."

In addition to the time that the depth charge fell off Krost's plane as he was attempting to land, Mardarello - with some embarrassment, recalls another loose ordnance incident:

> One of our TBFs was returning to land on the carrier and made a good landing. All TBF pilots on landing were ordered to open the bomb bay. Those of us who would not be flying at that time would usually stay on the gangway just below the carrier (flight) deck. This pilot opened his bomb bay and a 250 pound bomb fell on the deck. Sailors were running all over the ship (to get out of the way). As an Ordnanceman I should have known that the bomb cannot detonate until the fuse activates it.

While activities on the carrier's flight deck – launches and landings, were certainly the most dangerous and stressful times, ordinary life aboard ship can also produce some stress and anxiety. Mardarello relates how sleeping was even a "scary" time for him. He recalls, "We entered our below decks sleeping compartment aboard ship by crawling through a hatch. At night when the lights were turned out, the hatch was closed and dogged." In an emergency, it would have been hard to get out of the compartment. Being trapped below decks on a sinking ship is a common fear of many men who go to sea – as is falling overboard at night.

On 18 April 1944, ALTAMAHA's Commanding Officer turned over duty as Commander Task Group 11.1 to the Commanding Officer of the USS FANSHAW BAY (CVE-70) with VC-68 aboard. ALTAMAHA and her escorts then left the anti-submarine operating area for return to Pearl Harbor.

From the 19th through the 21st, the ships were en route to Hawaii. There were no flight ops. On the 22nd, at 0735, the squadron launched its still operational aircraft: five TBMs and thirteen FMs, to fly to NAS Ford Island. In the afternoon, ALTAMAHA reached Pearl Harbor and moored there.

On 25 April, VC-66 officially detached from ALTAMAHA and was ordered to report to the Commander Naval Air Force, U.S. Pacific for further assignment. The squadron's damaged aircraft: four TBMs and one FM-2, were unloaded and delivered to Ford Island.

During the ASW operation, VC-66 flew 282 combat flights with each averaging just over three hours. In general, the men of the squadron found their time aboard ALTAMAHA to be relatively dreary and boring – at least compared to the Marshalls Campaign. Both the squadron and the crew of the ship were glad the cruise was over.

As Y'Blood observes in *The Little Giants*, Pacific Fleet ASW experts would learn some lessons from the ALTAMAHA and VC-66 hunter-killer experience and use them to restructure ASW training and tactics. "Before long, dedicated hunter-killer groups built around an escort carrier would be on the prowl in the Pacific, with great success."

After offloading VC-66, ALTAMAHA continued operating in the Pacific. On 18 December 1944, while serving as part of Task Group 30.8 in the Philippine Sea, she was caught up in a powerful typhoon. The raging wind and mountainous seas caused her to roll as much as 25 to 30 degrees to either side making life miserable and very hazardous for all onboard. Imagine the room you are in turning 30 degrees on its side and then back 30 degrees the other way. Many things go flying about - including people. Moving about the ship is nearly impossible. Nearly half of the aircraft tied down on the flight deck broke loose and went over the side. The storm lasted a day and then subsided. ALTAMAHA was lucky. While sustaining considerable structural damage, no one was seriously hurt.

After detaching from ALTAMAHA, the squadron was granted some R and R time. Banks and the rest of the enlisted men were billeted at the plush Royal Hawaiian Hotel on Waikiki Beach for a few days. The pilots stayed at Alexander's Rest Home in Waikiki.

At the time, the Royal Hawaiian was probably the top hotel on Oahu. It remains one of the nicest in the early twenty-first century. Banks remembers, "We used the beach and swam in the ocean – after the Marine guards opened the barbed wire barrier that guarded the beach from invasion." Even after the Battle of Midway there was still concern that the Japanese might attack Hawaii again. Martial law was not lifted until 1944.

Banks recalls an incident involving some of the squadron's Sailors and a group of Marines that occurred while the VC-66 men were staying at the Royal Hawaiian. There was a narrow bridge on the hotel grounds. During the course of one evening's celebration, the Marines and Sailors both tried to cross the bridge at the same time – starting at different ends. They met in the middle. A colorful and animated "discussion" took place. Negotiations quickly broke down and a brawl ensued. One of the Sailors broke a finger. As punishment for being involved in the fight, his shipmates had to watch as the medical people set the finger by placing a wire through the end of it. Banks advises that "it was not pleasant to watch."

Why the occasional skirmish between Marines and Sailors? No doubt that part of it probably has to do with the volume of alcohol consumed on a particular evening's liberty, but part of it also has to be attributed to the friendly rivalry existing between the two services. The Marine Corps is actually part of the Navy Department, but the Marines don't like to admit it – and Navy men never stop reminding them of it. But beyond that, the Marines have a certain superior attitude or "esprit de corps" that defines them. They are proud of it - and it may have something to do with the rivalry. For example, in *Flags of Our Fathers*, James Bradley quotes PBS newsman and former Marine Corps officer, Jim Lehrer, as saying, "I learned that Marines never leave their dead and wounded behind, officers always eat last, the U.S. Army is chickenshit in combat, the Navy is worse, and the Air Force is barely even on our side."

For VC-66, the next few months after leaving ALTAMAHA – May through early August 1944, were devoted to squadron and aircrew training in and around Hawaii – and waiting for their next combat assignment. They spent time at NAS Ford Island, Oahu; NAS Barbers Point, Oahu (aerial photography and gunnery refresher training); NAAS Barking Sands, Kauai; and NAS Kahului, Maui (two weeks of gunnery ground training for the squadron's enlisted men). But to take advantage of the time away from the combat zone to maximize the opportunity for R and R, the training was at a somewhat "relaxed" pace. For example, the orders directing the enlisted men to the gunnery ground training at Kahului specified that, "Regularly scheduled days off will take precedence over school." And, "All men will take swimming trunks to school and swim for thirty (30) minutes immediately following secure, unless scheduled for a ball game."

Again, there were some lighter moments amidst the training and waiting for the next assignment. On 11 June, four of the pilots were apprehended for "illegally, unlawfully, and without authority, appearing on the public highway after the hour of curfew." They were each required to pay a ten dollar fine to the Provost Marshall. The squadron's enlisted men were amused.

And VC-66 Aviation Chief Metalsmith Chester M. Peart recalled, "One day Polski, with a large envelope in his hand, approached the Admiral's driver and told him that the Admiral wanted him to hand carry it down town." Peart didn't know the result of Polski's "borrowing" the Admiral's car or where Polski went with it, but he does know that the Admiral was waiting to "greet" Polski when he returned from his mission to town. Peart also remembers Polski having had three Saint Christopher medals blessed by his priest. Polski gave one of the medals to Peart and Peart feels that it got him through the war. Now, Peart's daughter wears it.

On 21 June, the squadron celebrated its 1st anniversary with an all hands beach party at the Fleet Recreation Area, Nimitz Beach on Oahu. Beer, charcoal broiled steaks, swimming, and softball ruled the day. During these times in Hawaii, Emidio Mardarello fondly remembers the squadron's officers versus enlisted men softball games. "As I remember it, we beat the officers more than they beat us."

On the 4th of July, the squadron was sent to NAS Kahului on Maui.

But even these relatively quiet times were not without their anxious moments. On 23 July – a Sunday, after attending a dinner party hosted by one of the local Maui ladies, Mamie Von Tempski, at her estate, several of the squadron's pilots decided to sleep in the estate's bunkhouse rather than return to the base that evening in a slightly "impaired" condition. At about 0200, they were awakened by the squadron duty officer who loaded them on a truck - "impaired" condition or not - and rushed them back to the airfield - and right to their planes on the flight line. When they got there, Stephens remembers seeing the TBMs being loaded with torpedoes and thinking, "it would be a real challenge making a torpedo run in the pilots' current condition."

The pilots and aircrews were told that President Roosevelt was visiting Hawaii and that the Japanese were about to launch another sneak attack. The situation eventually got sorted out after several hours while the pilots and aircrews sat in their planes. It was true that President Roosevelt was in Hawaii. Now that the allies had landed in France and were pushing toward Germany, he was in Hawaii to meet with Admiral Nimitz and General MacArthur to talk strategy about the war in the Pacific. But the information concerning another Japanese attack turned out to be wrong. The VC-66 pilots were not happy.

VC-66 was involved in another somewhat unusual incident during President Roosevelt's visit. As Bud Clark recalls:

…The squadron participated in a mock attack on Pearl Harbor for the benefit of President Roosevelt who was visiting there. Most of the military aircraft in the area participated, including the Army Air Corps. It was supposedly coordinated, but it was wild. Many planes were making simulated bombing and strafing runs from all directions. We didn't hear of any mid-air collisions, nor did we hear any response from President Roosevelt.

On 26 July, the squadron got some big news. They would be leaving NAS Kahului. They received orders to report aboard the USS FANSHAW BAY (CVE-70) – nicknamed "The Fighting Fannie Bee," for their next deployment. VC-66 would be supporting another invasion. The squadron had enjoyed its time on Maui. They had received good service from the local Carrier Aircraft Service Unit - CASU-32. And the beaches and clubs were good – as were the USOs. But before joining FANSHAW BAY, they would have a few more days on Maui - and they would not be boring.

Jack Dwight had a night to remember on the 27th. While doing nighttime field carrier landing practice (touch and go landings), his Avenger crashed into the water. Fortunately, Dwight's aircrew was not in the plane during the practice session and he was uninjured in the crash. Dwight vividly described his experience in a 12 February 2008 letter to me:

It was a devilishly dark night – no horizon, no moon. In fact, as we circled around to approach the runway, the only way I could keep track of the plane in front of me (and avoid a collision) was by observing his purple exhaust flame. But I still had to fly the "beast" and with no horizon, I had to resort to instrument flying. This is of course a decided flying "no no." Mixing the two usually leads to disaster. And so, in my case, it surely did. I don't to this day know how I got so disoriented, but the next thing I was aware of (not any sort of bump) was water coming up rapidly from the deck of the plane. I was conscious enough to realize that somehow I had flown into the water of the bay. I unstrapped and tried to get out but was impeded by the steel bar that fits over the cockpit front to back. But after getting by that – and now fully immersed in water, I ran into another obstacle (presumably the folded up wing). Thank God I had enough breath left to be able to get clear of that and pop up gasping.

It was so damn dark that not then or later could I determine whether the plane was upside down or rightside up (the perfectly rounded engine cover didn't help at all in this). In any event, I quickly swam away in case the plane should sink and carry me down with it. Interestingly enough, it stayed afloat for about an hour or so. In any event, I soon discovered that I was well offshore (about two miles), into the bay, and did not know the tide situation nor the shark one. This latter really worried me as I had no raft nor shark repellant. I soon lopped off my shoes since they really held me back. Then I decided the Mae West (life jacket) while keeping me afloat, was holding me back from swimming to shore. I was glad of my past water activities in high school and college as water did in no way disconcert me. But then I got one hell of a stomach cramp. My body turned hard as stone. Fortunately I knew what to do, so I just forced myself to relax and stretched out in the water and "willed" it away. It worked!!

Then I was "attacked" by a Portuguese Man-O-War. In a frenzy, I ripped his tentacles off my neck and in the process actually had the frenzied strength to rip off my 3 strand braided dog tag rope!

This accomplished, I proceeded to strip down for the long swim. First, however, there was a searchlight playing out over the bay so I took my t-shirt and tried to wave at them to attract attention. But to no avail. So then I buckled down to the business at hand. I was most anxious to get to land, not in fear of exhaustion, but of sharks.

I did keep my skivvies on as there were houses lining the shore and I figured to ring one of their doorbells for help. It occurred to me on the way in that one of the houses was occupied by Kay Spreckels - the heiress to the sugar fortune and future wife of Clark Gable. I could just imagine me ringing her doorbell, standing there "bare ass naked," and hear her scream at this apparition showing up at her door in the middle of the night.

In any event, I got nearer to shore and saw a coral reef. Fortunately for me the water there was neck high so I was pretty confident going over the sharp coral. I did get over with a minimum of discomfort and reached the lagoon. Now it was easy and I got to the beach in short order. But then I encountered barbed wire meant to stop infiltrators. But I managed to get through with only a few superficial scratches. I made my way through a small copse of trees to come out at the end of the airbase runways.

In those days there was no central lighting system, so they used individual lighted sections. An enlisted man was on a motorbike making his rounds to turn out each light as air operations had secured for the night (with me on the missing list).

I scared the hell out of the guy as I emerged from the woods in the total darkness, wet and disheveled. He had no weapon (thank God!) or he might have done me in right then. I identified myself and hitched a ride with him back to the hanger where I was greeted with joy and disbelief. I got back to the BOQ, dried off, and hit the sack thankfully.

The next day I got the full medical exam treatment and they found (to their surprise) that I was OK. They grounded me for one day and then it was back to work.

Since then I've thought of my adventure and my destruction of about $100,000.00 of government property which (thankfully) the Navy never billed me for. I did escape sharks and Kay Spreckels (darn it).

Even after some sixty-four years, it is pretty clear that Dwight has not forgotten much about that evening. He did have some extra incentive to make that long swim as he had become a new dad just a few months earlier.

On 3 August, Charlie Edwards also had a "memorable" experience. He was flying back from Pearl Harbor in an F4F that had just been reconditioned and as he recalls:

> Apparently a plastic plug containing a desiccant melted and between Molokai and Maui I lost oil pressure completely. The prop froze. I was below a low cloud cover and immediately elected a water landing rather than a parachute. Just off the coast of Maui I dead sticked to a water landing that would be parallel to the beach. I had a choice between landing in blue or green water. I chose the deeper blue with the thought that if I landed in the shallow green water and flipped I would be trapped. It was a good landing, wheels up, and I had no trouble getting out. I would have landed on a nearby golf course, but was concerned that I might flip over and be killed. About halfway to the beach I was joined by a young Hawaiian who swam out to meet me and escorted me ashore. I had signaled distress and minutes after I was ashore I was in an ambulance though totally unhurt.

The good news was that Edwards was also able to swim away from the mishap. He prides himself in the fact that, "I really strapped myself in the airplanes. I didn't want to bounce around and hit my head if I crashed." The bad news was that he was bringing several weeks worth of back mail to the squadron and it went down with the malfunctioning plane. As a result Edwards recalls, "I was greeted with less than enthusiasm by my buddies."

While it was exciting, Edwards does not feel that the emergency water landing was his "most memorable" Navy experience. He recalls feeling "totally confident with the water landing – and I made a good one." He feels that his "most memorable" experiences were the "near death" ones – combat and landing on a carrier at night. He recalls, "Landing on a carrier at night when the sea was rough pretty much equals combat. It never gets to be routine. Every nerve in your body is on edge and tingling when landing on a carrier – especially at night." Edwards advises that he has occasionally been accused of being a little "cocky," but he says, "I feel that I am entitled to it after landing on CVEs. It is not an easy thing to do."

Edwards was one of the original VC-66 pilots who joined the squadron in June 1943. He was born in January 1919. After graduation from Lehigh University in Pennsylvania – where he had been an intercollegiate lightweight wrestling champion, he went to work for the Bethlehem Steel Corporation working at the open hearth furnaces. It was tough, dirty, and hot work.

When the war started, although draft deferred because of his employment in the steel industry, Edwards too had been a member of the Civilian Pilot Training Program and volunteered for and was accepted into the Navy's V5 aviator training program. He, along with a good buddy of his, was sent to the University of North Carolina at Chapel Hill for pre-flight training. As Edwards recalls,

> One day our unit was lined up in formation and we were told to count off.
> An officer then told us that all of the "odd" numbers were going to be

Marine Corps pilots and all of the "even" numbers were going to be Navy pilots. My buddy and I were standing next to each other. He was an "odd" number and I was "even." He went to the Marines and I went to the Navy. That's how our service selection was made, but we both had good experiences in our respective services.

Following pre-flight, Edwards went to the Philadelphia Navy Yard for early flight training in the "beloved yellow perils." He remembers them as "good planes. You couldn't hurt it. You couldn't knock the wings off."

After Philadelphia, he was sent to NAS Pensacola, Florida, where he was commissioned and got his Wings. Next it was on to NAS Miami, Opa-Locka, for advanced fighter training. As he was driving up to the air station at Opa-Locka, Edwards remembers seeing a flatbed truck loaded with six coffins driving away and wondering, "What have I gotten myself into?" He also remembers engaging in "a good dog fight" with Gerry Trapp while in training. Trapp was an instructor at the time. Edwards recalls, "We really got into it. Trapp was very good." He remembers flying Brewster Buffaloes at Opa-Locka and recalls, "They were slow planes and clumsy – unlike the other Navy planes I would fly which were good."

While at Opa-Locka in March 1943, Edwards married Marnie. Marnie had taken the train alone from Bethlehem, Pennsylvania to Florida. As Marnie recalls - and as was mentioned in their 65th wedding anniversary announcement in the *Washington Post* on 16 March 2008, "We were married with no family within a thousand miles." They had found a Presbyterian minister who would marry them. Charlie was twenty-four. Marnie was twenty-one. For those days, they had a relatively long engagement – six months. They had a good time at Opa-Locka. Edwards remembers Opa-Locka having a good Officers' Club with a good orchestra. He recalls, "It was a good romantic place."

After Opa-Locka, Edwards was sent to Chicago to do his carrier landing qualifications on Lake Michigan - and then on to VC-66. Marnie traveled with him around the country as he and the squadron trained. She would sometimes travel by car with Gerry Trapp's wife and ENS Maurice W. "Marty" Barrett's wife, Irene. Marnie and Edwards would rent an apartment or small house near the base. Edwards would join her on weekends when he was not training. In December 1943, when the squadron left for Hawaii and the war, Marnie went back to Pennsylvania. She got a job doing secretarial work at Lehigh University. And like the Banks brothers, she and Edwards had devised a code involving a map of the world so that she could keep track of where he was in the Pacific.

VC-66 officers and men on the deck of USS ALTAMAHA (CVE-18). (Official U.S. Navy Photograph courtesy D.A. Banks collection)

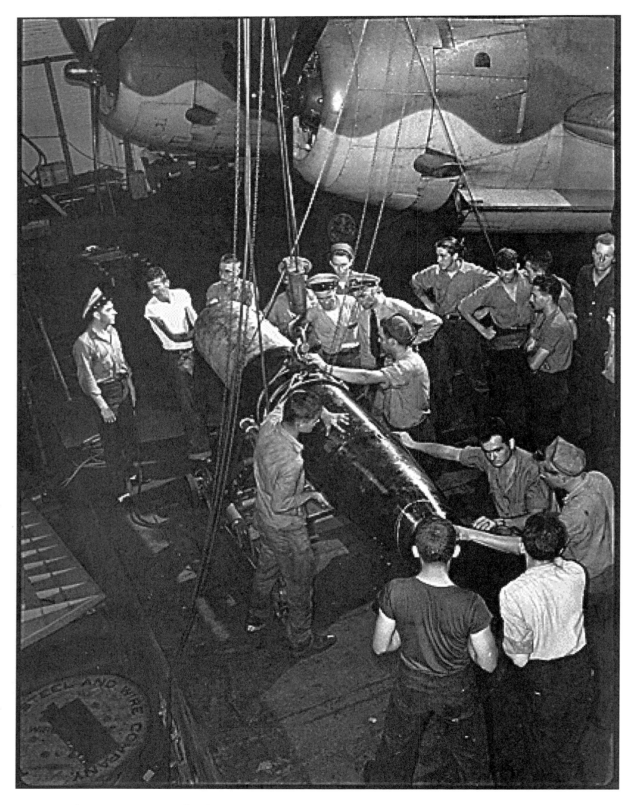

Men work on a TBM torpedo aboard a carrier in the South Pacific. (Photo: courtesy National Archives)

VC-66's Joseph N. "Jobbo" Polski. (Official U.S. Navy Photograph courtesy W.D. Cope)

VC-66 TBM on patrol in the Pacific. (Official U.S. Navy Photograph courtesy D.A. Banks collection.

VC-66's Charles T. "Charlie" Edwards standing on the wing of his FM Wildcat after successful attack on a Japanese submarine. (Official U.S. Navy Photograph courtesy C.T. Edwards)

The Air Medal awarded to Charlie Edwards for his participation in an attack on a Japanese submarine. It is one of many Air Medals awarded to VC-66 pilots during their combat deployments. (Photo: courtesy S.A. Banks)

A breeches buoy highline transfer between two underway ships – similar to what VC-66's Richard F. "Dick" Krost, Vincent T. Ruthman, and Charles S. Riffle went through after their TBM went into the water and they were rescued by the destroyer escort USS CABANA (DE-260). (Photo: courtesy National Archives)

The Royal Hawaiian Hotel, Oahu, Hawaii. VC-66's enlisted men spent a few good days of R & R there. (Photo: courtesy D.A. Banks collection)

13

To the Moluccas Islands, Western New Guinea, and Morotai

On 5 August 1944, the squadron detached from NAS Kahului and flew its planes - seven TBM-1Cs and fourteen FM-2s - to the FANSHAW BAY. At the time, FANSHAW BAY was underway in a training area south of Oahu. She had recently come out of the Pearl Harbor Naval Ship Yard where she had been getting repair work done.

The FANSHAW BAY had been built in Vancouver, Washington. She was commissioned in December 1943. Unlike VC-66's other carriers, NASSAU and ALTAMAHA, FANSHAW BAY had not been built on a merchant ship hull. She was one of the CASABLANCA class CVEs – named after the USS CASABLANCA (CVE-55). The CASABLANCA class consisted of fifty ships that were built using mass production techniques and prefabricated parts. The mass production of aircraft carriers – even small ones, was a pretty radical concept, but the people at Kaiser Shipbuilding in Vancouver made it work.

While a relatively new ship, FANSHAW BAY had already seen plenty of combat action. And it was that action that resulted in the need for the shipyard work. On 17 June 1944, she had been supporting the invasion of Saipan in the Mariana Islands when she got caught up in a series of raids by an estimated seventy Japanese planes. While her anti-aircraft gunners and fighters knocked down many of the attackers, a bomb did find its mark. It penetrated the elevator and exploded above the hangar deck. Fourteen men were killed and twenty-three were wounded. Fires broke out and several compartments were flooded. Once the situation was brought under control, FANSHAW BAY went back to Pearl Harbor for repairs.

In addition to a new ship to ride and a new combat operation, VC-66 had a new CO. It was their former XO - LT Gerry Trapp, who fleeted up to CO when LCDR Herb Bragg received orders for duty back in the states. It was a nice vote of confidence for Trapp, who was liked and respected by his men.

The squadron spent the 5th through the 8th of August training at sea with FANSHAW BAY, USS MARCUS ISLAND (CVE-77), and their destroyer escorts. In addition to flying ASP and CAP sorties, the squadron flew simulated attacks against the ships.

On 6 August, one of the TBMs missed the arresting wire and crashed into the barrier while landing. There were no injuries to personnel and only minor damage to the aircraft. On the 7th, an FM crashed the barrier. Again, no injuries to the pilot or shipboard personnel, but the Wildcat suffered "moderate" damage.

At 0603 on the 8th, flight operations began for anti-submarine patrol and to help search for a pilot from another squadron who was lost during night carrier landing qualifications on the MARCUS ISLAND. Flight ops were secured at 0921. The lost pilot was not found.

In the afternoon, FANSHAW BAY returned to Pearl Harbor and moored at the Pearl City Peninsula where she remained for the next three days while taking on stores, gasoline, fuel oil, and ammunition – including large numbers of 100, 250, and 500 pound bombs. VC-66 was about to take a long trip to the Southwest Pacific.

On 12 August 1944, FANSHAW BAY got underway with the MARCUS ISLAND and their escorts as part of Task Group 32.4. Altogether there were forty ships in the convoy. The initial destination was Guadalcanal in the Solomon Islands. The Solomons are approximately 3300 miles southwest of Pearl Harbor. The ultimate objective was Morotai Island in the Moluccas Islands, Dutch East Indies. The Moluccas are approximately another 2400 miles beyond the Solomons. Thus, the Task Group would be steaming almost 6000 miles to get to its objective.

The Moluccas Islands were part of the Japanese National Defense Zone and within the so-called "Tojo Line" – the Japanese main line of defense named after Prime Minister and War Minister, General Hideki Tojo. The Japanese would not give them up easily.

Morotai is approximately twenty-five miles wide and forty miles long. More important, it is about half way between the Philippine Islands – three hundred miles from Mindano - and New Guinea, and was big enough to build an airfield to support an invasion of the Philippines. And it was not as heavily defended as its bigger neighboring island - Halmahera.

Morotai was to be the final island invasion in the Dutch New Guinea area before the invasion of the Philippine Islands. Liberation of the Philippines would be the fulfillment of the famous promise Army General Douglas MacArthur made after President Roosevelt ordered his evacuation from Corregidor Island in February 1942. MacArthur promised the Philippine people, "I shall return" to drive the Japanese out.

The Philippines fell in May 1942 with the surrender of Corregidor – which followed by about a month the surrender of the cut off, out of ammunition, and starving American and Filipino troops at Bataan. Those "Battling Bastards of Bataan" were then subjected to the infamous "Bataan Death March" - during which hundreds of American and thousands of Filipino troops were shot, bayoneted, or beheaded by the Japanese. They marched sixty-five miles in three days without food or water to Japanese freighters known as "hell ships" that would take them to prison camp. And when they got to prison camp, their life continued to be hell. Ambrose in *To America* quotes a Death March survivor as saying, "While most Americans during the war thought of the Japanese as beasts, they really were not. A beast is an animal, and animals kill only to eat. The Japs killed for fun." Another Bataan survivor, Melvin H. Rosen, is quoted in his obituary written by Yvonne Shinhoster Lamb in the 31 August 2007 *Washington Post*:

> It was war, after all, and what I was trained for, but we had every right to assume we would be treated humanely and in accordance with international law. War or not, we could never imagine the racism, the cruelty, the torture, the savagery we would and did experience.

MacArthur would keep his promise. On 20 October 1944, as Commander in Chief of the Southwest Pacific, he would step off an American landing craft with the President of the Philippines onto a Philippine beach. The Americans had returned and while there would be heavy fighting for several months, Japan's remaining days of occupying the Philippines were numbered.

But before the Philippines could be liberated, some other things had to happen – including the taking of Morotai. Some of MacArthur's troops – the 31st Infantry Division, would be assigned the job. They would be supported by VC-66 flying from FANSHAW BAY- and a whole lot of other American naval units.

VC-66's trip to the Solomons lasted from the 12th until the 24th of August. While en route, the squadron flew anti-submarine patrol sorties and made several simulated attacks on Task Group ships. Mardarello remembers some of the time being passed by enlisted men versus officers basketball games on the hanger deck. He enjoyed them a lot and as in the softball contests back in Hawaii, he recalls, "We did very well against the officers."

15 August 1944 was a big day for Banks. He was advanced to Aviation Metalsmith First Class (AM1c) (pay grade E-6 and equivalent to a Staff Sergeant in the Marine Corps and Army). He was now one step below a Chief Petty Officer. His base pay went from $96 per month to $114 per month. There was also an appropriate raise in his flight pay. He was now earning more than $2000 per year. It was pretty good money in those days.

As always, some of the en route time was used for various shipboard drills and training such as damage control, general quarters, and abandon ship. In an abandon ship drill, the crew would be directed to muster on one of the weather decks wearing their life jackets. They would then be given helpful survival instructions over the ship's public address system such as "the nearest land is ten miles off our port bow," and the best and safest way to get from the ship to the water either by ladder or jumping. Typically, there would not be enough lifeboats or rafts for everyone.

Banks remembers that during one abandon ship drill, it dawned on him and Stoops that there was a life raft in their TBM that was just sitting there tied down on deck. They decided that they would make the plane their mustering spot and if they ever had to actually abandon ship, "We would grab the torpedo bomber's raft and jump over the side with it. It also had emergency flashlights and other emergency supplies." According to Banks, the word about their survival plan quickly got around and during the next drill, it was hard to find a plane and its raft that had not been claimed by some of the guys from the squadron. Banks does not know who "leaked" their idea, but he has suspicions.

On the 22nd of August, nine of the squadron's FMs were involved in a fighter scramble exercise. While landing, one of the FMs missed the arresting wire and crashed into the barrier causing slight damage to the plane, but no injuries to personnel.

Also on the 22nd, the Task Group crossed the Equator bringing about the traditional convening on each ship of King Neptune's Royal Court and the initiation and transformation of all first time crossers - "pollywogs," into "shellbacks." While a few of the "saltier" VC-66 old hands were shellbacks, most of the men were pollywogs.

The men of FANSHAW BAY and the squadron would soon be engaged in some pretty fierce combat with the Japanese, but for now, they were going to have a little "fun" amongst themselves.

FANSHAW BAY's Court was convened by the issuance of a "SUBPOENA & SUMMONS EXTRAORDINARY" to each pollywog. The pollywogs were invited to appear before "The Royal High Court Of The Raging Main." DeLoach Cope kept a copy of his subpoena. It reads in pertinent part:

GREETINGS AND BEWARE

WHEREAS, The aforesaid ship (FANSHAW BAY) carries a large and slimy cargo of landlubbers, swabs, haytossers, park-bench warmers, chicken-chasers, soda-inhalers, dancehall engineers, strap-hangers, tea slingers and sand crabs, falsely masquerading as seamen, of which low scum you are a member, having never appeared before us; and

WHEREAS, The ROYAL HIGH COURT OF THE RAGING MAIN has been convened by us on board the good ship FANSHAW BAY on the 22nd day of August 1944, in Latitude 00 00' 00", Longitude (Censored), together with surgeons, dentists, barbers, police, and executioners as may be necessary to execute its judgments; and

BE IT KNOWN, That we hereby summon and command you …to appear before this Royal High Court and Our August Presence on the aforesaid date at such time as may best suit our pleasure to be examined as to fitness to become one of our trusty shellbacks and to answer to the following charges:

CHARGE I. In that … has hitherto willfully and maliciously failed to show reverence and allegiance to our Royal Person, and is therein and thereby a vile landlubber and pollywog.
CHARGE II. In that he showed disrespect to all Loyal Shellbacks.
CHARGE III. In that he knowingly helped conceal the identity of "ELMER."

DISOBEY THIS SUMMONS UNDER PAIN OF OUR SWIFT AND TERRIBLE DISPLEASURE. OUR VIGILANCE IS EVER WAKEFUL, OUR VENGEANCE IS JUST AND SURE.

Signed NEPTUNIS REX, King

Signed DAVEY JONES, Scribe

Banks recalls the initiation as being pretty rough. In his words, "They beat hell out of us." Among other things, the pollywogs were subjected to hair cuts, black paint, electric shocks, dunking, and beatings with canvas socks soaked in salt water. Many of the guys could not sit down afterward and as a result, some could not fly.

Mardarello admits that he was looking at the initiation from the perspective of a teenager and someone relatively new to the squadron who was still enjoying the new adventure of life at sea. To him, "Even the shellback initiation was fun."

Charlie Edwards remembers the initiation as being a "wild time." As he recalls:

Most of the crew were pollywogs, but the shellbacks really knew what they were doing and beat on us hard. They blasted us with hoses and I thought we would be knocked into the Pacific. I was surprised that the ship's CO would allow it. The ship would be out of luck if a sub attacked us during the initiation.

In any case, VC-66's new skipper was not happy with the fact that after the initiation, some of his men were temporarily on the "binnacle list" - disabled or sick and excused from duty.

During the afternoon of 23 August, the winds were exceptionally light – only 2.5 miles per hour or less. Bud Clark feels that the light winds contributed to two of the squadron's planes – an FM and a TBM - missing the arresting wire and crashing into the barrier as they tried to land. Clark recalls:

> While operating near the equator on the Fanshaw Bay one of the ship's turbines failed or had to be shut down. Maximum speed that the carrier could get with only one engine was about 13 knots. At the same time we had a period of dead calm wind speed. It was desirable to have a wind speed of at least 25 knots over the deck for landing. With no wind and a crippled carrier, landings were a little too fast, which contributed to barrier crashes.

The FM suffered moderate damage while the TBM was only slightly damaged. Neither crash landing resulted in any personnel injuries.

On 24 August, after nearly two weeks of steaming, the Task Group reached the Solomons and anchored in Gavutu Harbor near Tulagi Island. Among other things, Tulagi had been home base to future president LTJG John F. "Jack" Kennedy and his PT-109 - before it was cut in half by a Japanese destroyer.

Being at Tulagi brought back some vivid memories for one of the squadron's "elders" – TBM Pilot, LT Albert J. "Al" Mayer from Fresno, California. Mayer was twenty-six years old. He had received his Navy pilot's wings ten days before the attack on Pearl Harbor and had already spent eighteen eventful months in the South Pacific before he joined VC-66 in July 1943.

After he got his wings, Mayer was assigned to the heavy cruiser USS NORTHAMPTON (CA-26) as one of six pilots on board flying little scout observation bi-planes - SOCs. As Mayer recalls, "They did 90 MPH in any position of flight."

Mayer was aboard NORTHAMPTON when she was part of Task Force 16 – the famous Doolittle Raid Task Force. On 18 April 1942, led by LTCOL James H. "Jimmy" Doolittle, sixteen Army B-25 medium bombers took off from the USS HORNET (CV-8) on a one way trip to give Tokyo a taste of the young Pacific war. While it did not do a great deal of damage, the raid gave American morale a boost and embarrassed the Japanese military.

Mayer was also on board NORTHAMPTON the night of 30 November 1942 when disaster struck. The cruiser was hit by two torpedoes from the Japanese destroyer

OYASHIO and sunk during the fierce battle of Tassafaronga near Guadalcanal. As Mayer recalls, "The Japanese torpedoes were good and they killed us that night."

After the NORTHAMPTON went down, Mayer and nine other pilots and their scout planes were left at Florida Island to work with the PT boats operating out of Tulagi and the Marines on Guadalcanal. Mayer advises, "I spent over five months existing on Florida Island at a Seaplane base we hacked out of the jungle. Bananas and Spam was our diet! Our pilot losses were terrible during this period."

When the war was over, Mayer stayed in the Navy. After he retired, he went to Optometry College, passed the California State Board exam, and practiced until he was seventy-nine years old.

But on 24 August 1944, he was twenty-six years old and back at Gavutu Harbor near Tulagi with VC-66 getting ready to do battle with the Imperial Japanese Navy and Army again.

FANSHAW BAY spent much of 25 August refueling. She took on 360,000 gallons of fuel oil and 22,000 gallons of aviation gasoline before leaving Tulagi in the evening to begin the transit to the next stop – the Admiralty Islands. Three destroyer escorts – USS BUTLER (DE-339), USS RAYMOND (DE-341), and USS ROWELL (DE-403), went with her.

There were no flight ops on the 26th and 27th because of light air.

During the evening of 28 August, FANSHAW BAY and her escorts arrived at Seeadler Harbor, Manus Island - about 300 miles off the north coast of New Guinea. They had come in from the southeast through the Coral Sea and Bismarck Sea. VC-66 flew its aircraft - eleven TBMs and fourteen FMs - from the FANSHAW BAY to Ponam Field on Ponam Island in the Admiralties.

Ponam Field was a single airstrip that had been built by the Navy's 78th Construction Battalion ("Seabees") working day and night for ten weeks earlier in 1944. The Seabees had lived up to their motto: "The difficult we do at once, the impossible takes a bit longer."

The squadron's introduction to the Admiralties was a tough one. While doing a fly-away take off in an FM for the flight to Ponam, ENS William J. "Bill" Johnson from Saint Paul, Minnesota, one of the squadron's newer pilots, was killed when his plane failed to develop enough power to gain altitude and crashed into the sea off FANSHAW BAY's starboard bow. The plane with Johnson still in it, sank "immediately."

On the 29th, the squadron launched eleven TBMs and eleven FMs from Ponam Field to make simulated attacks on FANSHAW BAY while she was underway in a training area north of Manus Island. The carriers and their escorts were now training in preparation to support the invasion of Morotai.

After the exercises of 29 August, the VC-66 planes returned to Ponam Field where the squadron remained for several days while FANSHAW BAY was at anchor in Seeadler Harbor. The carrier was making minor repairs and taking on stores, fuel oil, and aviation fuel.

In addition to flying and training, the squadron spent its time at Ponam by relaxing – including: hunting for shells, swimming, drinking beer, trading with the natives for carvings, and exploring the area. Mardarello found some Japanese pamphlets that some of the guys kept for souvenirs. The men of VC-66 knew they were going into a fight. Accordingly, they wanted to take advantage of the time they had left to enjoy themselves.

Banks has some good memories of the time at Ponam. He recalls, "I bartered with a Navy yeoman for several bottles of red ink. I used the ink to dye my mattress cover red. I then traded the red mattress cover to a native for a dugout canoe." Aside from providing enjoyable personal use for Banks and his buddies as a platform for shell diving in the Ponam lagoon, the dugout became a source for some nice "rental" income from other Sailors and officers. When the squadron left Ponam, Banks gave the dugout back to the native. He also remembers that some of the guys "drilled holes in ammo shells (machine gun, pistol) stringing them into necklaces and traded with the native islanders for dugout rentals, art work, or their jewelry. It went over big." He also remembers going swimming while an armed Marine stood shark guard on a bluff over the beach.

While at Ponam, each man was given a ration of two bottles of beer per day. On one of the days, Jobbo Polski had the officer of the day duty and somehow "confused" the Ponam supply Petty Officer who was responsible for distributing the beer. Instead of two beers per man, Polski was given two cases of beer for each man in the squadron! From that point on, according to Banks, "Polski was the best friend of all of the enlisted men." The squadron's sudden treasure of beer was hidden in an empty Quonset hut. Word got around, however, that there was to be a surprise building inspection. And according to Banks, "We quickly grabbed the cases of beer and hid them in the jungle where it was safe. We used evaporating gasoline to cool the beer before drinking it." Life on Ponam was good – and the men were making the most of it.

The VC-66 men were not so successful in "protecting" an ice cream machine that they had somehow obtained for squadron use. To their chagrin, the CO confiscated it and donated it to the ladies running the Red Cross Center. From then on, to get ice cream, the men had to pay for it. The skipper did not enamor himself with his men with that decision.

On 30 August, the Bob Hope USO Show paid a visit to entertain the troops at Ponam. VC-66 was given the job of meeting the entertainers' plane and transporting them to their quarters. Banks remembers that assignment being carried out with "great enthusiasm." He also remembers a couple of the pilots "kidnapping" one of the star dancers, Patty Thomas, and taking her on an unscheduled jeep tour of the island. Apparently she was good natured about the whole event since no one ended up in the brig.

Based on the kinds of things that went on at Ponam Island, one can see how James Michener – a former Navy Lieutenant Commander who served in the Solomon Islands during the war, could be inspired by his experiences to write the Pulitzer Prize winning *Tales of the South Pacific.* Rodgers and Hammerstein, along with Joshua Logan, then took Michener's book and turned it into a hit musical. "South Pacific" opened on Broadway in April 1949 and stayed there a long time. Subsequently, it has been performed countless times and enjoyed by millions of people – including my wife, Carol, and I. In 1966, we saw a performance at the old Fisher Hall on the campus of Miami University during our student days. It was our first date - and yes, it was "some enchanted evening."

Ponam Island was a brief, pleasant interlude for VC-66.

On the morning of 4 September, the squadron flew ten TBM-1Cs and twelve FM-2s back to the FANSHAW BAY. As one of the FMs was landing, it missed the arresting wire and crashed into the barrier causing moderate damage to the plane, but no personnel injuries. After landing the planes, FANSHAW BAY anchored in the harbor.

The squadron's first ship, the NASSAU, was also anchored in the same harbor and her officers invited the VC-66 officers to the local Officers' Club for a reunion. The participants talked over old times and by the VC-66 skipper's account, the evening ended on a high note. "The squadron drank a toast to the NASSAU, the 'fightingest ship in the Navy,' and was answered by the NASSAU's new Skipper, who said, 'We wish we had our old squadron back aboard.'" It was a fine compliment for the men of VC-66.

From 5 through 9 September, FANSHAW BAY remained at anchor in Seeadler Harbor, getting briefed and making final preparations for the Morotai invasion.

On 10 September, the squadron got underway aboard FANSHAW BAY with Task Group 77.1. The Task Group was made up of two escort carrier divisions totaling six CVEs and eight destroyer escorts. RADM Thomas L. "Tommy" Sprague, Commander Carrier Division 22, was overall Task Group Commander and was aboard the USS SANGAMON (CVE-26). RADM Clifton A.F. "Ziggy" Sprague (no relation to Thomas Sprague), Commander Carrier Division 25, was aboard FANSHAW BAY. CAPT D.P. Johnson was CO of FANSHAW BAY. The Task Group was en route to the objective area east of Morotai. The squadron's mission: to provide air support for the invasion of Morotai and otherwise as needed.

From the 10th to the 13th, the squadron flew anti-submarine patrol and combat air patrol sorties. The ships practiced anti-aircraft defense. Given FANSHAW BAY's previous experience during the Marianas campaign, every man aboard her appreciated the need to have a good anti-aircraft defense. During this time, the Task Group rendezvoused with the troop transports, cargo ships, landing ships, cruisers and other ships that would be taking part in the invasion. The convoy totaled approximately 135 ships and was about ten miles long. There were no flight operations on 14 September as the Task Group steamed toward its objective. The squadron rested and received final briefings.

15 September 1944 was D-Day for the invasion of Morotai. FANSHAW BAY was on station ten to thirty miles east of Morotai in company with the SANGAMON, USS CHENANGO (CVE-28), USS SUWANEE (CVE-27), USS SANTEE (CVE-29), USS MIDWAY (CVE-63), and their eight destroyer escorts. It was a potent force with which to hit Morotai.

The aircrews were called to flight quarters early. Flight operations began at 0516 and lasted all day - until 1900. The TBMs flew air support over Morotai while the FMs flew combat air patrol sorties. VC-66's Avengers dropped four tons of bombs on Gotalamo village which was in the path of the landing troops. In the meantime, U.S. troops landed on beaches adjacent to Japan's Pitoe Airfield in the southern part of Morotai. They quickly drove the Japanese defenders into the hills.

Since he was still in the training pipeline when VC-66 was involved in the Marshalls Campaign, the missions over Moratai would be Emidio Mardarello's first real taste of combat. He recalls, "The bombing and strafing was new to me as a replacement and I found it exciting." He was somewhat embarrassed, however, when he reported to his pilot and radio operator what he thought was anti-aircraft fire coming toward them. "I was quickly overruled and advised that what I saw was actually what we were sending down."

15 September was also D-Day for the invasion of Peleliu Island in the Palau Island group. These islands were about 500 miles northeast of Morotai and 500 miles east of the Philippines. The 1st Marine Division would assault Peleliu. The island was eventually taken, but the battle lasted two and a half months and was one of the most brutal and costly in terms of dead and wounded in Marine Corps history.

While returning to FANSHAW BAY on the 15th, an FM missed the arresting cable and hit the barrier. The plane suffered moderate damage, but neither the pilot nor any ship's personnel were injured. Two other FMs had to make emergency landings because of fuel line problems, but all in all, the invasion had gotten off to a good start.

By the end of D-Day, American troops had moved four and a half miles inland from Morotai's west beach and almost three miles inland from the southern coast. Casualties were light, and within a week work would start on the airfield that would help support the invasion and liberation of the Philippines.

In addition to the occasional air support mission over Morotai, the squadron would spend much of its time during the next three weeks neutralizing the Japanese airfields on neighboring Halmahera Island..

Banks remembers one mission when they were providing air support for attacking troops and Stephens flew the TBM lengthwise along the beach. Banks' turret was turned sideways so that he could strafe ahead of the advancing ground troops. The turret only moved sideways, not up and down. The .50 caliber machine gun could move up and down, but it could not shoot directly to the rear for fear of hitting the plane's tail. The radioman's .30 caliber machine gun faced the rear and could shoot up and down if necessary.

Banks recalls that they flew along the beach several times following instructions from a Navy pilot who was embedded with the attacking troops on the ground. The liaison officer on the ground would identify targets that were bothering the Marines and the planes would neutralize them. "We bombed and strafed villages, huts, artillery positions, and troop concentrations – anything that could be of use to the enemy. It went on all day." For Banks, "Morotai was a nightmare. I sat in that glass bubble after a bombing dive, climbing and watching ack ack burst around us and machine gun bullets reaching up for us."

Banks also remembers that they sometimes engaged in a little "psychological" warfare:

In addition to our normal explosive ordnance load, we would occasionally load the plane's tunnel area and radioman's space with empty bottles from the ship. After dropping our bombs, we would drop the bottles. The bottles sounded like bombs as they fell. It would scare hell out of the Japanese.

In addition to the stress and fatigue caused by the long hours of flying in combat conditions, it was hot and humid and the sun was intense in the Southwest Pacific. There was no air conditioning, no high tech synthetic clothing, and no special hydration packs. The aircrews wore one piece cotton flight suits. Banks remembers "the suits turning black from the sweat and beginning to rot." To keep the sun off his face, he doctored his cloth flight "helmet" with the brim of a baseball cap – which soon became fashionable with others in the squadron. Some of the fellows wore a piece of leather over their blistered noses or used zinc oxide on them to block the sun. They had to be creative in dealing with the tough conditions. Generally they just "sucked it up" and did the job.

Between missions, everyone tried to relax as best they could. Mardarello recalls going into the squadron's ready room between missions and observing the pilots listening to music from Gilbert and Sullivan's "The Mikado" and "HMS Pinafore." He thought it a somewhat unusual choice and remembers, "I and the other aircrewmen wished they would listen to something else." Today, at age eighty-two, Mardarello advises somewhat ironically, "Now, I like Gilbert and Sullivan and listen to their music often."

A TBM on the deck of a carrier with a destroyer in plane guard station astern of the carrier. In addition to providing ASW and anti-air defense, it is the destroyer's job to race in and pick up any survivors if a plane goes into the water. (Photo: courtesy National Archives)

A basketball game at sea in a carrier's elevator well. (Photo: courtesy National Archives)

Sailors enjoy some liberty on a South Pacific island. (Photo: courtesy National Archives)

Bob Hope and Frances Langford entertain VC-66 and other troops on Ponam Island in the Southwest Pacific. (Official U.S. Navy Photograph courtesy W.D. Cope)

Actress Frances Langford (left) and dancer Patty Thomas (right) on Ponam Island for the USO show. Thomas was briefly "kidnapped" by two VC-66 pilots and given a tour of the island in their jeep. (Official U.S. Navy Photograph courtesy W.D. Cope)

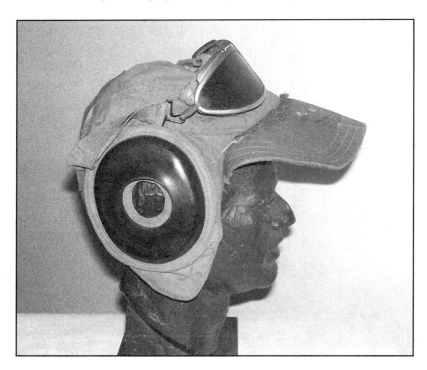

Banks' VC-66 flight helmet as modified by his adding a baseball cap brim for additional protection from the sun while sitting in the turret. (Photo: courtesy S.A. Banks)

14

VC-66's Finest Hour – Saving Ensign Thompson

D-Day plus one - 16 September 1944, was a long, hard day for the men of the squadron, and arguably their most memorable. Flight operations began at 0515. The TBMs again flew air support sorties over the Morotai landing area. The FMs flew CAP sorties protecting the TBMs and the ships. At 0653, while flying combat air patrol in an FM-2, LTJG Reynold "Rod" Rodriquez from Forest Hills, New York, made an overhead pass at a Japanese "Zero" fighter from approximately 1000 feet above the water. Rodriquez was unable to pull out in time and was killed when his plane hit the water and exploded.

At 0655, Rodriquez's VC-66 shipmate and fellow FM pilot, LTJG George W. "Brownie" Brown from Stockton, California, caught up with the Zero and shot it down ten miles south of Cape Gila, Morotai. The Zero burst into flames when it hit the water. Banks recalls the next day's news cast reporting: "General MacArthur's forces shot down a Zero on the 16th." Evidently, they didn't bother to mention Brown or the squadron's involvement in the matter.

At 0900 on the 16th, four of the squadron's TBMs were flying air support over the southern Morotai beaches when they were fired on by American LSDs (Landing Ship Dock) and destroyers. Fortunately - even though it was one of the heaviest anti-aircraft barrages that any of them had ever seen, the TBM crews suffered no casualties or damage to their planes from the friendly fire. But James Gander, who observed the whole incident from his turret, remembers it as probably the most frightening moment of the war for him. He recalls, "Our ships opened up and that was tense." He remembers thinking it "curious because the Japanese did not have any planes that looked like TBMs."

The VC-66 men did not make a big deal out of the matter when they got back to the carrier. The possibility of being shot down by your fellow Americans as well as the Japanese was just another on the list of dangers that the men of the squadron had to live with – including taking off and landing on a short, rolling, pitching deck; possible in flight mechanical failure; formation flying; high speed maneuvering; finding the carrier in poor visibility; and the threat of your ship being torpedoed while you slept. Each man dealt with the stress the best he could and got on with the job.

Later in the morning of 16 September, a VC-66 fighter group made strikes on Lolobata Airfield on Halmahera Island. They destroyed a Japanese "Sally" bomber and two Zeroes on the ground. But before returning to the FANSHAW BAY they got word that a pilot from another squadron had been shot down and was in serious trouble.

ENS Harold A. Thompson of FIGHTER SQUADRON TWENTY-SIX (VF-26) flying from the SANTEE had been shot down within a few hundred feet of Japanese held Wasile Bay, Halmahera. Halmahera was twelve miles south of Morotai. Thompson was in a tough spot. Halmahera was crawling with Japanese – 30,000 of them (by comparison, the soon to become famous island of Iwo Jima had a Japanese garrison of about 22,000).

Planes from Thompson's own squadron had been providing air cover for him, but they began running low on fuel and asked the VC-66 fighters for help. DeLoach Cope gives a nice first hand account of VC-66's role in the Thompson rescue in an issue of Joe Mussatto's *VC-66 (T-2) Newsletter*. Cope recalls:

We had fuel and ammunition enough to help out until others could come in and relieve us. While covering we strafed the beaches and made sure the enemy could not get to the downed pilot located behind a barge that had been sunk just off shore. Looking from the Bay the barge was to the right of a pier extending out into the Bay.

The VC-66 planes kept a "constant watch" and repeatedly strafed the pier "to make sure no one could make it out there to do harm to the downed pilot." The VC-66 fighters were eventually relieved and went back to the FANSHAW BAY. By now, arrangements were being made for a rescue effort by two PT boats – each with an all volunteer crew. VC-66 would help provide air support. In the meantime, Thompson - wounded in the hand and still being shot at by the Japanese, stayed in a life raft that had been dropped to him by a PBY. He hid as best he could - first near the pier and then by the sunken Japanese barge. It was sunk by the covering planes as it tried to attack Thompson.

At 1447, after refueling and rearming the fighters, VC-66 launched a special rescue covering strike group that involved virtually the whole squadron - seven TBMs and eight FMs. The skipper of one of the PT boats radioed to say that the Japanese fire from the beach was so intense that he had to turn back. J.P. Fox was the VC-66 flight leader. Fox told the PT boat skipper to hold on as they were on their way and would be there in just a few minutes. Fox recalls, "Then I gave him an invitation he couldn't refuse. Make another attempt and we will try to suppress the ground fire. He did a 180 degree and started his run in at full throttle while zig-zagging."

The squadron's planes arrived over the area and went to work bombing and strafing the Japanese positions. As Cope recalls, "All the Bay gun positions were bombed by the T-Bombers and the fighters strafed."

The VC-66 planes dropped nearly four tons of bombs. Three TBMs from another CVE also laid down an effective covering smoke screen. Anti-aircraft fire was heavy. Stephens recalls a plane from another carrier being hit and going down. It was an FM from the SUWANNEE that was hit while making a strafing run. It crashed only one hundred yards from where Thompson was trying to hide. The pilot, ENS William P. Bannister, died in the crash. Another SUWANNEE fighter was shot down and crashed farther out in the bay. Its pilot survived and was rescued by a PBY. The flak was so heavy that another PBY could not get close enough to Thompson to rescue him.

Fox recalls, "In the meantime, Thompson had drifted under a "T" pier extending into Wasile Bay. We strafed the Japs who were trying to come out to get him." Banks remembers circling the area and shooting at the Japanese end of the pier to keep them away from Thompson. Dean Birdsong recalls that some of the VC-66 planes ran out of ammunition. "But we continued to 'buzz' the Japanese to keep them down and from being able to fire at Thompson and the PT boats." The VC-66 guys were going to do whatever they could to keep Thompson from being killed or captured.

Thompson was saved late in the afternoon when one of the PT boats approaching within fifty feet of shore, dashed in and rescued him under heavy fire from the beach. The fire was especially intense near the bay entrance. As the PT boat got close to the pier, VC-66's J.P. Fox told the boat crew exactly where Thompson was hiding.

The planes continued to bomb, strafe, and lay down smoke while two swimmers from the PT boat went to get Thompson. Cope recalls, "It looked like the beach was on fire from the tracer bullets....bombers, that were loaded with smoke, made their run along the shore line – the breeze came to a stand still and the smoke settled along the shore line making it impossible to see the PT boat from shore."

After Thompson was in the PT boat and it was backing out into the bay, a second smoke run was made. Cope describes it as being "almost like a movie, everything was done with such perfection." Once back out in the bay, however, the PT boat still had to get back through the bay mouth to the open sea and safety. In Cope's words:

> The Japs had reloaded and were waiting for the little boat. The fighters and bombers and the smokers were also ready to put this daring crew and their little boat and the rescued pilot through that outlet. As the PT boat approached the outlet the fire began. The fighters and bombers had spotted the gun positions going through and were right on target. The smokers again were perfect with their part and the little boat made it back out to sea to join the other PT boat that was waiting to see if it was needed.

In his report of the mission, Fox indicated that while the PT boats were making their run out of the bay, the FMs split up with the VC-66 fighters covering the east shore and the other fighters covering the west shore. Fox continues:

> At this point our 7 VT (TBMs) and 3 Smokys (TBMs from another squadron) split up and bombed, strafed, and fired rockets with excellent results on both sides of the channel. In spite of all of this the shore batteries put up heavier fire than had previously been encountered by the PTs. The fire was inaccurate and was almost impossible to tell where it was coming from.

The PT boats had been under fire for over two hours, but suffered no casualties. Fox advises, "When he (the PT boat skipper) was safely out I gave him a 'Well Done' and we returned to the FANSHAW BAY. I wrote up the whole incident and said he should be given a high medal for risking his boat and crew to pick up one of our pilots." The Lieutenant who led the rescue mission was awarded the Congressional Medal of Honor. Several members of his crew were awarded Navy Crosses, and others – including the crew of the second boat, received Silver Stars.

Bob Kennon recalls how he felt during the rescue mission as he looked down from his radioman's position and saw what the PT boat crews were going through and what they were doing (Kennon's pilot was fellow Mississippian LTJG James O. "J.O." Mayo from Quitman, Mississippi, and his turret gunner was Aviation Machinist's Mate Second Class John Hart from Los Angeles, California). Kennon thought "how brave those shipmates were that were manning the PT boats." Today, Kennon relates, "I'm so glad to hear they received the awards and recognition they so much deserved."

As for the rescued ENS Thompson, his Wasile Bay experience lasted about eleven hours. According to Y'Blood in *The Little Giants*, Thompson's comment when it was over was, "Sure was a wonderful show to watch."

The VC-66 rescue support strike group landed on FANSHAW BAY at 1831. Commander Task Unit 77.1.2, RADM C.A.F. Sprague, gave squadron personnel "high praise" for their part in the operation. The men of the squadron were justifiably proud of their role in Thompson's rescue. It has become known as one of the more dramatic if not the most dramatic rescue of the war in the Pacific. The magnitude, intensity, and precision of the effort to save a fellow airman was truly impressive. Cope's flight log shows that he was in the air eight hours that day. And that was some tough flying. For it, he was awarded an Air Medal (Cope believes, "All on that flight received Air Medals"). The citation was signed by Secretary of the Navy, James Forrestal, and read:

> For meritorious achievement in aerial flight as Pilot of a Fighter Plane during operations against enemy Japanese forces in the vicinity of Halmahera Island, September 16, 1944. Participating in strafing attacks against enemy shore batteries and installations as wingman to the flight leader, Lieutenant (then Lieutenant, Junior Grade,) Cope pressed home his attacks to help destroy three enemy aircraft on the ground, and aided in the successful rescue of a fellow pilot from capture by the enemy. His airmanship, courage and devotion to duty were in keeping with the highest traditions of the United States Naval Service.

Cope agrees that supporting the rescue of Thompson was the squadron's finest hour. He states, "It is hard to conceive of the effort that went into it – and all of those planes flying around with no one running into each other."

The extent of the Thompson rescue effort – involving the risking of hundreds of lives, as well as many aircraft and boats, to save one man provides a sharp contrast to the way the Japanese regarded their soldiers and airmen. In *Flags of Our Fathers*, Bradley refers to an incident described in Saburo Ienaga's *The Pacific War: A Critical Perspective on Japan's Role in World War II* (1978). A captured Japanese officer saw American medical personnel treating badly wounded Japanese soldiers. "He expressed surprise at the resources being expended upon these men, who were too badly injured to fight again. 'What would you do with these men?' a Marine officer asked. 'We'd give each a grenade,' was his answer. 'And if they didn't use it, we'd cut their jugular vein.'"

As for the Japanese airmen, their planes – particularly their famed Zero fighter - unlike American planes, had little to no armor plating, no self sealing fuel tanks, and often no parachutes for the pilots. The Japanese were prepared to sacrifice much to gain a little speed and maneuverability advantage - which they had early in the war. As the war progressed, however, the Americans developed tactics and aircraft that could beat the Zeros, but the Japanese never really improved them even while building over 20,000. As a result of failing to provide basic protection for their planes and pilots, the Japanese lost a lot of good, experienced airmen that they could not easily replace. The American kill ratio against Zeros went from 1:1 early in the war to eventually 10:1.

Moreover, the Americans involved in the Thompson rescue may have been thinking about how the Japanese treated the American airmen that they pulled from the water during the Battle of Midway. Two of them, an Ensign and an Aviation Machinist's Mate Second Class were interrogated and then blindfolded, weighed down with five gallon cans of water, and thrown overboard. Another young pilot was also killed after being picked up by a Japanese ship and interrogated. His body was then either thrown overboard or fell into the sea.

No American on or over Wasile Bay on 16 September wanted to risk Thompson being captured. In *Flags of Our Fathers,* Bradley states well the difference between the Japanese and American fighting men: "The Japanese enemy would fight to the death for the Emperor. That motive made them formidable. But these boys (Americans) would fight to the death for one another. And that motive made them invincible."

Cope recalls that years later, after the war was long over, Kip Kiplinger – who had been one of the VC-66 TBM pilots involved in the Thompson rescue - told of once having lunch in Washington, D.C. with a fellow by the name of A. Murray Preston. Kiplinger at the time was Editor in Chief of *Kiplinger's Personal Finance* magazine. Preston was a banker. But during the war, as Commander of PT Squadron 33, he led the mission that rescued ENS Thompson and received the Medal of Honor for it. At the time of their lunch meeting, neither Kiplinger nor Preston knew the other had been involved in Thompson's rescue. Too bad. They probably would have had a pretty good time swapping sea stories. Kiplinger did not find out about Preston's involvement in the Thompson rescue until after Preston had died and Kiplinger read his obituary.

Bud Clark recalls a somewhat similar experience:

About 50 years after the war, at a family get-together, I was listening to my son's father-in-law telling a war story about participating in the rescue of a downed pilot. The story was familiar. It turned out that he had been a radioman in a TBM from the USS Sangamon which was laying down a smokescreen for the rescue of Ensign Thompson while we were making bombing runs. It was the first time that either of us knew that we had both been involved in that rescue.

VC-66's DeLoach Cope prepares to launch in his FM for a dawn mission. (Official U.S. Navy Photograph courtesy W.D. Cope)

VC-66's Charlie Edwards climbs into his FM. (Official U.S. Navy Photograph courtesy C.T. Edwards)

VC-66's Sam Takis after a successful landing in his FM. (Official U.S. Navy Photograph courtesy W.D. Cope)

One of Banks' squadron shipmates in a TBM turret. (Official U.S. Navy Photograph courtesy D.A. Banks collection)

15

The Battle Continues

From 0543 until 1804 on 17 September, the squadron flew ASP and CAP sorties – some locally over the Task Group ships and some over the target area. Sorties continued to last as long as four hours. Squadron aircrews reported that the Japanese runways on Halmahera at Galela and Miti were still in good condition. They also reported seeing at least eleven Japanese bombers and two fighters possibly still operational. In fact, earlier in the day, Japanese planes had attacked American troops on Morotai. Squadron aircrews also reported seeing three Japanese boats and fifteen barges in Wasile Bay, Halmahera.

Banks recalls:

> Over one of the bays, squadron planes were taking some heavy anti-aircraft fire from a big gun that nobody could spot. The CO asked for a volunteer to fly around and draw fire from the gun while other planes from the squadron tried to locate muzzle flashes so as to be able to neutralize it. Stephens volunteered us to be the target. We took off and circled the bay at low altitude watching the little puffs of smoke getting closer to us. At that time, I was reminded of the old saying that "there are no atheists in foxholes" and thought to myself, "that goes for turrets also." The other guys from the squadron spotted the gun – which turned out to be located in a church that we had deliberately not targeted previously. Bombs were dropped and the church and gun destroyed. Back on the carrier, one of the TBF pilots involved in the mission grounded himself saying if he had to bomb churches, he did not want to fly anymore. He became one of the landing signal officers (LSOs) who stood on the carrier and guided the planes with two hand held flags as they were making their landing approaches.

VC-66 flew a lot of missions in and around Morotai and Halmahera. Banks recalls sometimes not even being able to get out of the plane once it landed if they were doing multiple missions because of the combat situation. "The plane landed, refueled, and was launched again." Landing at night was particularly "scary." And when flight operations were going on fast and furious, sleep was at a premium. Banks remembers one of his fellow aircrewmen who could never be awakened. "The only way we could do it was to grab him out of his bunk then stand him up."

Charlie Edwards recalls dropping napalm – a very flammable jellylike substance, during one mission on Halmahera. He does not remember the target, but remembers it as being "nasty, nasty stuff." He recalls, "We carried it in a big tank under the plane. It burst into flames on impact."

Dean Birdsong also recalls flying a lot during that time – "96 hours in 14 days" – an average of about 7 hours per day. "And part of it was at night and I was never night trained." He remembers that it was always hot. "We had heat rash often over the upper body because of the flight suits. The Corpsmen set up a massage room for us. They would rub us down and put balm on us and then we would get back in the planes and go on another flight."

Birdsong was one of the earliest members of the squadron. He arrived just a week after it was commissioned in June 1943. VC-66 was his first assignment right out of flight training. When he went through fighter training, his Chief Flight Instructor was Gerry Trapp – who would be his XO and eventually CO with VC-66. Like Stephens, Birdsong did his final flight training carrier qualifications on Lake Michigan aboard the WOLVERINE.

And like Stephens, Birdsong was a Kansas man – having been born in the town of McCracken on 26 March 1921. He too had been a member of the Civilian Pilot Training Program in college at Fort Hayes State. Birdsong recounts, "I knew the war was coming and had a long time interest in flying, so I started pilot training. The military was the way to go to get flying experience." He recalls that the day after Pearl Harbor was attacked, "I went to the Navy recruiter to start the pilot selection process. You needed sixty hours of college credit to be eligible for the Navy pilot program." He chose the Navy out of a desire to fly the new F4U Corsairs which he says, "I finally got to do after VC-66 when I went to a squadron of F4Us." Birdsong remembers VC-66 as "a good group who liked each other."

Banks remembers the time when Birdsong got word that his brother was killed in action. His brother was in the Army. According to Banks:

> Birdsong told the ordnance men on the carrier to put on the maximum ordnance that his plane could carry for his next mission. During the mission when the initial strike was complete, Birdsong broke from the formation and went back and strafed the Japanese again at low altitude. After running out of ammunition in his machine guns, Birdsong opened his cockpit canopy, inverted his plane, took out his .45 caliber pistol, and blasted away at the Japanese with it. The rest of the squadron circled up above and watched in amazement; we never mentioned it.

While Birdsong does not remember the alleged inverted plane incident described by Banks, he does agree that it is a "good story." And he does confirm that he did get a report that his brother, who was serving in the Army in North Africa, was killed. But later to Birdsong's great relief, he got another report that his brother was still alive. The brother survived the war. Birdsong also recalls running out of ammunition during the ENS Thompson rescue, but continuing to "buzz" the Japanese to keep them down.

Flight operations began again on 18 September at 0526 with CAP and ASP sorties, and strikes against targets on Morotai. The planes searched for a Japanese radar site and strafed two beached medium oilers. While returning to FANSHAW BAY one of the FM's tailhook missed the arresting cable. The plane crashed into the barrier and overturned on top of another Wildcat. Both fighters were seriously damaged, but luckily there were no injuries to the pilot or ship's personnel. Flight ops secured at 1829 with a total of 27 sorties for the day.

Banks remembers an embarrassing incident from one of the missions:

> My .50 caliber machine gun jammed and I raised the gun cover to clear it – using the wrench that I had been awarded in school. I cleared the jam, but committed a mortal sin for a turret gunner when I forgot to close the gun cover. Later during the flight, I swung the turret up and proceeded to drive the gun cover through the turret top jamming it in that position. I made the rest of the flight in the upside down position and landed on the carrier on my back – not the most desirable position.

On another occasion, Banks remembers feeling especially proud of himself after a strafing run. "I thought I had done great damage to some significant targets - only to be called by Stephens over the intercom and given a 'well done' for shooting a couple of wild pigs. Upon landing, the plane captain painted two pigs on my turret."

The action started early on 19 September. FANSHAW BAY sounded General Quarters at 0348 and sent the crew to their battle stations. Hearing the GQ alarm is an awful way to be awakened. You are sleeping, when over the 1MC you suddenly hear the Boatswain's Mate of the Watch on the ship's bridge blow his pipe (whistle) and then announce loudly, "This is not a drill. This is not a drill. General Quarters! General Quarters! All hands man your battle stations!" A loud annoying alarm is then activated for a minute or so. It gets your attention. And then all hell breaks loose as men start running to their assigned battle stations not really knowing what is going on.

FANSHAW BAY went to General Quarters that morning to defend against what was thought to be an incoming Japanese aircraft attack. The "bogey" (unidentified aircraft) eventually faded from radar. But again, based on past experience, FANSHAW BAY was not taking any chances with suspicious in bound aircraft.

After the ship secured from General Quarters, flight operations began at 0527 with more ASP and CAP sorties. The squadron also flew strike missions against the Halmahera air bases. While having decided not to invade the heavily defended Halmahera, the Americans wanted to impede the enemy's ability to use it to counter-attack the U.S. forces now on Morotai. Accordingly, American planes hit Halmahera often. On the 19th, VC-66 strafed, fired rockets, and dropped forty bombs on a wooden barracks area there. All of the ordnance fell in the target area.

While returning to the carrier in the afternoon of the 19th, one of the FMs missed the arresting cable, crashed through the barrier, and overturned causing serious damage to the plane, but again no injuries to personnel. Flight operations secured for the day at 1808 with a total of 29 sorties having been flown. The ship went to General Quarters again in the evening at 1954, when ten to twelve bogeys were picked up on radar. They were thirty-nine miles away traveling at 250 miles per hour. The bogeys orbited, then changed course and faded from radar – to everyone on FANSHAW BAY's great relief.

20 September 1944, was a very tough day for the squadron. Flight operations began as usual at or about 0525 with the usual combat air patrol and anti-submarine patrol sorties being launched. Strikes were also launched against targets on Morotai. The strike group dropped almost two tons of bombs and fired sixteen rockets trying to knock out a radar

site that was supposed to be there. As VC-66 skipper, Trapp, eloquently put it, "Four VT (TBMs) blew Hell out of a wild piece of Morotai jungle in another attempt to destroy that elusive Jap radar station at Gorango Point."

At 1208, disaster struck. Two of the squadron's TBMs collided while joining up to return to the carrier after a mission near Morotai. Banks recalls seeing the planes collide, but not seeing them go into the water. It was "a terrible experience." Four men died in the tragic accident. Pilot LTJG Francis J. M. "Moose" McCabe from Brooklyn, New York (who had given the squadron its "Dat's Fo' de Boids" motto); turret gunner Aviation Machinist's Mate Second Class Robert L. "Nose" Keough (Banks' buddy who was newly married - Banks wrote a letter of condolence to his wife); and radioman Aviation Radioman Second Class Hyram L. Shaffer from Inkom, Idaho, went down with their plane. And Turret gunner Aviation Ordnanceman Third Class Manuel V. Calderon from Los Angeles, California, was unable to get out of the other Avenger before it crashed.

ENS Robert E. "Gizmo" Holley from Gorsicana, Texas, and radioman Aviation Radioman Second Class Roger L. Plouffe from Chicoppe, Massachusetts, were able to bail out and parachuted into the water south of Morotai. They were picked up by Patrol Craft 1134 and taken to a seaplane tender near the island for medical observation and treatment.

According to Holley, the tender was also the "Mother Ship" for a group of PBYs known as the Black Cat Squadron that made a nightly habit of attacking Japanese shipping in the area. Holley and Plouffe remained on the tender for three days before being taken back to the FANSHAW BAY. After living through the nightmare of the collision, Holley recalls that getting back to the carrier was "quite a thrill." And the guys from the squadron were happy to see their shipmates alive and well and ready to get back into the fray. They knew that the awful mishap could have happened to any of them. The first person Holley saw once he was back on the carrier was Deloach Cope and the next was the CO of FANSHAW BAY, Captain D.P. Johnson, who gave him a cigar. Welcome back!

Notwithstanding the warm welcome back to the squadron and the FANSHAW BAY given to them by their shipmates, the accident was still hard to deal with for Holley and Plouffe. Plouffe's wife recalls:

> Roger did not talk much about the Navy over the years, but I remember his talking about parachuting after the accident and his feeling bad because the other fellow (turret gunner Calderon) did not make it. It bothered him the rest of his life. He wondered if he could have done more to help - if he should have gone back to try to help him get out.

Plouffe died on 7 October 2007. His concern for the death of his buddy is understandable, but the reality is that if he had stayed with the plane to try to help Calderon, both would likely have died. Once again, given the remote location of their parachutes, the cramped conditions, and the short time that they had as the plane was plunging toward the ocean, it was extremely difficult for turret gunners to successfully get to their parachutes, put them on, and bail out before the plane hit the water. And once they hit the water, TBMs sank quickly. In all likelihood, Calderon had no chance.

In the late afternoon of 20 September, FANSHAW BAY again went to General Quarters. Radar picked up another bogey at twenty miles from the ship. This bogey also changed course and headed back toward the island before the combat air patrol planes could get to it. Flight Quarters ended at 1812 with a total of 29 sorties. All hands were glad that this day was finished.

Notwithstanding the squadron's previous day's losses, the fighting on and over Morotai and Halmahera continued the next day, and missions had to be flown. From 21 to 23 September, the squadron flew 71 air support, ASP, and CAP sorties. There was a whole lot of flying going on. Because of the personnel losses and other problems, some of the pilots and aircrewmen were flying eight hours a day and standing by in the ready room for another four to six hours. It was particularly tough for the fighter pilots because of the loss of Rodriguez, three of the new pilots failing their attempted carrier qualifications, and a couple of the others being temporarily grounded.

On the 23rd, one of the TBMs crashed the restraining barrier while landing and demolished another TBM that had been spotted forward of the barrier. The landing TBM's damage while serious, was repairable. The other Avenger was wrecked. Banks indicates that given his metalsmith rating, he would occasionally "moonlight" and help the non-aircrew metalsmiths patch up the planes that needed it. In addition to squadron personnel suffering wear and tear, the planes were also taking a beating. Everyone was working hard.

The men of the squadron would help each other in other ways. An aircrewman would stand in for a shipmate if that fellow was unable to go on a mission. Emidio Mardarello remembers flying with several pilots including Polski, Stack, McCabe, Krost, and Keyser. And Banks recalls flying at least once with J.O. Mayo. Mayo's regular gunner was not feeling well so Banks volunteered to take his spot. Banks remembers Mayo as being a quiet and good man.

Mayo was one of three VC-66 pilots from Mississippi. The other two were DeLoach Cope and Bill Cook. Mayo had graduated from Mississippi State University in 1941 with a business degree. He had been the business college's first student body president. According to Cope, one of Mayo's unofficial squadron collateral duties was the awarding of squadron nicknames such as "Cookie" or "Bubbles."

After the war, Mayo would remain in the Navy and do very well. His jobs included CO of a carrier, Chief of Staff for the Naval Air Force Atlantic, and Naval Attache to the U.S. Embassy in the Soviet Union.

After retiring in 1975 as a Rear Admiral, Mayo went to work with his former VC-66 shipmate, Kip Kiplinger, as an editor and eventually Vice Chairman of the Kiplinger Washington Editors, Inc. Mayo died 18 August 2007 and was buried in Arlington National Cemetery with full military honors. His shipmates remember him as a good and "close friend." They could not recall him as "ever in an angry or combative mode." He was "always the southern gentleman." They called him "Gentleman Jim."

During the afternoon of 23 September 1944, FANSHAW BAY, MIDWAY, and the destroyers USS HARRISON (DD-573) and USS JOHN RODGERS (DD-574) detached from Task Group 77.1 and left the Morotai area to refuel at Mios Woendi, in the Schouten Islands just to the north of New Guinea.

The 24th was spent steaming toward Mios Woendi. The squadron flew 12 CAP and ASP sorties. The ships reached Mios Woendi Harbor in the morning of the 25th. FANSHAW BAY moored alongside fleet oiler USS SALAMONIE (AO-26) and began taking on fuel oil and aviation gasoline. At 0534, on 26 September, the refueling was completed and the ships got underway for the return trip to Morotai. The squadron flew ASP and CAP sorties on the way.

On 27 September, flight operations were suspended from 1100 – 1455 because of bad weather. In the afternoon, two TBMs launched from FANSHAW BAY on a special mission. One carried three VC-66 TBM pilots as passengers to be landed aboard the SANGAMON. Their mission was to fly three replacement TBMs back to FANSHAW BAY for use by the squadron. The second TBM was launched with three VC-66 fighter pilots as passengers to land aboard the SANTEE and fly back with three replacement FMs. The extended, hard flying had been rough on the squadron's planes.

FANSHAW BAY was back on station east of Morotai Island on 28 September. Flight ops began at 0529. The squadron flew CAP and ASP sorties - as well as strikes against Galela air strip on Halmahera. The strike aircraft dropped three tons of bombs on the runway rendering it temporarily unserviceable. They also strafed and damaged two Japanese single engine planes on the ground.

The strike against Galela had been launched because of intelligence received indicating that the Japanese were staging planes in the Philippines for possible counterattacks against American forces on Morotai or Palau Island – and in fact, the Japanese did send planes against Morotai later in the day.

Back aboard FANSHAW BAY, one of the landing TBMs missed the arresting cable and crashed the barrier. The plane sustained serious, but repairable damage. There were no injuries to personnel. Flight ops secured at 1756. It had been a busy day with a total of 38 sorties.

The next day – the 29th of September, flight ops began at 0538 with more air support, ASP, and CAP sorties. One TBM with two FM escorts was assigned to fly a photo reconnaissance mission over the Halmahera airfields. When the torpedo bombers and fighters went on a mission together, the fighters would generally fly above the TBMs to provide protection from air attack. In addition to taking photos, the planes strafed and bombed anti-aircraft positions at the Galela air strip.

During the mission - which was led by the squadron CO, Gerry Trapp, TBM gunner Jim Rathbun was hit by anti-aircraft fire. A round came through the bomb bay, hit the radio, ricocheted off, and pierced the allegedly bullet proof hard homo steel seat in his turret striking Rathbun in the kidney.

In a desperate effort to get immediate help for his wounded gunner, pilot LT Martin J. "Lucky" Stack from Seattle, Washington, flew to Morotai and did a risky landing on the rough, unfinished air strip that Army engineers were building. Brownie Brown flying one of the escort fighters followed Stack and landed on Morotai as well. They were the first American planes to land on Morotai. Notwithstanding Stack's efforts to help him, Rathbun was dead when they landed. He was buried on Morotai.

Rathbun had been a friend of Mardarello. They used to go on liberty together. Rathbun was married and was the father of a three year old daughter. His wife was pregnant with their second child at the time of his death. It was another hard to take loss for the squadron.

Lucky Stack was one of the more experienced VC-66 pilots. He had been a member of the NROTC at the University of Washington – class of 1942. In September 1941, he began his flight training at NAS Sand Point, Seattle. He received his pilot's wings in June 1942 as well as his commission as an Ensign, and was assigned to TORPEDO SQUADRON ELEVEN (VT-11) flying TBFs. His squadron was sent to Guadalcanal where it flew combat missions out of Henderson Field against New Georgia and Bougainville. They were in the thick of the action in some of the earliest and fiercest fighting in the Pacific.

On one mission on 30 June 1943, Stack and his aircrewmen were supporting the landing of a small force of Marines that were to join up with a coast watcher in the jungle near the Munda, New Georgia airstrip. Stack and his crew spotted twenty-two Japanese Bettys (bombers) low on the water headed for American ships in the area. They alerted the ships and then saw about thirty Japanese dive bombers above their TBF – and several fighters headed for them. Stack's turret gunner - a Sailor named Combs, shot down one and probably a second Japanese plane.

Several hours later during a second attack, Stack pulled along side the lead Japanese dive bomber and gunner Combs fired at close range setting it on fire. Stack's nickname resulted from his good fortune in being able to return in one piece from these encounters with multiple enemy planes. On another mission, Stack and his aircrewmen were credited with a 2000 pound bomb hit on a Japanese destroyer. After his tour of duty with VT-11, Stack joined VC-66 on 17 October 1943.

After landing on Morotai to try to get help for Rathbun, Stack, his radioman, and Brown were temporarily unable to take off due to the rough condition of the still under construction air strip. They remained on Morotai overnight.

Meanwhile on FANSHAW BAY, operations went on as usual. An FM missed the landing cable and crashed the barrier. While the plane sustained serious, but not irreparable damage, neither the pilot nor any of ship's personnel were hurt. Flight ops secured at 1808 on the 29th, after another long day of 38 sorties – and another VC-66 shipmate lost.

From 30 September to 2 October, the daily routine was much the same with FANSHAW BAY operating in an area thirty miles east of Morotai as part of Task Unit 77.1.2 - escort carriers FANSHAW BAY and MIDWAY plus destroyer escorts EVERSOLE, ROWELL, EDMONDS, AND SHELTON - in continuing support of the invasion forces. Daily flight operations began around 0530 with the squadron flying more air support, anti-submarine patrol, and combat air patrol sorties.

On 30 September, after the Army Engineers finished rolling an eight hundred foot strip of runway, Brown took off from Morotai and landed aboard FANSHAW BAY. By doing so, he became the first pilot to land and take off from Morotai. Stack and his radioman returned from Morotai on 1 October.

On the 2nd, the squadron flew a strike mission against land based torpedo tubes at Galela, Halmahera. Banks recalls that for that mission, Stephens, he, and Stoops were assigned the plane that Rathbun was killed in. Banks had the unpleasant job of cleaning up the turret and filling the hole from the bullet that had killed his shipmate. During the last three days, the squadron had flown 89 more sorties.

On 3 October, flight ops began at 0528. During the day, the squadron would fly a total of 37 ASP, CAP, and submarine hunter-killer sorties, but the real excitement for the day happened aboard the carrier that morning. At 0806, TBM aircrews and FANSHAW BAY lookouts reported a torpedo wake visible on FANSHAW BAY's port quarter. The carrier turned hard right, went to flank speed, and sounded General Quarters.

The torpedo, which had been fired by Japanese submarine RO-41, passed astern of FANSHAW BAY and just forward of MIDWAY (which within a few days would be renamed the USS ST. LO (CVE-63)) before striking the stern of the USS SHELTON (DE-407) causing a large explosion and fire. SHELTON had been part of the screen for the carriers. She eventually sank and 13 men were killed. 210 survivors were rescued by the USS ROWELL (DE 403).

J.P. Fox remembers the sinking of the SHELTON and advises:

> About 10 years ago (1998) I got a phone call from a gentleman who gave me his name and asked if I was on the FANSHAW BAY in the late summer of 1944? When I replied in the affirmative, he said, "You got me sunk!" He then proceeded to say he was on the SHELTON and the torpedo that sank his ship was supposed to hit the FANSHAW BAY. He was a postman in Navarre, Florida about 20 miles east of where I live. I never did meet him.

The men of VC-66 were being shot at not only from the ground, but also from the sea. Even when they made it back from a combat mission and survived the landing on the carrier, they were not safe. Not with enemy submarines lurking around. The stress and anxiety level was high – as well as the general fatigue level.

The sinking of SHELTON was bad enough, but things would get worse. In the effort to find the Japanese submarine that had torpedoed SHELTON, an American destroyer escort mistakenly identified the USS SEAWOLF (SS-197) as the Japanese sub and successfully attacked her. SEAWOLF went down with all hands – about 100 men. Civil War General William Tecumseh Sherman got it right when he said, "War is hell."

As had happened with the failed submarine attack on ALTAMAHA back in April, Tokyo Rose reported FANSHAW BAY sunk by Japanese torpedoes. This time her report was not amusing. She only misidentified the ship that was sunk. In any case, the squadron had "dodged another bullet" – or to be more accurate – torpedo.

DeLoach Cope and Dick Krost remember hearing the radio broadcast. Cope recalls, "One night we were listening to Tokyo Rose and she thought our ship had been sunk." Moreover, according to Cope, she went on to call out Guy Catterton's name "and said his wife was going to miss him. She had the names of members of our unit – how she got them we did not know." It was a good question.

The 1 December 1944 *Hattiesburg (Mississippi) American* quotes Squadron CO Trapp concerning allegedly being sunk while aboard ALTAMAHA and FANSHAW BAY, "Our biggest regret about this is that the Navy Department didn't receive word of the 'sinkings' and give us all 60 day survivors' leave."

The good news for the squadron was that during the evening of 3 October, FANSHAW BAY and Task Unit 77.1.2 received orders to detach from the Morotai operating area and set out for Seeadler Harbor, Manus Island, Admiralty Islands.

On 4 October 1944, the Morotai operation was declared complete and Army Air Force squadrons were permanently assigned to Morotai. General MacArthur would have his air support for the liberation of the Philippines.

From 4 through 6 October, en route to Manus Island the squadron flew 40 ASP and CAP sorties over and around the ships.

Al Mayer recalls his last landing aboard FANSHAW BAY, "Steve (Stephens) landed. I followed and missed a wire and plowed into his plane damaging the tail. Fortunately your dad (Banks), Steve, and the other crew member (Stoops) had already evacuated the plane." Mayer's experience shows once again that landing on a CVE was always a risky adventure – even for good pilots with a lot of experience.

During the evening of 6 October, LTJG Robert A. "Bob" Weaver from Hollywood, California, and his TBM aircrewmen – turret gunner Aviation Ordnanceman Second Class Raymond A. Shoemaker from Lima, Ohio, and radioman Aviation Radioman First Class Vernon A. Kelly from Rushville, Illinois, made the last carrier landing for VC-66. Kelly would soon be detached from the squadron to attend flight training back in the states.

On 7 October 1944, flight operations began early - 0423. Four TBMs flew anti-submarine patrol. At 0524, the remaining VC-66 aircraft were launched for transfer to Pityilu Island Field, in the Admiralty Islands.

Pityilu is a small island – three miles long and about one quarter mile wide - near Manus. The 140th U.S. Seabee Battalion built the airstrip after the island was taken from the Japanese. With the fly off, VC-66 officially detached from FANSHAW BAY to await its replacement squadron and transport to Hawaii.

From 7 to 16 October, the squadron stayed on Pityilu. Banks recalls the Pityilu time as "waiting around anxiously for word of a replacement squadron being on its way and confirmation that we were going back to the states. We were really beat up." A "Muster Roll of the Crew" dated 1 October 1944, shows that the squadron was down to a total of forty enlisted men. Banks feels that the Morotai, Moluccas – Western New Guinea operation had been tougher than the Marshalls campaign. Absent a fresh replacement squadron showing up, the thinking in the squadron was that they would be kept around for the looming invasion of the Philippines.

After VC-66 detached, FANSHAW BAY spent from 7 until 11 October 1944 refitting and replenishing. During that time, VC-66's replacement squadron, COMPOSITE SQUADRON SIXTY-EIGHT (VC-68), reported aboard for duty.

As fate, and a small world would have it, on 29 May 2004, at the dedication of the National World War II Memorial in Washington, D.C. – and almost sixty years after leaving the FANSHAW BAY, Banks literally bumped into his counterpart from VC-66's replacement squadron. The fellow had been a TBM turret gunner with VC-68 and was walking around at the Memorial wearing a hat with USS FANSHAW BAY embroidered on it. Banks was wearing his "TBF Avenger – WWII" hat. They met directly in front of the Battle for Leyte Gulf engraving. Several minutes worth of good sea stories were quickly swapped by the two old gunners.

By October 1944, the Navy had come a long way since the Pearl Harbor attack. In the 1 October 1945 issue of *Naval Aviation News*, an article entitled "Capture of Caroline Islands," tells how far:

> At the time when the Navy was poised for the Philippines thrust, Naval Aviation had 34,000 planes and 47,000 pilots available. Seventy of the 100 aircraft carriers had been built in the preceding year and had sustained little damage up to then from the aerial attacks launched by the Japanese.

VC-66's Bill Piper remembers Manus Harbor in early October 1944 as "being huge and full of ships getting ready for the Philippines invasion."

Early on 12 October 1944, FANSHAW BAY and her new squadron got underway as part of the Philippines Invasion Task Group. She was the Flagship for RADM C.A.F. Sprague's Task Unit 77.4.3 and COMCARDIV 25. It would be another memorable assignment for the carrier.

On the morning of 25 October, after launching all of her planes for an attack, FANSHAW BAY herself came under attack from Japanese surface ships – two cruisers and three destroyers. She was being straddled by shells. By 0855, she had taken three hits, but was lucky – "only" four crew members had been killed and four wounded. Sprague's quick response to the Japanese shelling was to put the carrier into a rain squall that provided temporary safety. His action is credited with limiting the damage and casualties.

Meanwhile, another Task Group CVE, the ST. LO (formerly the MIDWAY – her name was changed to allow a new, bigger carrier to be named MIDWAY), was torpedoed by a Japanese destroyer, but managed to stay afloat. Later in the morning, the Japanese launched a multi-plane kamikaze (suicide) attack against the ships. One of the planes got through the American anti-aircraft barrage and crashed the ST. LO sinking her. While FANSHAW BAY's escorts were picking up survivors, she steamed alone and recovered planes from the other carriers that were damaged or sunk. This engagement would be known as the Battle of Samar – part of the famous Battle for Leyte Gulf. Later in the war, FANSHAW BAY would also take part in the invasion of Okinawa. By the end of the war, she had survived attacks by Japanese aircraft, submarines, and surface ships. She finished with five battle stars. She truly showed what the under-appreciated CVEs could take and what they could contribute.

VC-66's Jack Dwight was particularly saddened to hear of the sinking of the ST. LO. Prior to joining VC-66 in March 1944, he had been assigned to VC-65, but when he heard that squadron might be transferred to the Atlantic, another pilot and he "opted out as we desired some real action." He was then assigned to VC-66. As it turns out, VC-65 did not go to the Atlantic. During the Battle of Samar it was assigned to the doomed ST. LO and it fought gallantly to defend her. VC-65 lost 31 men killed in action - including their CO, LCDR Ralph M. Jones. Dwight remembered the VC-65 CO, "They don't come any better." In addition to the men from the squadron, the ST. LO lost another 91 men.

On 16 October, VC-66 happily received the word to report to the USS MAKASSAR STRAIT (CVE-91) for return to Hawaii and then the mainland. A final muster was held on the pier before boarding MAKASSAR STRAIT. Needless to say, all hands were present and on time.

As for all hands being present at the final VC-66 muster, Ed Keyser looking back at his days with the squadron recalls something that the whole squadron was proud of, "We were all told it was 'hazardous duty.' And despite everything that happened we were all present or accounted for at every muster."

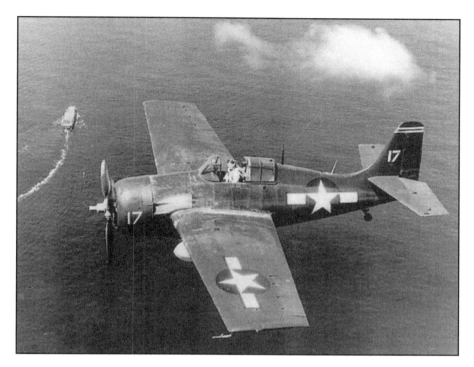

FM Wildcat flies combat air patrol over USS SANTEE (CVE-29). (Photo: courtesy Naval Historical Center)

VC-66's three pilots from Mississippi. Left to right: William E. Cook, James O. Mayo, and DeLoach Cope. (Official U.S. Navy Photograph courtesy W.D. Cope)

American born Iva Toguri – also known as Tokyo Rose. Twice she reported that carriers VC-66 was operating from were sunk. (Photo: courtesy National Archives)

A CVE at anchor. (Official U.S. Navy Photograph courtesy W.D. Cope)

16

Back to the States

On the 17th of October 1944, MAKASSAR STRAIT got underway for Pearl Harbor. In addition to VC-66, she was carrying seventy damaged planes being taken back to Hawaii. The squadron said goodbye to the Southwest Pacific. Spirits were high.

During its time aboard FANSHAW BAY, the men of VC-66 had flown 579 combat missions lasting 2109 hours against targets on Morotai and the Japanese airfields at Galela, Miti, Kaoe, and Lolobata on Halmahera. They also flew reconnaissance missions in the strait of Molucca, and numerous anti-submarine and combat air patrol missions.

For its combat accomplishments during the campaign, the squadron was awarded the nation's highest unit award – the Presidential Unit Citation, for "extraordinary heroism in action against enemy Japanese forces in the air, ashore, and afloat" during participation in the Western New Guinea operation from 15 September to 12 October 1944.

The men of VC-66 could and should be proud. Receipt of the Presidential Unit Citation is a very big deal. It demonstrates recognition by the highest levels of the Navy of a significant contribution reflecting the "highest credit" upon the men of the squadron and "the United States Naval Service." They are not given out lightly.

But out of a roughly sixty man complement, the squadron lost six men during the Morotai, Moluccas Islands - Western New Guinea action. VC-66 had deservedly earned a "well done" for its efforts and the operation was a success – but it had been costly.

The MAKASSAR STRAIT arrived at Pearl Harbor on 26 October and the squadron immediately began a short period of much needed rest and recreation. The men made the most of it. Banks recalls the preferred first meal in port to be steak and real milk. On the ship, they had to put up with powdered milk – "and worse yet, powdered eggs," and the traditional Navy creamed chipped beef on toast – or as it was affectionately known: "SOS" (shit on a shingle). It was tough for Banks to eat the steak, however, since he was still missing his two front teeth. Charlie Edwards recalls craving a fresh salad.

Also while in Hawaii, Banks bought Jean an engagement ring that he hoped to present to her during his anticipated upcoming re-assignment leave. And as he was told was a Navy tradition for returning Sailors - he purchased some black lingerie for her. It was a demonstration of great optimism.

On 29 October, VC-66 departed Hawaii aboard the troop transport USS GENERAL COLLINS (AP-147). The GENERAL COLLINS had a crew of 356 and a troop carrying capacity of about 2200. When VC-66 was aboard her, she was packed with troops returning to California. It had to be one crowded, but happy ship.

There was no more "officers' country" berthing and no private mess cook now for the squadron's enlisted men. Instead, they were berthed in a large compartment with many nine high rows of bunks and a lot of seasick Marines. To get out of the crowded berthing compartment, some of the VC-66 men would go up and sleep on the weather decks. They were served two meals a day with no seconds – but no one in the squadron was complaining. They were going home.

On 3 November, the GENERAL COLLINS arrived at NAS Alameda, San Francisco. At that time, the officers and men of the squadron were detached for leave and most for reassignment elsewhere in the Navy. While five of the pilots - DeLoach Cope, Brownie Brown, Bob Holley, Dick Krost, and Jobbo Polski, as well as a few of the enlisted men including Russ Jensen and Aviation Machinist's Mate Second Class Ulyse R. Borel, were reassigned to the "new" VC-66 that would be re-formed on 5 December 1944 and would be known as VC-66 Tour 2 (T-2), most of the VC-66 officers and enlisted men were sent to other places to help form new squadrons or re-form old squadrons for the final push against Japan.

As VC-66 (T-1) broke up, some of Emidio Mardarello's Aviation Ordnanceman buddies tried to talk him out of continuing as an aircrewman. They argued that he could still do his part by working with the ordnance aboard the carriers as they did, without flying in the planes. It was safer. But Mardarello still wanted to fly. He did, however, request assignment to an all TBF/TBM squadron rather than trying to stay with the new VC-66 (T-2) or another composite squadron. He figured that by joining an all TBF/TBM squadron, he was likely to fly from the bigger carriers instead of the CVEs. He thought he would like to give that a try.

Somewhat surprisingly the Navy eventually gave Mardarello what he wanted. After spending almost a month at Alameda, he was sent to NAS Jacksonville, Florida to be a gunnery instructor for gunners assigned to PB4Y-1s. They were the Navy's version of the B-24 Liberator bomber. Next, he was sent to Norman, Oklahoma for advanced training at the Aviation Ordnanceman "B" School, and then back to Jacksonville for additional gunnery training. Finally, he got his wish and was assigned to the newly formed all TBM squadron VTB-2. It was made up of twenty-four TBMs and was then training in Miami, Florida. Mardarello was happy.

James Gander got orders to instructor duty at the Naval Air Technical Training Center in Chicago, Illinois. While there he was advanced to Aviation Machinist's Mate First Class. He would remain as an instructor in Chicago until his discharge in April 1946.

Charlie Edwards was sent to an all fighter squadron, VF-93, flying F6F Hellcats. VF-93 was assigned to the brand new USS BOXER (CV-21). They went on a shakedown cruise in the Caribbean and then through the Panama Canal on to San Francisco. In San Francisco the BOXER would have its guns upgraded. At this time the Navy was concerned about the kamikaze threat and wanted more fire power on the carriers. The BOXER's 20-mm gun mounts were removed and replaced with quad 40-mm mounts. As Edwards puts it, "The goal was to be able to knock the Japanese planes down rather than just hit them."

Before the work on the BOXER was completed, the war ended. VF-93 was directed not to board her as she sailed for post-war duty in China. Edwards recalls that the squadron went to the top floor of the Mark Hopkins Hotel in San Francisco and watched the BOXER sail under the Golden Gate Bridge. After several weeks, Edwards was sent back to Philadelphia for separation. He was anxious to get home to see his new baby daughter.

Because he had served two tours of duty outside the U.S. – Panama and VC-66, Bill Piper had a priority in requesting his next duty station. He chose Fort Lauderdale, Florida. He spent the rest of the war in charge of maintenance at a pilot training base.

A few of the VC-66 aircrewmen – Vernon Kelly; Chief Aviation Radioman Dean K. Mitchell from Portland, Oregon; Aviation Radioman First Class Robert P. Muse from Fayetteville, Tennessee; and Tom Stoops, were offered and accepted the opportunity to go to flight school and become pilots. Banks thought about it, but decided against applying because it could involve an additional service obligation beyond the war if the war should end sooner.

Dean Birdsong remembers Chief Mitchell's desire to fly and his applying to flight school:

> Subsequently, he received an appointment and won his "Wings of Gold."
> I believe he remained an enlisted pilot, but of that I am not sure. After the War I used to run across him on cross countries. He was usually ferrying planes from East to West during the Korean War. Saw him most often at NAS Dallas which was a usual fueling stop for cross country travel. Your father (Banks) should remember him. He was an outstanding member of the Squadron. We always reminisced and lifted a beer at these meetings.

Prior to splitting up to go their own ways after VC-66, Banks, Stephens, and Stoops got together for a last beer. Banks remembers it not so much as any kind of celebration, but talking over all of the experiences that they had together. And they had a few.

Before being allowed to leave NAS Alameda, the Shore Patrol gave each enlisted man a one inch by five inch lead bar to sew into his uniform neckerchief. It was to be used to defend against "muggers" who were preying on recently paid Sailors coming back from the war. "Welcome home," Banks thought. He still has the lead bar.

But most civilians treated the returning Sailors well. Mardarello recalls a bartender near Alameda who took a liking to him and invited him, a Marine, and a WAC (Woman's Army Corps) over for Thanksgiving dinner with the family – "And we had a good time."

Even though the drinking age was "officially" twenty-one, most places were not very strict with the troops. When he was only nineteen, Mardarello could get served most of the time when he wanted. He recalls thinking it kind of funny that "nineteen was good enough to go to sea, fly, and fight, but not to drink."

The reassignment of most of the squadron personnel to other Navy units effectively terminated the original VC-66 or VC-66 (T-1) as it later came to be known.

From 21 June 1943 through 3 November 1944, COMPOSITE SQUADRON SIXTY-SIX (VC-66 (T-1)) amassed 14,891 hours of flight time including 5866 flight hours at sea. All of that flying included over 2000 carrier landings; numerous combat bombing and strafing missions; many spotting, photographic, and long range fleet patrol missions; and over 600 anti-submarine patrol and combat air patrol missions. During that period, the squadron was credited with destroying or doing significant damage to Japanese aircraft, ships, and airfields where it flew.

While squadron personnel earned a Presidential Unit Citation and numerous personal decorations, they had lost twelve shipmates and friends. But those twelve men did not die in vain. They and the surviving members of VC-66 had made a major contribution to victory in a war that had to be won. While it had been a sobering and maturing experience, it was also one for which they could rightly take - as President Kennedy would say years later - "a good deal of pride and satisfaction." Not only had they done everything asked of them and more, but along the way they had come to trust and respect one another – and enjoy each other's company. They were shipmates in the truest sense of the term. Thus, the many friendships that still exist more than sixty years later. The enlisted men respected the squadron's officers and trusted them with their lives and the officers respected and appreciated the enlisted men. Ed Keyser sums it up well:

> After 64 years dealing with hundreds of people on active duty, the reserves and civilian life, I do recall your father's name. He and all our enlisted men – aircrew, maintenance, and the ships' companies did an outstanding job. They worked around the clock to keep the aircraft in an "UP" status.

Now it was time for Banks and the surviving members of the original squadron to move on – within the Navy and their personal lives.

And as they moved on, the men of VC-66 (T-1) could rest assured that the men taking their places in the new VC-66 (T-2) were ready, willing, and able to carry on the proud traditions and maintain the high standards that their predecessors had set. VC-66 (T-2)'s performance during the intense training and preparation for the anticipated invasion of Japan would be outstanding in all respects. They did the old squadron proud.

VC-66 Sailors on liberty after their last combat cruise. Left to right: Raymond A. Shoemaker, Emidio J. Mardarello, William A. Summers, Walter W. Molash, and Donald R. Swenson. (Photo: courtesy E.J. Mardarello)

Four of VC-66's Chief Petty Officers. Left to right: Bernald H. Stoffer, James H. Sheridan, Frederick L. Bisson, and Chester M. Peart. There is an old Navy saying that "the Chiefs run the Navy." (Official U.S. Navy Photograph courtesy D.A. Banks collection)

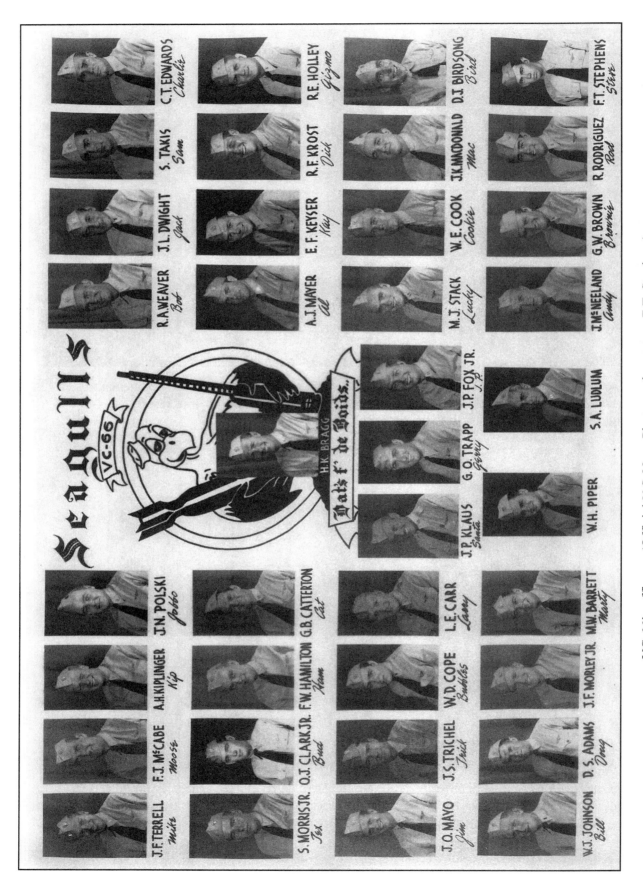

VC-66's officers. (Official U.S. Navy Photograph courtesy F.T. Stephens)

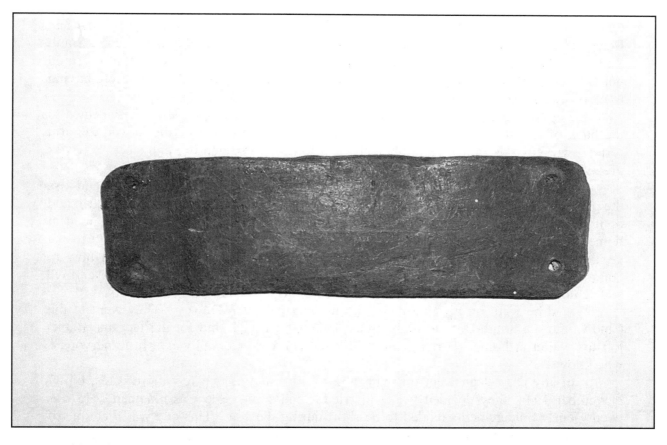

Lead bar given to Banks and other Sailors by the Shore Patrol at NAS Alameda. The Sailors were to sew the bar into their uniform neckerchiefs to help defend against "muggers" as they left the base. Banks felt it was a strange way of being welcomed home. (Photo: courtesy S.A. Banks)

17

Leave and Marriage

On 10 November 1944, Banks went down to the Railway Express Agency office in San Francisco and sent a box containing personal gear to his mother's home at 2584 South Park Avenue in Buffalo. He then went to the airport and caught the first flight he could get back to Buffalo. He had been authorized a substantial amount of leave before having to report to his next duty station.

On the flight home, Banks recalls that the stewardesses moved the servicemen to the back of the plane "where there were quite a few empty seats. She moved the arm rests down, gave us pillows and blankets, and told us to stretch out and sleep." It was great.

He remembers landing in Buffalo and feeling like, "I wanted to get down and kiss the ground." It had been two years since he had been home. The things he had seen and done during that time were incomprehensible to most of the people who remained at home. He spent the first days visiting friends and relatives, trying to acclimate to the civilian world again. It was quite a culture shock. He even had to re-learn how to communicate. The language he was used to in the Fleet was somewhat more "earthy" and "colorful" than the folks at home were used to. Banks had to watch himself.

And he went on his first date with his pen pal, Jean Dewey. They went to the Club Como – a South Buffalo night club. Things went well, but for the fact that Banks left his wallet at home. Perhaps the "hardened combat veteran" was a little nervous – who knows?

In any case, Jean went out with him again – and after a few more dates, on 27 November 1944, they decided to get married – and soon. She was nineteen. He was twenty-one. Engagements tended to be short during the war. This one was a couple of weeks. It is hard to imagine in the twenty-first century, but that is the way it was – and pretty much had to be given the uncertainty in the world and everyone's lives.

Finding a "best man" was a problem. All of the potential candidates were in the service. Jean's cousin, Geraldine "Sis" Scuto, volunteered her husband, Joe "Scotty" Scuto, to fill the role. Scotty was home on medical leave from the Army. He was recuperating from an injury he had received when an amphibious vehicle that he was riding in sank and he had to swim a long distance to save himself.

Although he did not know Banks at the time, Scuto was game and agreed to be "best man." They would go on to become good friends. One of Jean's other cousins, Rita Beeny, was the "maid of honor." For whatever reason, Bea Banks was not enthusiastic about the wedding and would not attend the ceremony nor greet the wedding party afterward. Bea would later come to accept and love Jean, but for now she was being stubborn.

Nonetheless, after a lot of snow and a bit of a delay – Banks left the marriage certificate at home and had to go back to get it - the Banks/Dewey wedding took place on 14 December 1944. The ceremony was held in the priests' parlor of the rectory at Our Lady of Victory Basilica, Lackawanna, New York.

After the wedding ceremony there was no reception, so "best man" Scuto decided that the wedding party needed a car so that they could do some celebrating around town. He took Banks and they hopped a bus to travel across Buffalo to borrow a car from a pal of Scuto's. They got the car and after a "little celebrating," Banks and his new wife spent their wedding night at the Tourine Hotel – now an apartment building – on Delaware Avenue in downtown Buffalo. As Scuto was dropping them off at the hotel, he reminded Banks to sign the hotel register as Mr. and Mrs. Donald Banks. Banks recalls that he was so nervous, he forgot Scuto's advice and signed in as Donald Banks – but then quickly added "and wife."

After a couple of days at the hotel, they stayed with Jean's cousin, Rita's, family. The newlyweds spent the rest of the time in the Buffalo area visiting with friends and family before Banks had to leave for his new duty assignment in Florida. He remembers well - but not fondly - the time he was visiting with his new in-laws and was proudly showing everyone his survival pack and the gear it contained. He forgot that most of the gear was placed in condoms to keep it waterproof. He cringes remembering offering that explanation to his new mother-in-law.

In most instances Banks wore his uniform when visiting people. "I didn't have many civilian clothes." But even in the midst of the war, his grandmother had not changed her beliefs and he was not allowed to wear his uniform in her house.

Before Banks left for Florida, the couple made plans for Jean to join him there for a real honeymoon as soon as the opportunity presented itself. As a combat aircrewman, Banks was relatively well paid – and he had been able to save most of his money. Other than for a little "gedunk" (snack food) now and then on the carrier, there had not been a lot of opportunity to spend it.

It is noteworthy, that while the Banks/Dewey marriage came together somewhat helter-skelter, it is still going strong after sixty-three years.

Banks and Jean sitting on the Dewey's front porch. (Photo: courtesy D.A. Banks collection)

18

Starting Over

In late December 1944, Banks took the train out of Buffalo and reported to the Navy Transfer Unit at NAS Jacksonville in northeast Florida. He had been sent there for reassignment. Stephens had also been sent to Jacksonville. The two VC-66 shipmates would be paired up again. As things turned out, this arrangement was very fortuitous for Banks.

Stephens recalls that Banks showed up at Jacksonville without his orders. That was not a good thing. As a result, the base command was ready to put him in the brig. They thought he was an unauthorized absentee from some command and was "playing games" to get out of an assignment or deployment. As Stephens puts it, "I stood up for him and saved his butt. I told them he had just gotten married, had left Buffalo in a hurry with a lot on his mind, and forgot the orders." The base command said "okay." Banks was off the hook and back to work. He owed Stephens.

At around the same time Banks was having his problems, another Jacksonville Sailor whose marriage was also preceded by a quick engagement followed by a short honeymoon was having some problems of his own. His experience was reported in the 15 December 1944 issue of *Naval Aviation News*:

> A sailor approached the Travelers' Aid desk and explained reluctantly that his bride of 1942 was arriving by bus in a few minutes, and that he was afraid he would be unable to recognize her. He had married a girl after a whirlwind courtship of four hours and had been shipped out the morning after the marriage. "I've been out of the States for two years," he added. The Travelers' Aid representative met the bus. "Yes, I'm Mrs. Joe Doaks," answered a pretty, well-dressed girl. "Your husband had to leave the station," said the representative, "and he asked me to meet you and take you to my desk." Seaman Doaks waited three minutes, rushed up to the desk, opened his arms to the girl and exclaimed, "Mary, darling, its like heaven to see you again!"

While at Jacksonville, Stephens and Banks were joined by their new radioman – Seaman First Class Aviation Radioman Marvin R. Sherrod. Sherrod was very junior – only pay grade E-3 and probably just out of radioman school. They were soon sent to NAS Miami, at Opa-Locka in Southeast Florida to be part of a new TBM combat team.

Banks was not unhappy about leaving Jacksonville. He had narrowly avoided the brig and to this day recalls very little about the time he spent in Jacksonville. He even denies ever having heard of the somewhat unusual and famous NAS Jacksonville mascot of the time – a pet duck named "Fubar." One wonders what the duck looked like or did to warrant that particular name? But apparently, Fubar had the run of the station and would waddle around begging doughnuts from all hands. A heinous, but thwarted attempt to kidnap (ducknap?) him was described in the 1 August 1945 issue of *Naval*

Aviation News. Banks claims to have been out of the area at the time, but admits that he does enjoy a good duck dinner.

The formation of combat teams was a relatively new development in Naval aviation operational training. The team consisted of one experienced Fleet pilot with actual combat experience – Stephens, one assistant instructor pilot from the training command, six new pilots ("nuggets"), and their aircrewmen - for a total of eight aircraft. The idea was that they would train together with the experienced aircrewmen obtaining refresher training and the new men gaining from the benefit of the experienced men's combat knowledge. The team would then be assigned to a new or existing squadron. Banks remembers, "I felt like an "old man – the others were all kids.""

NAS Miami was a busy place. It was made up of three separate fields – with Opa-Locka or Mainside being an important one of them. It was a major training base during the war for fighters, dive bombers, and torpedo bombers. There was also a Navy air gunnery school there. When Stephens, Banks, and Sherrod were there in early 1945, the place was at its peak with 7,200 active duty personnel and 3,100 civilian employees.

The new combat team would do operational training at Opa-Locka until March 1945. The training included ship and aircraft recognition, communications, sighting, turret familiarization, ordnance, and survival. Banks recalls having it pretty good during this early phase of training. As a combat experienced aircrewman and a relatively senior First Class Petty Officer, he was basically excused from most of it. He was required to report to the base once a day for muster and then was allowed to go his own way. "Not a bad deal," he thought.

It was not all fun and games though. Stephens remembers one training flight in particular:

> The planes at Miami were "well used" and some were in tough shape. One day, we took off and I soon felt moisture on my right leg. I knew from the smell of it that it was aviation gasoline. Talk about being scared! I thought one spark could blow us up. I made one quick radio transmission telling them we were going to land. We made an emergency landing right in the midst of all of the other traffic. The air controller was not happy, but we had to get down. There was a leak in a gas line causing the gas to spew out.

It was during the time at Opa-Locka that Jean took the train down to Miami – about a sixteen hundred mile trek that lasted a couple of days. She recalls the train ride as being "horrible." It was her first time traveling alone away from home. She remembers:

> The train was crowded with people standing in the aisle. You were afraid to get up to go to the restroom for fear that someone would take your seat. It was also smoky – from people smoking and from locomotive smoke blowing back into the passenger cars.

Jean did have a little excitement on the trip south. At some point, "A Marine that looked an awful lot like the famous movie actor Tyrone Power tried to sit down next to me. He asked if the seat was taken. I told him that it was – that the lady sitting there went to the restroom. He moved on." Banks would be relieved. Tyrone Power was hugely popular with the ladies at the time – sort of a Brad Pitt of his day.

To break up the trip, Jean spent the night in Washington, D.C. with a lady friend of one of her cousins. They had a good time. It was the first time Jean had seen Washington. She got back on the train the next day and went on down to Miami, but not before sending her mother a postcard saying that everything was going well. Before leaving Buffalo, her mother made her promise to send a postcard from every place that the train stopped long enough to mail one.

In Miami, Banks had rented a room in a nice rooming house. He and Jean stayed there as they enjoyed their real honeymoon. They would stay out late some nights beyond curfew for the Sailors. Jean recalls, "On a few occasions we would have to hide in alleys and dark places from the Shore Patrol so they wouldn't throw Donnie in jail – but we had a good time in Miami."

One of Jean's favorite memories involves an evening at a night club when one of the new aircrewmen – a fellow nicknamed "the Russian," did a Russian dance for her. She also recalls seeing the famous band leader, Sammy Kaye, and his band while in Miami. Kaye had a popular NBC radio show at the time called "Sunday Serenade." His theme was "Swing and sway with Sammy Kaye." Kaye was a big deal and the ladies loved him. Jean also enjoyed Biscayne Bay. "I would sometimes walk over a bridge to watch the dolphins swim while Donnie was working."

After several days, Jean had to go back to Buffalo and Banks and the combat team had to go west – to San Diego. It was March 1945. While the war in Europe was nearing its end, the war in the Pacific was still going strong. The fierce battle of Iwo Jima was still raging. And some of the worst fighting was yet to come. The invasion of Okinawa would take place on 1 April. And plans were going forward for the ultimate invasion of Japan - where it was estimated that American casualties might be as high as one million! The outlook was grim and the thinking at the time was that the war could well go on through 1946.

Prior to leaving Opa-Locka, as part of their training syllabus, the turret gunners had to shoot at a sleeve being pulled by a plane. They were scored by the number of holes they put in the sleeve.

Banks recalls a beforehand bet with Stephens as to the number of likely hits. He also recalls the actual shoot as being a really poor one for him and losing the bet. He says that he began to focus on how little distance there was between the tow plane and the sleeve - and remembering how his brother, Warny's, PBY had been accidentally shot down while pulling a similar sleeve. As a result, Banks feels he was a little too cautious. He remembers Stephens yelling to him over the plane's intercom, "Hit the damn thing!" And his response being, "Fly the plane right and I will!" In any case, he says, "I was embarrassed by the score."

DeLoach Cope says he can relate to Banks' concern about missing the sleeve and hitting the tow plane, "I occasionally flew tow planes and was worried about the ships' gunners hitting me."

As Stephens tells it, "I deliberately made it hard for Banks by giving him a maneuvering shot which was much more difficult. I would not give him an easy shot as the other pilots were doing for their gunners, by for example slowing down." Stephens felt the exercise should be realistic. After counting the number of holes in the sleeve, the instructors were not going to let Banks graduate. Stephens stepped in and explained what had happened and said, "I wanted Banks - and that he was a helluva gunner." It worked. They were off to San Diego.

Former VC-66 TBM pilot, Lucky Stack, had also been assigned to Opa-Locka. He was serving as a flight instructor. Shortly after Stephens, Banks, Sherrod, and their combat team left for San Diego, Stack had a once in a life time experience that again showed why he is called Lucky. He took off in a TBM and was airborne over the middle of the runway checking his instruments when he heard his propeller "biting" at the runway. Stack described what happened next in an excellent article by Ed Rombauer published in the July 2005 issue of *Warbird Flyer* – the newsletter for the Cascade EAA Warbirds Squadron 2:

> Suddenly everything was quiet. The engine had fallen off! I heard the WAVE in the tower let out a scream as she was giving landing instructions to another plane. I remember pushing the control stick forward and banging it there trying to get the nose down. All I could see was sky. Without the weight of the engine, the plane zoomed up. Witnesses said about 200 feet. I did a kind of falling leaf back to the runway, landing three point. Except for the engine, the plane was undamaged. The crewman in the turret (ARM2c J.L. Cote) was a bit shook! A propeller blade had broken off causing the engine to break loose. A rare experience.

As Stack observes, "Not many pilots have landed a plane without an engine – backwards!"

Stack went on to serve twenty-eight years in the Navy and retired as a Captain (O-6). During his career he served in a variety of important positions including CO of ATTACK SQUADRONS NINETY-FIVE (VA-95) and FORTY-TWO (VA-42); CO of the USS MARIAS (AO-57); and CO of NAS Jacksonville.

During his NAS Jacksonville tour, he was able to find and obtain a TBM that he put on display in front of the administration building. Unfortunately, his successor – apparently not being very appreciative of fine historic aircraft, had the TBM removed from public view and put in storage. I am happy to observe, however, that today that TBM is very much back in public view looking good as part of an outstanding static display of venerable Navy aircraft in NAS Jacksonville's "Heritage Park."

When they got to NAS San Diego, Stephens, Banks, Sherrod, and the rest of the fresh trained combat team were temporarily assigned to TORPEDO SQUADRON NINETY-EIGHT (VT-98). VT-98 was responsible for providing TBM aircrew replacements to any squadron that needed them.

Among those who had previously passed through VT-98 on his way to another squadron was Aviation Radioman Third Class Paul L. Newman. After the war, Newman went on to have a reasonably good civilian career as an actor starring in such movies as "Cool Hand Luke," "Butch Cassidy and the Sundance Kid," and "The Sting."

VT-98 left San Diego in April 1945 and headed a couple of hundred miles up the coast to NAAS Oxnard, California for training.

Meanwhile, on 3 April, on the other side of the Pacific, the USS CORONIS (ARL-10) arrived off Okinawa to support the invasion of that island. It would be the largest invasion of the Pacific War. CORONIS was an LST that had been converted to a landing craft repair ship. Banks' older brother, John, was a Molder Second Class serving aboard her.

The CORONIS remained near Okinawa until 18 June. And they were in the thick of that horrific battle that resulted in over 50,000 Americans killed or wounded – including almost 5000 Navy dead, and over 200,000 Japanese killed – including over 100,000 civilians.

In addition to their repair work – and there was a lot of it, CORONIS operated a fog generator to provide cover from the hundreds of swarming kamikazes that descended on the American ships. On 6-7 April – just three days after the CORONIS arrived on the scene, one attack on the U.S. Fleet involved 355 kamikazes! And that was only the first of ten such mass attacks during the long battle for Okinawa. Besides making fog, the crew of CORONIS also used her 20 and 40 mm guns to help with air defense. John Banks was a member of a gun crew that helped shoot down one of the kamikazes.

In May 1945, VT-98 went to NAF Thermal, California for desert training. Banks recalls being curious as to why the Navy was sending them for desert training when as far as he could tell, "There were no deserts in the Pacific area where we were likely to be operating for the rest of the war."

But the big news was that on 7 May, while the squadron was in Thermal, Germany surrendered and the war in Europe was over. Japan, however, continued to demonstrate a desire to fight to the death. Even the civilians - including women, were being trained for hand to hand combat using wooden spears. An invasion would be brutal and bloody.

The town of Thermal is located twenty-five miles southwest of Palm Springs. The airfield with its two 5000 foot runways was located two miles southeast of the town at an elevation of 119 feet below sea level. The place is hot – 120 degrees Fahrenheit in the shade in summer! Because of the heat, flight operations took place between 0300 and 1300. The Army built the base early in the war and General Patton used it to train his army troops before the invasion of North Africa. The Navy took it over in December 1944. Aircrews used the facilities for rocket, gunnery, and bombing training.

Banks remembers the living conditions in the desert to be "austere:"

We lived in Quonset huts with broken windows, holes in the screens, and spaces between the floor boards. For amusement, someone would throw a smoke bomb under a hut and watch as the inhabitants came leaping through windows and doors thinking the place was on fire. Eating utensils were in short supply. As a result, we had to guard any utensils that we had acquired lest someone "borrow" them. As the only metalsmith in the outfit, I made metal cups for the guys from tin cans and wire – I still have one. I also made metal knee boards for the pilots. They clamped them onto their thighs when they were flying so that they had a surface to write on.

Stephens and Banks next to their TBM. (Official U.S. Navy Photograph courtesy D.A. Banks collection)

Beach during invasion of Okinawa in April 1945. Banks' older brother, John, was part of the invasion Task Force aboard the USS CORONIS (ARL-10). (Photo: courtesy National Archives)

19

To VC-92 and Beyond

In June 1945, VT-98 reported to NAAS Los Alamitos, California. Los Alamitos is just southeast of Los Angeles and just east of Long Beach. They were there for more operational training while still waiting to be assigned to a Fleet squadron.

With time to kill in the evenings - and now as a married man, Banks opted to do less "steaming" with the guys and instead to take in a little culture. On 8 June, he attended a performance of the Woman's Symphony Orchestra of Long Beach in the Long Beach Concert Hall.

And on 25 June, he bought a war bond and attended a war bond show in the Long Beach Municipal Auditorium. This was the country's seventh war bond drive and tour – the so-called "Mighty 7th." The goal was to raise fourteen billion dollars to finish the war. That meant that almost one hundred dollars would need to be donated by every American. This was the bond tour whose symbol was the famous Iwo Jima flag raising photograph and whose headliners were the three surviving flag raisers: Marines Ira Hayes and Rene Gagnon, and Sailor John Bradley. Banks kept the ticket stub for the show in his "Sailors Log." The bond drive was a huge success. Americans bought twenty-six billion dollars worth of war bonds to continue funding the war.

In July, VT-98 returned to NAS San Diego and while there, Stephens, Banks, Sherrod and their combat team were assigned to COMPOSITE SQUADRON NINETY-TWO (VC-92).

As had happened with VC-66, VC-92 was being re-formed after recently returning from its last long combat deployment. The squadron had been aboard the USS TULAGI (CVE-72) from December 1944 until June 1945, providing air support for the Marines and protecting the fleet during the invasions of the Philippines, Iwo Jima, and Okinawa.

In late July, now with Stephens, Banks, Sherrod, and the other replacement aircrews on board, the re-formed VC-92 flew up to NAAS Oxnard to begin squadron training in preparation for participation in the final operation of the Pacific war - the invasion of the Japanese home islands.

As to the invasion of Japan, VC-66 (T-2)'s Joe Mussatto describes the plan in his history of the re-formed VC-66, i.e., *History of Squadron VC-66 (T-2)*:

> The first Amphibious assault was scheduled to take place on Kyushu, November 1, 1945, followed by a second landing at Honshu, March 1, 1946. Estimated casualties, 250,000 to 1,000,000. 500,000 Purple Hearts were ordered by the Pentagon. USS Anzio and VC-66 were part of the 66 Carrier Task Force.

And the Japanese knew what was coming and were getting ready as evidenced by Radio Tokyo comments published in the "Tokyo Talks" section of the 1 August 1945 edition of *Naval Aviation News*:

The people of Kyushu are definitely of the opinion that the enemy will surely attempt to land on their island, and are solidly determined to strike them with a special attack spirit. Touched by the heroic fighting on the part of the People's Volunteer Corps of Okinawa, the entire people of Kyushu now anxiously await the chance to be converted into a combat unit to deal a crushing blow to the enemy invaders.

The eleven weeks of fighting on Okinawa had been brutal. In addition to the many thousands of American and Japanese military personnel killed, over one hundred thousand civilians were killed – one-third of the Okinawan population. Radio Tokyo went on to advise:

Combat units of the Civilian Volunteer Corps have been organized with the object of placing the entire Nation under the personal command of the Emperor as armed forces in the Imperial fighting services. In the event that the decisive battle is fought on our soil, these units will be called on to take part in the actual fighting and to carry out rear duties for the regular troops. Members of the Civilian Volunteer Corps combat units will not leave their assigned duties without orders however intense the fighting becomes. They have orders not to be taken prisoner alive or die dishonorably.

But there would be no invasion of Japan. On 6 August 1945, the United States dropped the first atomic bomb on the city of Hiroshima. VC-92 was still at Oxnard. Notwithstanding incredible devastation, Japan did not surrender. On the 9th, another atomic bomb was dropped - this time on the city of Nagasaki. More horrible devastation. The big question was would Japan surrender now or was the country prepared to fight to the last man, woman, and child?

Everything was up in the air. It was possible that the war could end at any moment – or not. On 12 August, Jean sent Banks a Western Union Telegram via the USO at Oxnard saying she was going to stay home in Buffalo rather than visit him in Oxnard as she had hoped to do. It was probably a good call. She was twenty years old and five months pregnant. Everything was too uncertain.

On 15 Aug 1945, reason prevailed and Japan surrendered. The war was over – just like that. Since no one had known what was going to happen after the atomic bombs were dropped, training had continued. Prior to the A-bombs being dropped, American carriers and their escorts had been cruising off the Japanese coast. It was not unusual for raids on Japanese targets to involve hundreds of planes.

Stephens, Banks, and Sherrod were on a practice bombing mission with a flight of eight planes on the 15th of August. Stephens was the section leader. He recalls, "We got a mysterious radio message on the guard channel directing all planes in the air to return to the base immediately. No explanation was given. When we landed, we were told the war was over." Just like that.

161

Few in the country knew about the development of the atomic bomb. As far as anyone in VC-92 knew, the only way Japan would be beaten was by invasion – hence all of their training to support it. Now, 3 years and 250 days after Pearl Harbor was attacked, suddenly the war had ended. FLEET ADMIRAL Ernest J. King sent out an ALNAV message marking the occasion. It read:

> The day of final victory has at last arrived. Japan has surrendered. Her fleet which once boasted that it would drive us from the seas has been destroyed. The U.S. Naval Services played a major role in this mighty triumph; therefore we observe this hour with special pride and satisfaction in our achievements. Especially do we remember the debt we owe our comrades of the Navy, Marine Corps, and Coast Guard who are absent today because they gave their lives to reestablish a world in which free peoples might live. Our sympathies go out to their relatives and friends. At the same time we extend thanks and appreciation to our companion services of the Army and to the gallant allies who fought beside us and to the millions of people on the home front who supported us with their labors and their prayers.
>
> It is as a team we have worked and fought to the victorious conclusion of the war. As we turn now from the vital tasks of war I call upon all members of the Naval Services to rededicate their efforts with the same courage, devotion to duty, and united spirit to the work of resolving the great problems of peace. Only by so doing can we fulfill our obligations in preserving that freedom which has been gained at such great cost and effort. I am proud to have served with every one of you.

While the victory celebration by an estimated two million people back in Times Square may have been loud and wild, Banks does not recall doing much celebrating. His thoughts were quickly focused on getting discharged, returning home to his expectant wife – and moving on with his life. Stephens also recalls not celebrating. He admits that he "felt let down after all of the training." It was a sudden shock.

With the war over, Banks stayed at Oxnard. He remained with VC-92 until shortly before it was decommissioned on 18 September 1945. While he was awaiting re-assignment, he helped out in the base metal shop. Just before the squadron was disestablished, he and most of the VC-92 enlisted men were assigned to work with CASUs 8 and 17 providing maintenance and other support duties for the planes, and standing watches. While only with VC-92 for a short time – less than three months – Banks did make some buddies among his new shipmates. In addition to Marvin Sherrod, a few others were: ARM3c Thomas M. Scott, ARM3c William Erny, S1c (ARM) Artie R. Fields, and AMM3c Vernon E. Thielmann – who Banks would by accident meet again years later in Whittier, California. In September 1945, they were all basically marking time until the Navy could figure out what to do with them.

But one of the more significant and noteworthy events of Banks' Navy service happened while he was assigned to CASU 8. It was determined that as a result of his time with VC-66, he had qualified to receive the Combat Aircrew Insignia with the maximum of three combat stars. The Combat Aircrew Insignia was roughly equivalent to the Army's Combat Infantryman Badge. It showed that the wearer had actually been in combat. And it was considered a mark of distinction for the men who wore them. To be awarded the Combat Aircrew Insignia, the recipient had to have served for at least three months as a member of the aircrew of a combatant aircraft that: "engaged enemy aircraft, or engaged armed enemy combatant vessels, or engaged in bombing or offensive operations against enemy fortified positions."

At the beginning of October 1945, Banks got orders to report to the Reclassification Center, Coronado Heights Annex, NAS San Diego. On 3 October, at the Reclassification Center, it was determined that he had accrued enough demobilization points to be eligible for "immediate release" from active duty. Points were awarded for certain "Demobilization Factors" such as age, number of months on active duty, number of months served outside the U.S., and dependents. Banks was a happy man. As it turns out, about the same time - 12 October 1945, his old squadron - VC-66, was being decommissioned. The Navy was beginning a big downsizing - and doing it quickly.

On 19 October, Banks was given orders to proceed to the U.S. Naval Receiving Station, Pier 92, New York City, New York for discharge processing. His life was now on fast forward. Just two months ago he had been training to support the invasion of Japan and now he was on his way to being a civilian again.

Banks got a flight to New York. He reported to the Receiving Station and was billeted in a large barracks with a lot of other guys waiting to be discharged. His high spirits suffered a temporary setback when the watch that Bea had given him when he left for Boot Camp - and that he worn throughout the war - was promptly stolen when he accidentally left it in the head after washing.

On or about 6 November, after finishing processing in New York City - including his discharge physical, Banks took the train upstate to Sampson – which was now a U. S. Naval Separation Center. He was back where it had all started. It was a strange feeling. He had come full circle in the Navy.

As he was reporting in at Sampson, he passed his service record through a window to a Yeoman on the other side. As fate would have it, the duty Yeoman was his good friend from South Buffalo, Jim Linden. Again, it was a small world and a small Navy. That evening, Linden and his wife, Betty, invited Banks to their base quarters for a welcome home spaghetti dinner. Banks remembers it as a great evening and great way to start his new life.

The Navy wasted no time in moving the men through Sampson. Once anxious to get them to the Fleet as soon as possible, now the emphasis was on getting them out as soon as possible. After only two days at Sampson, on 8 November 1945, Donald Austin Banks was honorably discharged from the United States Navy. His total service was 3 years and 12 days. His total payment at time of discharge was $95.54 with a mustering out bonus of $100.00.

During those 3 years and 12 days, Banks had earned the Victory medal, American Campaign medal, Asiatic-Pacific medal with three combat campaign stars, Combat Aircrew Insignia with three stars, Good Conduct medal, and the Presidential Unit Citation.

He also would receive a letter from James Forrestal, the Secretary of the Navy, which summed it all up pretty well. It read in part:

You have served in the greatest Navy in the world.

It crushed two enemy fleets at once, receiving their surrenders only four months apart.

It brought our land-based airpower within bombing range of the enemy, and set our ground armies on the beachheads of final victory.

It performed the multitude of tasks necessary to support these military operations.

No other Navy at any time has done so much. For your part in these achievements you deserve to be proud as long as you live. The Nation which you served at a time of crisis will remember you with gratitude.

Stephens relates that right after the war, "I went back to Kansas, looked around, and decided to stay in the Navy. By doing so, I knew the Navy would at some point allow me to finish college." He considers himself "lucky that he had the opportunity to go regular Navy." As it turns out, he remained in the Navy thirty-one years - having "a good career and a wonderful time." He married and raised three "terrific" daughters. He and his family ultimately settled in Texas. Among others, his Navy assignments included: CO of FIGHTER SQUADRON 103, CO of Carrier Air Wing 3, CO of USS THOMASTON (LSD-28), CO of USS PRINCETON (LPH-5), and CO of NAS Moffett Field, California.

Earlier in his post-war career – 1954-57, Stephens had been assigned to the Navy's Test Pilot School (TPS) and Flight Test Division at Patuxent River, Maryland. His shipmates in TPS Class 12 included future Astronaut and Senator John Glenn and future Vietnam POW and Medal of Honor recipient Vice Admiral James Stockdale.

As one of the top graduates in the TPS class, Stephens was assigned to the Carrier Suitability Section of the Flight Test Division where he recalls:

We had some very interesting experiences as the various new aircraft arrived. It was our job to test for structural integrity as well as the minimum speeds they would fly off the catapult and land aboard safely. We had many interesting experiences with bad cat shots, broken arresting wires, etc.

In addition to serving in World War II, Stephens also made combat deployments during the Korean and Vietnam Wars. He earned numerous personal awards during his career. After retirement from the Navy, he went to work for a large savings and loan organization and was eventually promoted to vice president. Of his post-Navy career, Stephens says, "I enjoyed it. It was a good outfit." After fifteen years, he retired again. He still maintained ties to the Navy by serving as President of the Corpus Christi, Texas Council of the Navy League.

In October 2007, Stephens turned eighty-five. He still enjoys living in Texas and playing golf regularly – and proud that at age seventy-eight he shot his age. In a 1992 Christmas card, he related to Banks, "We are in pretty good health, but have a few aches and pains from too many cat shots and hard landings and gray hairs from running down errant gunners, etc."

As Banks recalls, Stoops stayed in the Navy and went to flight school to become a pilot. He eventually left the Navy and finished college with an advanced degree in chemistry. He married and had a son and daughter. According to his son, Thomas A. Stoops, Stoops "worked for many years for the Tucson Medical Center running the nuclear medicine lab. He spoke often of his days in the Navy and was an avid pilot and restorer of antique aircraft after the war." Tom Stoops died from cancer at the age of sixty-four.

Charlie Edwards thought about staying in the Navy, but decided against it. He recalls,"I loved flying, but did not want to be away from my family." He and Marnie had four children and still live in Falls Church, Virginia. After a long career, Edwards retired from the Atomic Energy Commission where he had worked in the Intelligence Section. He advises that he enjoyed working for the AEC. He also always enjoyed driving sports cars and today drives a Mazda Miata. He and Marnie have done a lot of traveling and have been back to Hawaii several times – including Barking Sands. The only flying he did after the Navy was in his personal one seater "ultralight" aircraft. He enjoyed teaching his son how to fly it, but admits teaching was more stressful than flying himself.

For his eighty-fifth birthday, Edward's children gave him a thirty minute ride in an SNJ – one of the planes that he had trained in. It was a highlight of his post-Navy life. Edwards advises, "It all came back to me. I loved it! I feel like I could have landed it." Marnie observes, "He even walked like a fighter pilot again. They had a certain walk – a swagger." Edwards adds, "The girls loved our walk."

When VC-66 returned to California from Hawaii in November 1944, unlike most of the men who were reassigned elsewhere, Russ Jensen remained to help re-form the squadron and become part of VC-66 (T-2). One of his most vivid memories is being at sea with the re-formed squadron aboard the USS ANZIO (CVE-57), and being caught in a Typhoon between Guam and Korea.

Jensen was discharged from the Navy on 9 February 1946. He went home to Oregon, bought some land, built a couple of log houses with his dad, and went to work driving cement mixer trucks. He got married in April 1947. The Jensen's daughter was born in September 1948 and a son in August 1951. They bought some more land and built their own home on it. In 1969, Jensen became part owner of a sand and gravel plant while still driving his own truck. The Jensens ran their business until 1984. Today, Jensen and his wife, Katy, own and live on eighty acres of land in Eagle Point, Oregon. Jensen refers to it as "God's country!" They have enjoyed traveling and hunting. And Jensen got his deer this year even while engaged in a battle with cancer. After more than sixty years, he and Banks recently renewed their friendship via telephone and letter writing.

When Jack Dwight left the Navy after the war, he took his wife and little son, John Jr., back to Pennsylvania where he eventually bought and operated a printing business for many years. He retired to Mexico where he lived for ten years in a "colony" of other Americans and enjoyed the weather and playing golf. After a heart attack, he moved back to the U.S. Today, he lives in a retirement home in Lawrence, Massachusetts where he describes himself as "happy as health and emphysema will allow."

After his discharge, James Gander went back to Madison, Wisconsin. He married in 1946 and he and his wife raised seven children. He worked as an automobile mechanic for a number of years before opening his own repair shop.

Today, Gander and his wife live in Minnesota where he still works part time in his son's eye glass business. In his spare time, he enjoys hunting and fishing. One of the highlights of his post-Navy life was a 1985 trip to Hawaii with his wife. Among other things, he enjoyed going back to Kauai and visiting Barking Sands.

Gander did much of his VC-66 flying with Jobbo Polski and was sorry to hear of Polski's death. Gander would have liked to talk with Polski again.

Emidio Mardarello was on thirty days leave in between duty stations when the war ended. His new squadron had finished training in Florida and had orders to report to Coronado Heights in San Diego. Mardarello had completed refresher aerial gunnery training in grand style by scoring forty-five hits on a towed sleeve. As he recalls, "The next closest gunner only got nineteen hits. And many were below ten hits." Mardarello was a heck of a good shot.

With the end of the war, Mardarello got a break and was ordered to Shore Patrol duty at the 3rd Naval District. He remained on active duty for about three months serving as an SP in New York City and Hoboken, New Jersey. He was born in Hoboken and it had been his hometown before the war – so he too had come full circle. He was discharged from the Personnel Separation Center, Lido Beach, Long Island, New York.

After his discharge, Mardarello went back to New Jersey. Before the war, he had worked at Macy's department store making "good money" – forty-five dollars a week as a seventeen year old supervisor. But rather than returning to Macy's, his father – who along with Mardarello's mother had been born in Italy - and other family members who had worked for years on the New Jersey docks, talked him into working with them on the waterfront. As Mardarello tells it, "I got a job doing clerical work and stayed for fifty-one years until I retired ten years ago at age seventy-two." He married and raised a family. Today, he is a great grandfather. He and his wife were together for fifty-seven years until her death.

As to his time in the Navy, Mardarello like many others who served in World War II advises:

> I didn't think or say much about it for years. I remember meeting a girl who asked me why I never talked about what I did? She said I had lots of ribbons, so I must have done something. I said I was on a carrier. She said her brother was on a tanker and asked if that was like a carrier? I decided to say no more. She would not understand.

Mardarello is enjoying retirement. He does volunteer work at a hospital and serves as an usher for his church. He remembers Banks well, "He was one of the most pleasant fellows I met – always had a smile on his face, and was the only metalsmith gunner that I ever knew."

Of his time with VC-66, Mardarello says, "It was the proudest moment of my life – next to my marriage and the birth of my children."

Banks' VC-92 buddy and fellow turret gunner, William Erny, in a TBM Turret. (Official U.S. Navy Photograph courtesy D.A. Banks collection)

Stephens leads a section of TBMs on a training flight similar to the one he, Banks, and new radioman Marvin R. Sherrod were on when the war in the Pacific ended. (Official U.S. Navy Photograph courtesy D.A. Banks collection)

Banks and a group of his new VC-92 shipmates at NAAS Oxnard, California shortly after the war had ended. (Photo: courtesy D.A. Banks collection)

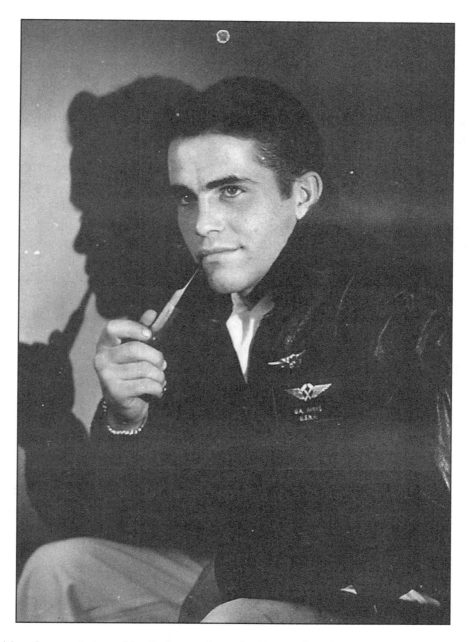

Banks waiting for word about his discharge from the Navy after the war ended. (Photo: courtesy D.A. Banks collection)

20

Going Home and Moving On

With his discharge papers in hand, Banks took the next train leaving Geneva, New York for Buffalo. Jean, and her parents, Nora and Elmer, met him at the Buffalo train station.

Elmer Dewey was a proud veteran of the 1916 Pancho Villa Punitive Expedition and World War I in France. He saw combat as part of Battery B, 106th Field Artillery, 52nd Field Artillery Brigade, 27th Infantry Division. And a little over twenty-six years earlier, after being discharged from the Army, he had returned to Buffalo via the same train station where he now greeted Banks.

The Banks and Deweys went home to the Deweys' house at 100 Roseview Avenue in Windom (now Blasdell), New York. Windom in late 1945 was a town "in the country" about ten miles south of Buffalo. "In the country" in those days, among other things, meant no indoor plumbing. People still used "out houses" and got their water from a hand operated well pump in the kitchen. They cooked on coal stoves. Telephones were relatively rare. Windom was also in the "snow belt" area of western New York. In the winter after storms – which were not uncommon - Elmer would muster all of the neighborhood men at one end of the road with their shovels, and they would shovel the length of the road so that the cars could use it. The road was approximately one mile long.

After settling in and being given a warm welcome by the whole Dewey family - including Jean's younger sisters Frances and Ann – brother Dan was still on his way home after serving with Patton's Third Army in Europe, Banks was somewhat surprised that no one really wanted to hear about his war experiences. Apparently everyone wanted to move on - as did Banks. He decided not to join the American Legion or the Veterans of Foreign Wars. Jean was expecting in December and his first priority was to get a job.

While listing commercial drawing as his post-Navy employment preference on the official Notice of Separation that went to the Veterans Administration, Banks had no experience in that field. But he did put his Navy metalsmith training to good use and got hired as an apprentice welder with the Bethlehem Steel Company in Lackawanna, New York. One can imagine all of the men looking for work right after the war, so Banks was fortunate.

And it was a good thing that he did find work because on 15 December 1945, in the midst of a raging snow storm, I was born. My parents named me Stephen – after LTJG Franklin T. "Steve" Stephens. I have considered it an honor ever since. Now, Banks was not only a full time civilian and husband, but also a new father.

The steel plant job was interrupted by a labor strike whereupon Banks, in need of an income, went to work for the Gas Company in Buffalo in the meter repair shop. He considered it a good job – and better than the steel plant environment, but recalls, "I didn't see myself doing it for the rest of my life."

In March 1946, Jean's mother, Nora, died after a relatively sudden illness. She was only forty-five years old. At age twenty, Jean suddenly became the mother of an extended family: Banks, me, Elmer, Frances, Ann, and Dan - who was now home from the Army. It was a lot of responsibility and a lot of work.

Like so many other World War II vets, Banks soon came to feel that the GI Bill was an opportunity too good to pass up. Jean agreed. While it would mean sacrifice in the short run, it was a wise and life changing decision. According to the Fall 2004 issue of *The National D-Day Museum Newsletter,* Stephen Ambrose called The GI Bill of Rights (officially "The Servicemen's Readjustment Act of 1944"), "The best piece of legislation ever passed by the U.S. Congress, and it made modern America." Nearly eight million World War II veterans would take advantage of the educational opportunity. The number of college graduates would double.

Banks decided to pursue his artistic interest – first expressed by his VC-66 ready room cartoons. He enrolled at Buffalo State College in the Art Education Department.

Banks credits his acceptance by the College's Art Education Department to Dr. Stanley Czurles – the Department chairman. Banks did not have an outstanding high school record. Bea had made him take Latin – and re-take it, which was a real problem for Banks. He couldn't pass it. And the business courses he took did not impress the other members of the Art Department. But after a long interview and a review of Banks' Navy record, Czurles decided to take a chance. He allowed Banks to enroll in the Department. To say that Czurles' decision had a significant impact on Banks' life would be a huge understatement.

While it was not easy beginning college at age twenty-three when most of the other freshmen were eighteen - and having been about as far away from academic work as you can get for years, Banks persisted. He quit the job at the gas company. The GI Bill gave him and Jean $120 per month to live on plus payment of tuition, books, and supplies – which was important for an art major. To make extra money, he worked summers and vacations as a short order cook and other odd jobs. He took extra courses when he could and spent a lot of time on buses between the house in Windom and the college, but he graduated in January 1950 after three and a half years. It was a major accomplishment. He was the first one in either the Banks or Dewey families to get a college education.

Ambrose was right, the GI Bill was a great thing – both for the veterans and for the country. My parents certainly came to appreciate the value of a college education. As far back as I can remember, they made it clear to me that there was no question, I would go to college.

After graduation, Banks accepted an offer from the Niagara Falls, New York, Public School Department. They liked his creativity. The starting salary for a first year teacher was $2700 per year. My parents and I moved out of the Dewey home and into a small upstairs apartment on Lockport Street in Niagara Falls.

Many other changes were taking place at the Dewey home. At around the same time as the Banks family moved to Niagara Falls, Frances married Bill Finken – who had also served in the Navy in one of the engineering ratings. Bill would soon teach Banks and Jean how to drive the new powder blue 1950 Studebaker Champion that they had just bought.

Dan had also married and he and his wife, Florence, had a place of their own. And Elmer soon remarried and moved into the city. Ann, who was only eleven, stayed with Frances and Bill in the Dewey house.

Bill would die from heart disease in his late twenties and Frances would eventually marry another former Navy man, John Mowell. Mowell had been a PBY aircrewman during the war. Ann would eventually marry Dick Kruszka, who had spent some time in the Marine Corps. Thus, in addition to sharing good looks, it appears that the Dewey women also shared a significant amount of good judgment as they apparently made prior Naval service (again, the Marine Corps is part of the Navy Department) a prerequisite for marriage. Although Frances did waiver from the "Navy rule" and consented to her son, Bill Finken Jr., joining the Air Force. Bill went on to make Frances and the rest of the family proud by his service in Vietnam. And Ann and Dick's grandson, Nicholas Kruszka, joined and is still serving in the Air Force.

Banks went on to have an outstanding career as an art teacher. He enjoyed working with the kids, and the kids enjoyed his classes. While very comfortable in the classroom, he also put a lot of thought and preparation into his lessons. He was considered a good example and role model for young teachers and those college students aspiring to be teachers. As a result, many "student teachers" were assigned to work with him.

Banks spent summer "vacations" working temporary jobs to supplement the relatively meager teacher's salary. He did such things as house painting and putting roofs on houses, and later serving as a U.S. Customs Inspector on the Niagara Falls area bridges between the U.S. and Canada.

In 1953, Banks and Jean used the GI Bill again – this time to buy a small two bedroom home in Kenmore. Kenmore is a northern suburb of Buffalo and about fifteen miles south of Niagara Falls. The newly built house cost ten thousand dollars. They still live in it.

In the mid-50s, Banks earned a Master's Degree from Buffalo State. In the meantime, Jean pursued a career in secretarial work. She ultimately became the Secretary to the Head of the Math Department at Buffalo State – a job that she enjoyed and eventually retired from – and for which her services were much appreciated. She also served as a homemaker, a Scout leader, and the keeper of the family purse strings – and did a good job with it all. For example, in the summer of 1954, when I was eight years old, we took a weekend trip to see the Gettysburg Civil War battlefield in Pennsylvania. Our budget for the entire trip was twenty-five dollars! Today, you can't fill your gas tank for twenty-five dollars. But we didn't miss anything. We slept in our little Nash Rambler stationwagon and had a great time. I credit that trip as sparking my life long interest in history – especially military history.

After several years of teaching, Banks was selected to be the Supervisor of Art Education for Niagara Falls. He ultimately retired as the Supervisor of both Art and Music Education. It was a good, rewarding career. When Banks looks back, he admits without hesitation that he liked the classroom teaching and working with the kids the best. Dealing with the bureaucracy and funding issues wore him down as a Supervisor.

In addition to his day job working with the young people of Niagara Falls, Banks spent many an evening and weekend working with boys as a Scout leader. He led us on some great adventures and treks. On one occasion, we backpacked up New York's highest mountain, Mount Marcy, in three feet of snow – without snowshoes. It was a tough, character building grind, but we made it. At least a couple of his former Scouts have written to him over the years thanking him for his inspiration and contribution to their lives.

Today, Banks and Jean enjoy working in their yard, traveling, and spending time with friends and family – especially their four grandchildren: Ken, Erin, Christopher, and Shannon who are spread out all over the country, and their great-granddaughter, Ava Hope Banks. They are proud of all of them. Most recently they are very proud of Jean's cousin, Madonna Mahoney, who is just back (May 2008) from a tour of duty as an Air Force nurse in Afghanistan (Madonna's brother, Jim Jr., served with the Marines in Vietnam and her dad, Jim Sr., was wounded at Normandy while serving with the 82nd Airborne Division in World War II).

Thus, like so many of his former Navy shipmates, Banks went on to have a very productive and successful post-Navy life. It is an accomplishment that seems a common thread among that group of young men who came together from such diverse civilian backgrounds to form VC-66 and go on to become outstanding pilots, gunners, radiomen, or mechanics during the war - and then afterward continued to excel in whatever they chose to do.

Several of them – including Stephens, Birdsong, Stack, Cook, Fox, and Mayer, chose to make the Navy a career. They ultimately achieved positions of much responsibility such as commanding officers of squadrons, ships, and bases, and retired as senior officers – including a Rear Admiral (Mayo).

Most of them left the Navy and went on to have successful civilian careers in such diverse fields as education (Banks, Kennon, and former fighter pilot LT Lawrence E. "Larry" Carr), the trades (Chaz Jones and AMM1c Robert B. Muzzy), engineering (Stoops), medicine (Mayer), communications (Dean Summers), publishing (Kiplinger), public service (Cope), auto repair (Gander), business (Krost, Piper, Jensen, and Dwight), shipping (Mardarello), law (Catterton), real estate (Takis), and so on. Many had two careers.

Some like Krost, Takis, Catterton, Carr, Keyser, and Dean Summers stayed in the Reserves so that they could continue to fly and serve in addition to having civilian careers. Their love of flying was strong and fortunately they were able to combine it with their regular jobs and family life. For example, Keyser flew with Ready Reserve squadrons VS-931 and VS-935 at NAS Willow Grove, Pennsylvania until July 1966. And Catterton's son, G. Berry Catterton, Jr., describes his dad who died in 1984:

> He was a wonderful man, leader, husband, and father – what you would expect from the "Greatest Generation" as were all the members of the squadron….After World War II he graduated from the Univ. of California School of Law and became a JAG…before opening his private practice. He remained in the US Navy Reserve (VS-872) into the 1960's so he could fly his plane and enjoy the camaraderie of the aviators. I grew up many a weekend accompanying him to NAS Oakland and NAS Alameda. These are memories I will never forget.

Larry Carr, in addition to pursuing his career as a math professor and remaining in the Reserves, participated in the "1000 Aviator Study." The study was begun in 1940 by The Naval School of Aviation Medicine in Pensacola. The goal was to investigate the process of aging by tracking a selected group of 1,056 aviators through their lives. The group would be evaluated at various intervals and the data recorded. Carr had gotten involved at the time of his commissioning. The project was to last until the deaths of the participants, but according to Carr's wife, Jean Carr, "It was disbanded several years ago for lack of funds." Too bad. These were tough, strong men and the results probably would have been interesting.

And concerning Carr, DeLoach Cope advises that he flew wing for Carr and liked him. Cope recalls, "Carr was a good friend of Bing Crosby's. No one knew how, but we kidded him about it."

Over the years, some of the VC-66 (T-1) pilots got together in a few informal mini-reunions. They had a good time telling sea stories and catching up. In a January 1990 letter to Banks, Stephens described one of the pilots' reunions:

> Well as you surmised we had a lot of fun at our little VC-66 reunion, mostly remembering various old adventures. But all in all it was very sedate and nobody was thrown into the cold beer trough. There were no Marines or submariners to start a fight with. Also no one lost their travel orders so we didn't have to bail anyone out of trouble. Also a careful check showed we all had the same spouses we started out with 40 odd years ago. I thought this pretty remarkable as we all married at rather tender ages and have had a lot of tough times in between.

The men of VC-66 and the others who served in the Pacific during the war were - and still are - a remarkable group. They served in a time of giants and legends: Chet Nimitz, Bull Halsey, Frank Fletcher, Ray Spruance, and Howlin Mad Smith – and fought alongside them. They are best defined by their willingness to serve, sacrifice, and contribute throughout their lives. As Banks tells it, "Now, I wear my World War II hat with pride of my service, but more so for the guys that didn't come back – we all did our best and that's good enough." It sure was.

June Hartman-Banks (Banks' brother John's wife), Banks, and Jean. (Photo: courtesy D.A. Banks collection)

Jean, Banks, Jean's sister Frances, and Frances' husband Bill Finken, celebrate Banks' graduation from college at the Town Casino night club in Buffalo. (Photo: courtesy D.A. Banks collection)

The author, Banks, and Jean outside Kleinhans Music Hall in Buffalo after Banks received his Master of Arts degree. (Photo: courtesy S.A. Banks)

Banks leading a group of students on a tour of the Albright-Knox Art Gallery in Buffalo. It was a long way from the battles of the South Pacific. (Photo: courtesy D.A. Banks collection)

Some of the VC-66 officers at a mini-reunion in 1989. From left: Franklin T. Stephens, Dean J. Birdsong, Martin J. Stack, John P. Fox, Albert J. Mayer, Austin H. Kiplinger, Joseph S. Trichel, James O. Mayo, and W. DeLoach Cope. (Photo: courtesy F.T. Stephens)

Banks (in the middle) swaps war stories with a TBF turret gunner from VC-68 – the squadron that replaced VC-66 aboard FANSHAW BAY after the Moluccas Islands – Western New Guinea Campaign. The two "old" gunners literally bumped into each other at the dedication of the National World War II Memorial in Washington, D.C. (Photo: courtesy S.A. Banks)

IN MEMORIAM

(VC-66 shipmates who died while serving with the squadron)

BENNETT, William A., LTJG – Los Angeles, California.

CALDERON, Manuel V., AOM3c (CA) – Los Angeles, California.

DAVIS, Ben E., ENS – Danville, Illinois.

DEGANKOLP, E. B., ENS – Home of record unknown.

HEBERT, Edward J., AMM3c – Home of record unknown.

JOHNSON, William J., ENS – Saint Paul, Minnesota.

KEOUGH, Robert L., AMM3c (CA) – Colville, Washington.

LAVIN, Martin T., ARM3c – Home of record unknown.

McCABE, Francis J. M., LTJG – Brooklyn, New York.

RATHBUN, James A., AMM3c (CA) – Cincinnati, Ohio.

RODRIGUEZ, Reynold, ENS – Forest Hills, New York.

SHAFFER, Hyram L., ARM2c – Inkom, Idaho.

When you go home
Tell them for us and say
For your tomorrow
We gave our today.*

*As chiseled on the Iwo Jima cemetery wall, See: James Bradley with Ron Powers, *Flags of Our Fathers*, Bantam Dell, New York, N.Y, 2000, page 247.

COMPOSITE SQUADRON SIXTY-SIX (VC-66) ROSTER

(PERSONNEL ATTACHED DURING THE PERIOD
21 JUNE 1943 – 3 NOVEMBER 1944)

ADAMS, Douglas S., ENS;
BANKS, Donald A., AM1c (T) (CA);
BARRETT, Maurice W., LTJG;
BENNETT, Maynard W., AMM1c;
*BENNETT, William A., LTJG;
BIRDSONG, Dean John, LTJG;
BISSON, Frederick L., ACMM;
BOREL, Ulyse R., AMM2c (CA);
BOWDISH, William J., AMM1c;
BRAGG, Herbert K., LCDR;
BROWN, George W., LTJG;
*CALDERON, Manuel V., AOM3c (CA);
CARR, Lawrence E., LT;
CATTERTON, Guy B., LT;
CHAMBERLIN, Leo P., ARM2c (CA);
CLARK, Otha J., LTJG;
COOK, William E., LTJG;
COPE, William DeLoach, LTJG;
*DAVIS, Ben E., ENS;
*DEGANKOLP, E. B., ENS;
DEGASIS, Alphonse J., LTJG (MC);
DeLOACHE, Hebert E., ACOM;
DeVORE, Albert A., AOM2c (CA);
DWIGHT, John L., LTJG;
EDWARDS, Charles T., LTJG;
FERNANDEZ, Joe, AMM2c (CA);
FOX, John P., LT;
GANDER, James, AMM2c (CA);
GIBSON, Homer A., ACOM (PA);
HAMILTON, Fay W., LTJG;
HART, John, AMM2c (CA);
HAWBAKER, Melvin E., ARM2c (CA);
*HEBERT, Edward J., AMM3c;
HOLLEY, Robert E., ENS;
IRVIN, David R., ARM2c (CA);
JENSEN, Russell P., AOM2c (CA);
*JOHNSON, William J., ENS;
JONES, Charles R., ARM2c (CA);
JONES, Joseph J., ARM2c (CA);

KELLY, Vernon A., ARM1c (CA);
KENNON, Robert L., ARM1c (CA);
*KEOUGH, Robert L., AMM2c (CA);
KETCHAM, Lewis C., Y1c (T);
KEYSER, Edward F., ENS;
KIPLINGER, Austin H., LTJG;
KLAUS, Joe P., LT;
KROST, Richard F., ENS;
*LAVIN, Martin T., ARM3c;
LUDLUM, Samuel A. , LT;
MacDONALD, Jerrold K., LTJG;
MARDARELLO, Emidio J., AOM2c (CA);
MAYER, Albert J., LT;
MAYO, James O., LTJG;
*McCABE, Francis J. M., LTJG;
McNEELAND, John, LTJG;
MITCHELL, Dean K., ACRM (AA);
MOLASH, Walter W., AOM1c (CA);
MORLEY, John F., ENS;
MORRIS, Sidney, ENS;
MUSE, Robert P., ARM1c (CA);
MUZZY, Robert B., AMM1c;
NAYLOR, Robert J., ACRT (AA) (T);
PEART, Chester M., ACM;
PIPER, William H., LT;
PLOUFFE, Roger L., ARM2c (CA);
POLSKI, Joseph N., LTJG;
*RATHBUN, James A., AMM3c (CA);
REYNOLDS, William W., ENS;
RIFFLE, Charles S., ARM2c (CA);
*RODRIGUEZ, Reynold, ENS;
ROUSE, Jerome A., ENS;
RUTHMAN, Vincent T., AMM3c (CA);
SALMON, John L., ARM3c (CA);
SATTERTHWAITE, Norman D., ENS;
SCHILLER, Avner R., LT;
SCHLEICHER, Raymond O., PR1c;
*SHAFFER, Hyram L., ARM2c (CA);
SHERIDAN, James H., ACMM;
SHICK, George W., LT;
SHOEMAKER, Raymond A., AOM2c (CA);
SMITH, Roger W., AOM1c;
SPOONER, John H., AMM3c;
STACK, Martin J., LTJG;
STAMPER, Salkeld, AMM2c (CA);
STEPHENS, Franklin T., LTJG;

STOFFER, Bernald H., ACMM (PA);
STOOPS, Thomas D., ARM3c (CA);
SUMMERS, Dean H., ARM2c (CA);
SUMMERS, William A., ACEM (PA);
SWENSON, Donald R., ARM2c (CA);
TAKIS, Sam, LTJG;
TAPPAN, Rex A., ARM2c (CA);
TAYLOR, Leo V., AMM1c;
TERRELL, Joseph F., LTJG;
TRAPP, Gerald O., LT;
TRAYNOR, Raymond H., LTJG;
TRICHEL, Joseph S., LTJG;
WEAVER, Robert A., LTJG;
WHITLOCK, Ira W., AOM1c (T) (CA);
YAGODZINSKI, Thomas F., AMM2c (CA).

* Indicates died while serving with VC-66.

CHAPTER NOTES AND SOURCES

Sources cited here are listed in order of appearance of an individual quoted, or the author's statement of a fact, in a given chapter. Each note is numbered for ease of subsequent reference.

1. Joining Up

1. Details of the attack on Pearl Harbor are from: *The Pearl Harbor Memorial Fund* Web Site, <http://www.pearlharbormemorial.com/site/pp.asp?c=fqLQJ2NNG&b=239190>, accessed 29 June 2007; and *The USS Arizona National Memorial – People, U.S. National Park Service* Web Site, <http://www.nps.gov/usar/historyculture/people.htm>, accessed 29 June 2007.
2. All quotations from President Franklin Roosevelt are from his address to Congress on 8 December 1941.
3. All quotations and information from Donald A. Banks (Banks) in this and subsequent chapters are from one or more of the following sources: unpublished *LIFE IN THE SERVICE "The Sailors Log"* including significant dates, events, records, promotions, shipmates, assignments, miscellaneous paper souvenirs, and other personal information and experiences, dated 1942 to 1945, by Banks; "Gallantry Disclosed," *The Buffalo Evening News*, 22 March 1945; unpublished eighty-eight page memoir, circa 1997, by Banks; Donald A. Banks, "Wotje and Then Some," *Aviation History*, July 2001, pp. 8 and 63; interviews, Banks by Stephen Banks, 20 April 2003, 24 September 2004, 21 November 2006, and 24 November 2006; telephone interviews, Banks/Stephen Banks, March 2005, 10 June 2006, July 2007, 7 August 2007, 20 August 2007, 1 November 2007, 10 December 2007, and 21 January 2008; written notes, from Banks to Stephen Banks, June 2006, 20 December 2006, 15 January 2007, 8 June 2007, 30 July 2007, August 2007, September 2007, 20 November 2007, and 20 December 2007; completed questionnaire re Navy service, dated 17 November 2006, by Banks; and e-mail, Banks to Stephen Banks, 27 February 2007, 19, 21, 22, and 25 January 2008, 28 March 2008, and 13 May 2008.
4. Details re the Curtiss-Wright Corporation and its Buffalo plant are from *Wings over WNY – The Digital Collection of the Niagara Aerospace Museum* Web Site, <http://aerospace.bfn.org/DL/museum.htm>, accessed 28 June 2007.
5. On the Banks family: Banks, n. 3 above.
6. On Bea Banks: Banks, n. 3 above; Valerie Marrs, "BEATRICE BANKS – HAPPY 100TH BIRTHDAY! Hard work the secret to her longevity," *Whittier (California) Daily News*, 20 September 1997; and Stephen Banks' personal recollection.
7. On Banks' growing up: Banks, n. 3 above.
8. On Banks working at Curtiss-Wright: Banks, n. 3 above.
9. Details re Glenn Curtiss are from "WORLD WARS BOOM NAVAL PILOT TRAINING TO MEET FLEET NEEDS," *Naval Aviation News*, 15 October 1944, p. 22.
10. On the workload at Curtiss-Wright: See n. 4 above.
11. For the shape of the world in 1940-41: Stephen E. Ambrose, *To America: Personal Reflections of an Historian* (New York, N.Y.: Simon and Schuster, Inc., 2002), p. 82; and Stephen E. Ambrose, *The Victors – Eisenhower and His Boys: The Men of World War II*, (New York, N.Y.: Simon and Schuster, Inc., 1998), p. 15.
12. On Banks choosing to join the Navy: Banks, n. 3 above.
13. On the large number of men enlisting on 8 December 1941: Ambrose, *To America*, p. 94.
14. For Banks' enlistment processing: Banks, n. 3 above.

2. Training

1. Details of Boot Camp in general are from William J. Veigele, "WWII Navy Boot Camps," *Navy Knowledge Online – Astral Publishing Company* Web Site, <http://www.astralpublishing.com/wwii-navy-boot-camps.html>, accessed 29 August 2007.

2. Details of NTC Sampson are from: "Sampson Naval Training Base," *New York State Military Museum and Veterans Research Center, NYS Division of Military and Naval Affairs* Web Site, <http://www.dmna.state.ny.us/forts/fortsQ_S/sampsonNavalTrainingBase.htm>, accessed 27 July 2006; and "Anchors Aweigh," Plaque at Sampson State Park, New York museum, visited 1 October 2007.

3. On Banks' life as a Boot at Sampson: Banks, n. 3, ch. 1; and n. 1 above.

4. On graduation from Sampson and leave: Banks, n. 3, ch. 1.

5. Details of NATTC Norman are from: "Norman, Oklahoma," *U.S. Naval Activities World War II by State* Web Site, <http://www.ibiblio.net/hyperwar/USN/ref/USN-Act/OK.html>, accessed 30 August 2007; and "Norman Supplies Steady Flow of Mechs," "RUGGED PHYSICAL PROGRAM FITS NORMAN TRAINEES FOR COMBAT," and "AM'S SIMULATE REAL SQUADRON OPERATIONS AT NORMAN SCHOOL," *Naval Aviation News*, 15 November 1944, pp. 20, 21, and 26.

6. On Banks' life during "A" school: Banks, n. 3, ch. 1.

7. For WAVES at Norman: "Joan Holmes Crews Recalls Life and Times as WAVE – The Rare Breed – Recognizing Area Veterans of World War II," *Palacios Beacon* Online, Palacios, Texas Web Site, <http://www.palaciosbeacon.com/home/features-crews.shtml>, accessed 30 August 2007; "WAVES Aviation Metalsmiths," Department of the Navy, Naval Historical Center, Washington, D.C. Web Site, <http://www.history.navy.mil/photos/prs-tpic/females/wvw2-am7.htm>, accessed 30 August 2007; and "World War II Era WAVES – Overview and Special Image Selection," Department of the Navy, Naval Historical Center, Washington, D.C. Web Site, <http://www.history.navy.mil/photos/prs-tpic/females/wave-ww2.htm>, accessed 30 August 2007.

8. On liberty and recreation in Norman: Banks, n. 3, ch. 1; and "RUGGED PHYSICAL PROGRAM FITS NORMAN TRAINEES FOR COMBAT," *Naval Aviation News*, 15 November 1944, p. 21.

9. On Tex Beneke at Norman: Banks, n. 3, ch. 1; and "Gordon 'Tex' Beneke," *The Big Band Broadcast* Web Site, <http://www.bigbands.org/benekebio.htm>, accessed 30 August 2007.

10. On graduation from "A" school: Banks, n. 3, ch. 1.

11. Details of World War II enlisted pay are from: "U.S. Navy Enlisted Pay 1943-1945," *BlueJacket.com* Web Site, <http://www.bluejacket.com/usn_pay-scale_1943-1945_enlisted.html>, accessed 30 August 2007; and "WWII U.S. Navy Enlisted Base Pay," *Valor at Sea* Web Site, <http://www.valoratsea.com/paygrade.htm>, accessed 4 September 2007.

3. Learning To Be A Turret Gunner

1. On the trip to Seattle via Chicago: Banks, n. 3, ch. 1.

2. Details of NAS Seattle are from "Sand Point Naval Air Station: 1920 – 1970," *Historylink.org – The Online Encyclopedia of Washington State History* Web Site, <http://www.historylink.org/essays/output.cfm?file_id=2249>, accessed 31 August 2007.

3. On aerial free gunnery: "Pilot Weapons Training – Gunnery: U.S. Navy NATC No. 2667, Gunnery Manual, 1944: Free Gunnery," 10 July 1944, *WW2 Air Fronts* Web Site, <http://ww2airfronts.org/Flight%20School/transition/weaponsschool/natc-2667-44/pages/natc-2667-44-14.html>, accessed 19 October 2007.

4. Details of the gunnery school curriculum are from: "GOOD GUNNERY PROTECTS AVENGERS AGAINST ENEMY FIGHTER ATTACKS," *Naval Aviation News,* 15 July 1944, pp. 42-43; and "FREE GUNNERY TRAINING," "FIRST SCHOOL USED GUNS FROM PLANES WRECKED IN JAP ATTACK," "GUNNER MUST MASTER SIGHTS IF HE WANTS TO BECOME MARKSMEN," "SHIP AND PLANE RECOGNITION IS STRESSED IN GUNNER'S TRAINING," "STUDENT FIRES 6,500 ROUNDS IN MACHINE GUNS DURING TRAINING," and "STUDENT USES TRAINING DEVICES ALONG WITH ACTUAL RANGE FIRING," *Naval Aviation News*, 1 November 1944, pp. 14–16, and 20–22.

5. On Banks' pistol shooting at gunnery school: Banks, n. 3, ch. 1.

6. For Howard Alley re pressure during gunnery school: Howard Alley, "The Making of an Aircrewman: The Gunnery Range (Part 2)" *VC-66 (T-2) Newsletter*, April 2008, BACK SIDE, col. 1-2.

7. On Robert Stack as a gunnery instructor: "In Memoriam: Robert Stack," *Industry News* Web Site, <http://scoop.diamondgalleries.com/public/default.asp?t=1&m=1&c=34&s=259&ai=43284&ssd=5/17/2003&arch=y>, accessed 31 August 2007; and Jose Andres "Andy" Chacon, "United States Navy," *West-Point.org – The West Point Connection* Web Site, <http://www.westpoint.org/users/usma1951/18250/US%20Navy.htm>, accessed 31 August 2007.

8. On Banks' experiences at gunnery school: Banks, n. 3, ch. 1.

9. For Howard Alley re the difficulty of gunnery school: Howard Alley, "The Making of an Aircrewman: The Gunnery Range (Part 2)" *VC-66 (T-2) Newsletter*, April 2008, BACK SIDE, col. 1-2.

10. For Marine Corps recruiter's comment: Ken Burns, "THE WAR," Episode 1, Public Broadcasting Service, WETA, 23 September 2007.

11. On Banks' first flight experiences: Banks, n. 3, ch. 1.

12. For information re the SNJ: "SNJ Trainer," *Air Group 31* Web Site, <http://www.vf31.com/aircraft/snj.html>, accessed 22 February 2007; and "Mission and Description," Department of the Navy, Naval Historical Center, Washington, D.C. Web Site, <http://www.history.navy.mil/branches/hist-ac/snj-6.pdf>, accessed 22 February 2007.

13. For the description of the Boeing building: Banks, n. 3, ch. 1; "Boeing Military Aircraft in the 1930s and 1940s," *U.S. Centennial of Flight Commission* Web Site, <http://www.centennialofflight.gov/essay/Aerospace/boeing-1930s_1940s/Aero19.htm>, accessed 31 August 2007; and Erik Lacitis, "This is one of the places that won the war," *The Seattle Times* Web Site, 25 September 2006, <http://seattletimes.nwsource.com/html/localnews/2003274068_boeingplant25m.html?syndication=rss>, accessed 31 August 2007.

4. To The Fleet

1. On Banks' assignment to TBFs: Banks, n. 3, ch. 1.

2. For TBFs accepted by the Navy: "Grumman TBF/TBM Avenger," Display, National Museum of the Marine Corps, Quantico, Virginia, December 2006.

3. For information re TBF/TBMs: "Naval Aircraft: Avenger," 1 July 1943, Department of the Navy, Naval Historical Center, Washington, D.C. Web Site, <http://www.history.navy.mil/branches/hist-ac/tbf-1.pdf>, accessed 16 February 2007; Lou Drendel, *Walk Around TBF/TBM Avenger*, (Carrollton, Texas: Squadron/Signal Publications, Inc., 2001), pp. 2, 10, 38-39, 52, and 59; Robert F. Dorr, "TBF/TBM Avenger was Navy's Greatest Torpedo Bomber," *Navy Times*, 8 January 2001, p. 26, col. 4-6; and "Grumman TBF Avenger," *Pacific Aviation* Web Site, <http://www.microworks.net/pacific/aviation/tbf_avenger.htm>, accessed 26 October 2007.

4. On Navy belief in the quality of TBFs: "TBF TEAMWORK," *Naval Aviation News*, 15 July 1944, p. 41.

5. On how the Navy designates squadrons: "World War II Naval Aircraft Squadron Designations," *Bluejacket.com* Web Site, <http://www.bluejacket.com/usn-usmc_avi_ww2_squadron_desig.htm>, accessed 8 March 2007.

6. For information re F4F/FMs: "Naval Aircraft: Wildcat," *Naval Aviation News*, December 1971, pp. 20-21, Department of the Navy, Naval Historical Center, Washington, D.C. Web Site, <http://www.history.navy.mil/branches/hist-ac/f4f-4.pdf>, accessed 22 February 2007; "Grumman F4F-4 Wildcat," Display, National Museum of the Marine Corps, Quantico, Virginia, December 2006; "Grumman F4F 'Wildcat' Fighters," Department of the Navy, Naval Historical Center, Washington, D.C. Web Site, <http://www.history.navy.mil/photos/ac-usn22/f-types/f4f.htm>, accessed 22 February 2007; "General Motors FM-2 'Wildcat' Fighters," Department of the Navy, Naval Historical Center, Washington, D.C. Web Site, <http://www.history.navy.mil/photos/ac-usn22/f-types/fm2.htm>, accessed 22 February 2007; and "Grumman F4F (FM-1)," Display, National Air and Space Museum, Washington, D.C., December 2006.

7. On number of Avengers and Wildcats in a VC squadron: Lou Drendel, *Walk Around TBF/TBM Avenger*, (Carrollton, Texas: Squadron/Signal Publications, Inc., 2001), p. 78.

8. On number of Avengers and Wildcats built: "Aircraft, United States," *History of World War II* (CD-ROM), Multieducator (New York, N.Y., 1997); and Lou Drendel, *Walk Around TBF/TBM Avenger*, (Carrollton, Texas: Squadron/Signal Publications, Inc., 2001), p. 2.

9. On the commissioning of VC-66: "Squadron 'X'," *EASTERN AIRCRAFTSMAN*, November 1943, p. 1, col. 1–4, pp. 8 and 9, col. 1-5; Gerald O. Trapp, Lieutenant, A-V(N), USNR, VC-66, Commanding Officer, "UNITED STATES PACIFIC FLEET AIR FORCE COMPOSITE SQUADRON SIXTY-SIX (VC-66): An Informal Squadron History (June, 1943, to November, 1944)," 1944, pp. 1-2 (used with Navy Department approval); and Paul W. Austin , "COMPOSITE SQUADRON SIXTY-SIX" (hand drawn chart of Pacific Ocean prepared for Austin H. Kiplinger showing where VC-66 operated and annotated with statistics and summaries of the squadron's three combat deployments), 1953.

10. For the General Motors press coverage of VC-66: "Squadron 'X'," *EASTERN AIRCRAFTSMAN*, November 1943, p. 1, col. 1–4, pp. 8 and 9, col. 1-5.

11. On the makeup of the original sixty-five members of the squadron: See "Squadron 'X'," *EASTERN AIRCRAFTSMAN*, November 1943, p. 1, col. 1–4, pp. 8 and 9, col. 1-5; Gerald O. Trapp, Lieutenant, A-V(N), USNR, VC-66, Commanding Officer, "UNITED STATES PACIFIC FLEET AIR FORCE COMPOSITE SQUADRON SIXTY-SIX (VC-66) (June, 1943, to November, 1944)," 1944, pp. 1-2 (used with Navy Department approval); and Banks, n. 3, ch. 1.

12. All quotations and information from Robert L. Kennon (Kennon) in this and subsequent chapters are from one or more of the following sources: telephone interview, Kennon/Stephen Banks, 18 January 2008; and letter, 19 February 2008, from Kennon to Stephen Banks.

13. On Ben Davis: "Squadron 'X'," *EASTERN AIRCRAFTSMAN*, November 1943, p. 9, col. 2; and Banks, n. 3, ch. 1.

14. On the Davis, Banks, and Stoops team: Banks, n. 3, ch. 1.

5. Squadron Pre-Deployment Training

1. For the move to NAAS Shelton and description of life there for VC-66: Gerald O. Trapp, Lieutenant, A-V(N), USNR, VC-66, Commanding Officer, "UNITED STATES PACIFIC FLEET AIR FORCE COMPOSITE SQUADRON SIXTY-SIX (VC-66): An Informal Squadron History (June, 1943, to November, 1944)," 1944, p. 3 (used with Navy Department approval); Banks, n. 3, ch. 1; and "Port of Shelton," *Port of Shelton* Web Site, <http://www.portofshelton.com/about_port.html>, accessed 13 March 2007.

2. Re VC-66 and the USS Tripoli (CVE-64): Unknown author, "COMPOSITE SQUADRON SIXTY-SIX (VC-66) June, 1943 – Nov, 1944," six page history, circa 1944, p. 1.

3. All quotations and information from Charles T. Edwards (Edwards) in this and subsequent chapters are from one or more of the following sources: telephone interviews, Edwards/Stephen Banks, 24 August 2007, 1 February 2008, and 9 March 2008; e-mail, Edwards to Stephen Banks, 25 September 2007; and interviews, Edwards by Stephen Banks, 13 February 2008 and 10 March 2008.

4. On training at Shelton: Banks, n. 3, ch. 1; Gerald O. Trapp, Lieutenant, A-V(N), USNR, VC-66, Commanding Officer, "UNITED STATES PACIFIC FLEET AIR FORCE COMPOSITE SQUADRON SIXTY-SIX (VC-66) (June, 1943, to November, 1944)," 1944, p. 3 (used with Navy Department approval); Unknown author, "COMPOSITE SQUADRON SIXTY-SIX (VC-66) June, 1943 – Nov, 1944," six page history, circa 1944, p. 1; and Harold F. Ellsworth, *History of VC-82* Web Site, <http://home.comcast.net/~bmmelvin/warhero/wwiipac.htm>, accessed 8 March 2007.

5. On recognition training: Banks, n. 3, ch. 1; "SHIP AND PLANE RECOGNITION IS STRESSED IN GUNNER'S TRAINING," *Naval Aviation News*, 1 November 1944, p. 20; and Howard Alley, "The Making of an Aircrewman: The Real Training Begins (1944)" *VC-66 (T-2) Newsletter*, March 2008, BACK SIDE, col. 1-2.

6. All quotations and information from William H. Piper (Piper) in this and subsequent chapters are from a telephone interview of Piper by Stephen Banks on 30 January 2008.

7. For account of Ben Davis' death: Banks, n. 3, ch. 1; and Gerald O. Trapp, Lieutenant, A-V(N), USNR, VC-66, Commanding Officer, "UNITED STATES PACIFIC FLEET AIR FORCE COMPOSITE SQUADRON SIXTY-SIX (VC-66) (June, 1943, to November, 1944)," 1944, p. 3 (used with Navy Department approval).

8. On Stephens joining VC-66: Banks, n. 3, ch. 1; and Gerald O. Trapp, Lieutenant, A-V(N), USNR, VC-66, Commanding Officer, "UNITED STATES PACIFIC FLEET AIR FORCE COMPOSITE SQUADRON SIXTY-SIX (VC-66) (June, 1943, to November, 1944)," 1944, p. 3 (used with Navy Department approval).

9. All quotations and information from Franklin T. Stephens (Stephens) in this and subsequent chapters are from one or more of the following sources: log entry entitled "COMPOSITE SQUADRON SIXTY-SIX (VC-66)" including significant dates and events between 2 June 1943 and 3 November 1944, circa 1946, by Stephens; "Bio" of Navy duty assignments with inclusive dates, circa 1974, by Stephens; letters, Stephens to Banks, September 1977, December 1987, January 1989, 12 January 1990, December 1992, December 1995, 26 January 1998, 16 June 1998, 16 September 1998, 17 June 2001, 24 January 2002, and circa 2005; e-mail, Stephens to Banks, 25 April 2003; e-mail, Stephens to Stephen Banks, 12 May 2005, 7 July 2005, 16 July 2005, 9 September 2005, 8 March 2007, 29 June 2007, 20 July 2007, 1 August 2007, and 5 August 2007; telephone interviews, Stephens/Stephen Banks, 15 January 2006, 6 December 2006, 19 December 2006, 17 February 2007, 29 January 2008, 26 February 2008, and 4 March 2008; and "Franklin T. Stephens," *The Navy Log*, The United States Navy Memorial Web Site, <http://www.lonesailor.org/nl_log.php?search=yes&navy_log_id=848565&lname_search=STEPHE NS&fname_search=FRANKLIN&page=1&firstname=FRANKLIN&lastname=stephens>, accessed 21 October 2007.

10. For information about the CPTP: "Civilian Pilot Training Program – U.S. Air Force Fact Sheet," National Museum of the USAF Web Site, <http://www.nationalmuseum.af.mil/factsheets/factsheet.asp?id=8475>, accessed 4 September 2007.

11. On Stephen's flight training: Stephens, n. 9 above; "WORLD WARS BOOM NAVAL PILOT TRAINING TO MEET FLEET NEEDS," "AVIATION CADETS GET STIFF PHYSICAL COURSE," "PRIMARY SCHOOLS GIVE STUDENTS FIRST FLYING," "INTERMEDIATE TRAINING EXPANDS TO 20 WEEKS," and "OPERATIONAL TEAMS UP PILOT AND AIRCREWMEN," *Naval Aviation News*, 15 October 1944, pp. 22, and 24-27; and "THOROUGH TRAINING READIES PILOTS AND AIRCREWMEN FOR THE FLEET," and "IN OPERATIONAL TRAINING PILOTS LEARN FLEET TEAMWORK TACTICS," *Naval Aviation News*, 15 July 1944, pp. 41 and 44.

12. Re USS Wolverine (IX-64): "IX-64 WOLVERINE," *GlobalSecurity.org* Web Site, <http://www.globalsecurity.org/military/systems/ship/ix-64.htm>, accessed 14 August 2007; and Joe Mussatto, "TOP GUNS OF 1943," *VC-66 (T-2) Newsletter*, November 2007, p. 1, col. 1.

13. On the start of the Stephens, Banks, and Stoops relationship: Banks, n. 3, ch. 1.

14. For the move to NAAS Holtville and description of life there for VC-66: Edwards, n. 3 above; Stephens, n. 9 above; M.L. Shettle, Jr., "Naval Auxiliary Air Station, Holtville," *Historic California Posts*, The California State Military Museum, California State Military Department Web Site, <http://www.militarymuseum.org/NAASHoltville.html>, accessed 13 March 2007; and Harold F. Ellsworth, *History of VC-82* Web Site, <http://home.comcast.net/~bmmelvin/warhero/wwiipac.htm>, accessed 8 March 2007; Unknown author, "COMPOSITE SQUADRON SIXTY-SIX (VC-66) June, 1943 – Nov, 1944," six page history, circa 1944, p. 1.

15. On liberty in southern California: Banks, n. 3, ch. 1; and letter re taking photos of servicemen, from Alice Ignoff to Mrs. Ryder, 18 March 1944.

16. All quotations and information from Otha J. Clark (Clark) in this and subsequent chapters are from one or more of the following sources: telephone interviews, Clark/Stephen Banks, 26 January 2008 and 12 March 2008; and letter, Clark to Stephen Banks, 5 March 2008.

17. For getting 18 men into a TBM: Joe Mussatto, "THE 18 PASSENGER TBM," *VC-66 (T-2) Newsletter*, April 2008, p. 1, col. 1.

18. For the move to NAAS Brown Field, Otay Mesa and description of life there for VC-66: Banks, n. 3, ch. 1; Stephens, n. 9 above; and M.L. Shettle, Jr., "Naval Auxiliary Air Station, Brown Field," *Historic California Posts*, The California State Military Museum, California State Military Department Web Site, <http://www.militarymuseum.org/NAASBrownField.html>, accessed 13 March 2007.

19. On Banks' advancement in rate: Banks, n. 3, ch. 1.

20. Details of World War II enlisted pay are from: "U.S. Navy Enlisted Pay 1943-1945," *BlueJacket.com* Web Site, <http://www.bluejacket.com/usn_pay-scale_1943-1945_enlisted.html>, accessed 30 August 2007; and "WWII U.S. Navy Enlisted Base Pay," *Valor at Sea* Web Site, <http://www.valoratsea.com/paygrade.htm>, accessed 4 September 2007.
21. For the move to NAS San Diego and description of life there for VC-66: Banks, n. 3, ch. 1; Stephens, n. 9 above; Clark, n. 16 above; and M.L. Shettle, Jr., "Naval Air Station, North Island (NAS San Diego)," *Historic California Posts*, The California State Military Museum, California State Military Department Web Site, <http://www.militarymuseum.org/NASNorthIsland.html>, accessed 13 March 2007.

6.   To The Carriers

1.   On the MANILA BAY and carrier qualifications: Banks, n. 3, ch. 1; Stephens, n. 9, ch. 5; Clark, n. 16, ch. 5; and Gerald O. Trapp, Lieutenant, A-V(N), USNR, VC-66, Commanding Officer, "UNITED STATES PACIFIC FLEET AIR FORCE COMPOSITE SQUADRON SIXTY-SIX (VC-66): An Informal Squadron History (June, 1943, to November, 1944)," 1944, p. 7 (used with Navy Department approval).
2.   For information on CVEs: "Escort Aircraft Carriers," *DANFS Online* Web Site, <http://www.hazegray.org/danfs/carriers/cve.htm>, accessed 16 November 2006; William T. Y'Blood, *The Little Giants – U.S. Escort Carriers Against Japan* (Annapolis, Maryland: Naval Institute Press, 1987), pp. 10-17; Robert F. Dorr, "'Jeep' carrier Gambier Bay fought gallantly to the end," *Navy Times*, 13 January 2003, pp. 50 and 54, col. 4-6.
3.   For information on CVNs: "Aircraft Carriers – CV, CVN," *United States Navy Fact File* Web Site, < http://www.navy.mil/navydata/fact_display.asp?cid=4200&tid=200&ct=4>, accessed 4 April 2007; and Stephens, n. 9, ch. 5.
4.   On landing on a CVE: Banks, n. 3, ch. 1; Kennon, n. 12, ch. 4; Stephens, n. 9, ch. 5; Clark, n. 16, ch. 5; "Introduction to Life Aboard an Aircraft Carrier," four pages from Navy Manual, circa 1943, p. 26; "Hold-Off Barrier Crashes," *Naval Aviation News*, 1 October 1945, p. 25; Y'Blood, *The Little Giants*, p. 62; and telephone interview, Mrs. Charles R. Jones/Stephen Banks, 17 January 2008.
5.   All quotations and information from Edward F. Keyser (Keyser) in this and subsequent chapters are from letters, Keyser to Stephen Banks, 18 February 2008 and 20 March 2008.
6.   All quotations and information from James Gander (Gander) in this and subsequent chapters are from a telephone interview, Gander/Stephen Banks, 23 January 2008.
7.   All quotations and information from William DeLoach Cope (Cope) in this and subsequent chapters are from one or more of the following sources: William DeLoach Cope, "THE HALMAHERA RESCUE," *VC-66 (T-2) Newsletter*, undated; telephone interviews, Cope/Stephen Banks, 24 June 2007, 29 January 2008, 31 January 2008, 1 February 2008, and 10 March 2008; notes, Cope to Stephen Banks, 19 July 2007, 2 February 2008, 4 February 2008, and 15 February 2008; and e-mail, Cope to Stephen Banks, 29 January 2008, 30 January 2008, 31 January 2008, 1 February 2008, 2 February 2008, 6 February 2008, 7 February 2008, 8 February 2008, 11 February 2008, and 11 March 2008.
8.   For more on taking off: Edwards, n. 3, ch.5.
9.   On taking off from a CVE at night: Don Moore, "North Port Man Flew A Wildcat Off USS Tulagi In WWII," *Charlotte (Port Charlotte, Florida) Sun*, 8 April 2007; and Banks, n. 3, ch. 1.
10.   Re USS TRIPOLI and shakedown cruise: Banks, n. 3, ch. 1; Stephens, n. 9, ch. 5; "Tripoli," *Dictionary of American Naval Fighting Ships,* Department of the Navy, Naval Historical Center, Washington, D.C. Web Site, <http://www.history.navy.mil/danfs/t8/tripoli-i.htm>, accessed 26 February 2007; "Escort Aircraft Carriers," *DANFS Online* Web Site, <http//www.hazegray.org/danfs/carriers/cve.htm>, accessed 16 November 2006; and Unknown author, "COMPOSITE SQUADRON SIXTY-SIX (VC-66) June, 1943 – Nov, 1944," six page history, circa 1944, p. 2.
11.   On ENS Degankolp's death: Banks, n. 3, ch. 1.
12.   All quotations and information from John P. Fox (Fox) in this and subsequent chapters are from one or more of the following sources: after action report, Fox, "REPORT OF RESCUE MISSION SEPTEMBER 16, 1944," 16 September 1944; and letters, Fox to Stephen Banks, 18 August 2007 and 3 March 2008.

13. Re the WHITE PLAINS and on to Hawaii: Banks, n. 3, ch.1; Stephens, n. 9, ch. 5; and "White Plains," *Dictionary of American Naval Fighting Ships,* Department of the Navy, Naval Historical Center, Washington, D.C. Web Site, <http://www.history.navy.mil/danfs/w7/white_plains-i.htm>, accessed 26 February 2007.

14. For "America's War:" See James Bradley with Ron Powers, *Flags of Our Fathers*, (New York, N.Y.: Bantam Dell, 2000), p. 58.

15. All quotations and information from Dean J. Birdsong (Birdsong) in this and subsequent chapters are from one or more of the following sources: telephone interview, Birdsong/Stephen Banks, 17 July 2007; and e-mail from Birdsong to Stephen Banks, 29 January 2008 and 1 February 2008.

7.   The Marshalls

1. Re arriving in Hawaii and reporting to the NASSAU: Banks, n. 3, ch. 1; and Stephens, n. 9, ch. 5.

2. On the history of the NASSAU: "Nassau," *Dictionary of American Naval Fighting Ships,* Department of the Navy, Naval Historical Center, Washington, D.C. Web Site, <http://www.history.navy.mil/danfs/n2/nassau.htm>, accessed 26 February 2007; and Sam Moore, "The History of the USS Nassau (CVE-16) – 'The Princess' aka 'The Nasty Maru," March 2002, *USS NASSAU* Web Site, <http://www.ussnassaucve16.com/History/ussnassauhistory.htm>, accessed 15 November 2006.

3. For VC-66 personnel and their roles when reporting aboard NASSAU: *USS NASSAU (CVE-16) War Diary,* 4-31 January 1944; *USS NASSAU (CVE-16) Deck Log,* 4-31 January 1944; and Unknown author, "COMPOSITE SQUADRON SIXTY-SIX (VC-66) June, 1943 – Nov, 1944," six page history, circa 1944, p. 2.

4. Banks' recollection of life aboard ship: Banks, n. 3, ch. 1.

5. Re Petty Officer Dorie Miller: "Ship's Cook Third Class Doris Miller, USN," Department of the Navy, Naval Historical Center, Washington, D.C. Web Site, <http://www.history.navy.mil/faqs/faq57-4.htm>, accessed 5 September 2007.

6. For thoughts and experiences concerning life aboard ship: Banks, n. 3, ch. 1; Stephens, n. 9, ch. 5; Gander, n. 6, ch. 6; Gerald O. Trapp, Lieutenant, A-V(N), USNR, VC-66, Commanding Officer, "UNITED STATES PACIFIC FLEET AIR FORCE COMPOSITE SQUADRON SIXTY-SIX (VC-66): An Informal Squadron History (June, 1943, to November, 1944)," 1944, pp. 11-12, (used with Navy Department approval); Edwards, n. 3, ch. 5; Kennon, n. 12, ch. 4; and Cope, n. 7, ch. 6.

7. On Clark Gable and John Wayne and military service: Steven Agoratus, "Clark Gable in the Eighth Air Force," *Centennial Tribute to Clark Gable* Web Site, 1999, <http://www.geocities.com/cactus_st/article/article143.html>, accessed 29 December 2007; and Cecil Adams, "Was John Wayne A Draft Dodger?," *The Straight Dope* Web Site, 1998, <http://www.straightdope.com/classics/a5_004.html>, accessed 29 December 2007.

8. Re submarine sighting: *USS NASSAU (CVE-16) War Diary,* 5 January 1944; *USS NASSAU (CVE-16) Deck Log,* 5 January 1944.

9. David W. "Warny" Banks and PBY crash: Banks, n. 3, ch. 1.

10. The Banks Code: Banks, n. 3, ch. 1.

11. VC-66 and NASSAU pre-deployment training: *USS NASSAU (CVE-16) WarDiary,* 4-22 January 1944; *USS NASSAU (CVE-16) Deck Log,* 4-22 January 1944; Gerald O. Trapp, Lieutenant, A-V(N), USNR, VC-66, Commanding Officer, "UNITED STATES PACIFIC FLEET AIR FORCE COMPOSITE SQUADRON SIXTY-SIX (VC-66): An Informal Squadron History (June, 1943, to November, 1944)," 1944, p. 9 (used with Navy Department approval); and Banks, n. 3, ch. 1.

12. Getting underway and steaming to the Marshalls: *USS NASSAU (CVE-16) WarDiary,* 23-30 January 1944; *USS NASSAU (CVE-16) Deck Log,* 23-30 January 1944; Gerald O. Trapp, Lieutenant, A-V(N), USNR, VC-66, Commanding Officer, "UNITED STATES PACIFIC FLEET AIR FORCE COMPOSITE SQUADRON SIXTY-SIX (VC-66): An Informal Squadron History (June, 1943, to November, 1944)," 1944, p. 9 (used with Navy Department approval); and Paul W. Austin, "COMPOSITE SQUADRON SIXTY-SIX" (hand drawn chart of Pacific Ocean prepared for Austin H. Kiplinger showing where VC-66 operated and annotated with statistics and summaries of the squadron's three combat deployments), 1953.

13. Re the Marshall Islands and "Island Hopping" strategy: "MARSHALLS," *Naval Aviation News*, 1 March 1944, pp. 17 and 19; "The Gilberts and Marshalls Campaign," *Naval Aviation News*, 1

October 1945, p. 10; Gordon L. Rottman, *The Marshall Islands 1944 – Operation Flintlock, the capture of Kwajalein and Eniwetok* (New York, N.Y.: Osprey Publishing Ltd., 2004); "The Marshall Islands," Exhibit, National Museum of the Marine Corps, Quantico, Virginia, November 2006; Sam Moore, "The History of the USS Nassau (CVE-16) – 'The Princess' aka 'The Nasty Maru," March 2002, *USS NASSAU* Web Site, <http://www.ussnassaucve16.com/History/ussnassauhistory.htm>, accessed 15 November 2006; "The Bloody Battle of Tarawa, 1943," *EyeWitnessHistory.com* Web Site, <http://www.eyewitnesstohistory.com/tarawa.htm>, accessed 17 September 2007; and "U.S. Naval Chronology Of WWII, 1944," *NavSource History Naval* Web Site, <http://www.navsource.org/Naval/1944.htm>, accessed 16 November 2006.

14. On the loss of Bennett, Hebert, and Lavin: *USS NASSAU (CVE-16) WarDiary,* 30 January 1944; *USS NASSAU (CVE-16) Deck Log*, 30 January 1944; Banks, n. 3, ch. 1; Fox, n. 12, ch. 6; and Gander, n. 6, ch. 6.

15. For D-Day for the Marshall Islands invasion: *USS NASSAU (CVE-16) WarDiary,* 31 January 1944; *USS NASSAU (CVE-16) Deck Log*, 31 January 1944; Sam Moore, "The History of the USS Nassau (CVE-16) – 'The Princess' aka 'The Nasty Maru," March 2002, *USS NASSAU* Web Site, <http://www.ussnassaucve16.com/History/ussnassauhistory.htm>, accessed 15 November 2006; Banks, n. 3, ch. 1; Gerald O. Trapp, Lieutenant, A-V(N), USNR, VC-66, Commanding Officer, "UNITED STATES PACIFIC FLEET AIR FORCE COMPOSITE SQUADRON SIXTY-SIX (VC-66): An Informal Squadron History (June, 1943, to November, 1944)," 1944, p. 9 (used with Navy Department approval); and "The Army 27th Infantry Division," *National Park Service American Memorial Park, Saipan, Northern Mariana Islands World War II Virtual Museum* Web Site, <http://www.nps.gov/archive/amme/wwii_museum/preparation_for_war/preparations_for_war. html>, accessed 11 December 2007.

16. Re Harlon Block: James Bradley with Ron Powers, *Flags of Our Fathers*, (New York, N.Y.: Bantam Dell, 2000), pp. 33-36.

17. The Marshalls Campaign in general: William T. Y'Blood, *The Little Giants – U.S. Escort Carriers Against Japan* (Annapolis, Maryland: Naval Institute Press, 1987), pp. 45-47, and 53; "The Marshall Islands," Exhibit, National Museum of the Marine Corps, Quantico, Virginia, November 2006; Gordon L. Rottman, *The Marshall Islands 1944 – Operation Flintlock, the capture of Kwajalein and Eniwetok* (New York, N.Y.: Osprey Publishing Ltd., 2004); and Paul W. Austin, "COMPOSITE SQUADRON SIXTY-SIX" (hand drawn chart of Pacific Ocean prepared for Austin H. Kiplinger showing where VC-66 operated and annotated with statistics and summaries of the squadron's three combat deployments), 1953.

18. On "Howlin Mad" Smith: James Bradley with Ron Powers, *Flags of Our Fathers*, (New York, N.Y.: Bantam Dell, 2000), pp. 63 and 133.

19. VC-66's role during the Marshalls Campaign: *USS NASSAU (CVE-16) War Diary,* 1-21 February 1944; *USS NASSAU (CVE-16) Deck Log*, 1-21 February 1944; and Sam Moore, "The History of the USS Nassau (CVE-16) – 'The Princess' aka 'The Nasty Maru," March 2002, *USS NASSAU* Web Site, <http://www.ussnassaucve16.com/History/ussnassauhistory.htm>, accessed 15 November 2006.

20. On Banks' first combat mission: Banks, n. 3, ch. 1; Lou Drendel, *Walk Around TBF/TBM Avenger*, (Carrollton, Texas: Squadron/Signal Publications, Inc., 2001), p. 50; and "Introduction to Life Aboard an Aircraft Carrier," four pages from Navy Manual, circa 1943, pp. 24-25.

21. Re the .50 caliber machine gun: Lou Drendel, *Walk Around TBF/TBM Avenger*, (Carrollton, Texas: Squadron/Signal Publications, Inc., 2001), p. 10; ".50 Caliber Machine Gun," Exhibit, National Air and Space Museum, Washington, D.C., December 2006; and "Japanese Fighter Planes: Navy's Mitsubishi A6M Zero, Army's Ki-42 Oscar," *American Aces of WWII* Web Site, <http://www.acepilots.com/planes/jap_fighters.html>, accessed 22 February 2007; and Banks, n. 3, ch. 1.

22. VC-66 missions 1-5 February 1944: *USS NASSAU (CVE-16) WarDiary,* 1-5 February 1944; *USS NASSAU (CVE-16) Deck Log*, 1-5 February 1944; and Gerald O. Trapp, Lieutenant, A-V(N), USNR, VC-66, Commanding Officer, "UNITED STATES PACIFIC FLEET AIR FORCE COMPOSITE SQUADRON SIXTY-SIX (VC-66): An Informal Squadron History (June, 1943, to November, 1944)," 1944, p. 10 (used with Navy Department approval).

23. For VC-66 and assignment to support Operation Catchpole – the invasion of Eniwetok Atoll: Gerald O. Trapp, Lieutenant, A-V(N), USNR, VC-66, Commanding Officer, "UNITED STATES PACIFIC

FLEET AIR FORCE COMPOSITE SQUADRON SIXTY-SIX (VC-66): An Informal Squadron History (June, 1943, to November, 1944)," 1944, p. 10 (used with Navy Department approval); and Gordon L. Rottman, *The Marshall Islands 1944 – Operation Flintlock, the capture of Kwajalein and Eniwetok* (New York, N.Y.: Osprey Publishing Ltd., 2004), pp. 16-17.

24. VC-66 missions 6 February 1944: *USS NASSAU (CVE-16) WarDiary,* 6 February 1944; and *USS NASSAU (CVE-16) Deck Log,* 6 February 1944.

25. On the use of chaff: Banks, n. 3, ch. 1.

26. Re Taroa Island: Dirk H.R. Spennemann, "Taroa, Maloelap Atoll – A brief virtual tour through a Japanese airbase in the Marshall Islands," *Marshalls – digital Micronesia* Web Site, <http://marshall.csu.edu.au/Marshalls/html/japanese/Taroa/Taroa.html>, accessed 16 April 2007; and Gordon L. Rottman, *The Marshall Islands 1944 – Operation Flintlock, the capture of Kwajalein and Eniwetok* (New York, N.Y.: Osprey Publishing Ltd., 2004).

27. VC-66 missions 7 February 1944: *USS NASSAU (CVE-16) War Diary,* 7 February 1944; *USS NASSAU (CVE-16) Deck Log,* 7 February 1944; and Gerald O. Trapp, Lieutenant, A-V(N), USNR, VC-66, Commanding Officer, "UNITED STATES PACIFIC FLEET AIR FORCE COMPOSITE SQUADRON SIXTY-SIX (VC-66): An Informal Squadron History (June, 1943, to November, 1944)," 1944, p. 10 (used with Navy Department approval) .

28. Re Wotje Island: Dirk H.R. Spennemann, "The Japanese seaplane base at Wotje Island, Wotje Atoll," *Marshalls – digital Micronesia* Web Site, http://marshall.csu.edu.au/Marshalls/html/WWII/Wotje.html>, accessed 16 April 2007; and Gordon L. Rottman, *The Marshall Islands 1944 – Operation Flintlock, the capture of Kwajalein and Eniwetok* (New York, N.Y.: Osprey Publishing Ltd., 2004).

29. On Sam Takis' shoot down and rescue: *USS NASSAU (CVE-16) War Diary,* 7 February 1944; *USS NASSAU (CVE-16) Deck Log,* 7 February 1944; Gerald O. Trapp, Lieutenant, A-V(N), USNR, VC-66, Commanding Officer, "UNITED STATES PACIFIC FLEET AIR FORCE COMPOSITE SQUADRON SIXTY-SIX (VC-66): An Informal Squadron History (June, 1943, to November, 1944)," 1944, p. 10 (used with Navy Department approval); Sam Moore, "The History of the USS Nassau (CVE-16) – 'The Princess' aka 'The Nasty Maru," March 2002, *USS NASSAU* Web Site, <http://www.ussnassaucve16.com/History/ussnassauhistory.htm>, accessed 15 November 2006; Fox, n. 12, ch. 6; and Cope, n. 7, ch. 6.

30. John P. Fox: n. 12, ch. 6.

8.   Trouble Over Wotje

1. VC-66 missions 8 and 9 February 1944: *USS NASSAU (CVE-16) War Diary,* 8 and 9 February 1944; and *USS NASSAU (CVE-16) Deck Log,* 8 and 9 February 1944.

2. Re events of 10 February over Wotje Island: *USS NASSAU (CVE-16) War Diary,* 10 February 1944; Gerald O. Trapp, Lieutenant, A-V(N), USNR, VC-66, Commanding Officer, "UNITED STATES PACIFIC FLEET AIR FORCE COMPOSITE SQUADRON SIXTY-SIX (VC-66): An Informal Squadron History (June, 1943, to November, 1944)," 1944, p. 10 (used with Navy Department approval); Banks, n. 3, ch. 1; Stephens, n. 9, ch. 5; and Russell P. Jensen, telephone interview by Stephen Banks, 17 January 2008.

3. For requirements of Air Medal award: Robert F. Dorr and Fred L. Borch, "Air Medal Recognizes Heroism, Merit In Flight," *Navy Times,* 22 October 2007, p. 46, col. 4-6.

4. For newspaper write-up: "Gallantry Disclosed," *The Buffalo Evening News,* 22 March 1945.

9.   Continuing To Pound The Marshalls

1. VC-66 missions 11 and 12 February 1944: *USS NASSAU (CVE-16) War Diary,* 11 and 12 February 1944; and *USS NASSAU (CVE-16) Deck Log,* 11 and 12 February 1944; Edwards, n. 3, ch. 5; and Cope, n. 7, ch. 6.

2. Re Banks' next mission after Wotje incident: Banks, n. 3, ch. 1.

3. Re TBM's electric powered turret: Lou Drendel, *Walk Around TBF/TBM Avenger,* (Carrollton, Texas: Squadron/Signal Publications, Inc., 2001), p. 2.

4. Description of the TBF/TBM radioman's job: Robert F. Dorr, "Radioman-Gunner Flew Despite Silent Missions," *Navy Times,* 1 May 2006, p. 29, col. 4-6; Gerald Thomas, "A Tribute To Avenger

Air Crewman," *Air Group 4 "Casablanca to Tokyo"* Web Site, <http://www.airgroup4.com/crewmen.htm>, accessed 1 December 2006; "THOROUGH TRAINING READIES PILOTS AND AIRCREWMEN FOR THE FLEET," *Naval Aviation News*, 15 July 1944, pp. 41 and 45; "Flying Radioman," *Naval Aviation News*, 15 February 1944, p. 9; Banks, n. 3, ch. 1.

5. On TBM aircrew pranks: Banks, n. 3, ch. 1.

6. On bailing out of a TBM: Banks, n. 3, ch. 1.

7. For LTJG George H.W. Bush's bail out experience: "Lieutenant Junior Grade George Bush, USNR," Department of the Navy, Naval Historical Center, Washington, D.C. Web Site, < http://www.history.navy.mil/faqs/faq10-1.htm>, accessed 6 September 2007; Lou Drendel, *Walk Around TBF/TBM Avenger*, (Carrollton, Texas: Squadron/Signal Publications, Inc., 2001), p. 4; and Judith S.Gillies, "A Presidential Portrait," *The Washington Post (TV Week)*, 4 May 2008, p. 3, col. 1 and 2.

8. Re surviving a ditching: Banks, n. 3, ch. 1.

9. On post-mission stress: Banks, n. 3, ch. 1.

10. VC-66 missions 13 - 21 February 1944: *USS NASSAU (CVE-16) War Diary,* 13 - 21 February 1944; and *USS NASSAU (CVE-16) Deck Log*, 13 - 21 February 1944.

11. For VC-66 and USS NASSAU Marshalls Campaign accomplishments: Sam Moore, "The History of the USS Nassau (CVE-16) – 'The Princess' aka 'The Nasty Maru," March 2002, *USS NASSAU* Web Site, <http://www.ussnassaucve16.com/History/ussnassauhistory.htm>, accessed 15 November 2006; Paul W. Austin, "COMPOSITE SQUADRON SIXTY-SIX" (hand drawn chart of Pacific Ocean prepared for Austin H. Kiplinger showing where VC-66 operated and annotated with statistics and summaries of the squadron's three combat deployments), 1953; and Gerald O. Trapp, Lieutenant, A-V(N), USNR, VC-66, Commanding Officer, "UNITED STATES PACIFIC FLEET AIR FORCE COMPOSITE SQUADRON SIXTY-SIX (VC-66): An Informal Squadron History (June, 1943, to November, 1944)," 1944, p. 11 (used with Navy Department approval).

12. On the success of the Marshalls Campaign: Gordon L. Rottman, *The Marshall Islands 1944 – Operation Flintlock, the capture of Kwajalein and Eniwetok* (New York, N.Y.: Osprey Publishing Ltd., 2004), pp. 17 and 88.

10. Back To Pearl Harbor

1. VC-66 activities aboard NASSAU 22 February – 5 March 1944: *USS NASSAU (CVE-16) War Diary,* 22 February – 5 March 1944; and *USS NASSAU (CVE-16) Deck Log*, 22 February – 5 March 1944.

2. Re Japanese prisoners of war: *USS NASSAU (CVE-16) Deck Log*, 24 February 1944; Banks, n. 3, ch. 1; Sam Moore, "The History of the USS Nassau (CVE-16) – 'The Princess' aka 'The Nasty Maru," March 2002, *USS NASSAU* Web Site, <http://www.ussnassaucve16.com/History/ussnassauhistory.htm>, accessed 15 November 2006; and Gordon W. Prange, Edited by Donald M. Goldstein and Katherine V. Dillon, *Miracle At Midway*, (New York, N.Y.: McGraw-Hill Book Company, 1982) p. 342.

3. On the difference between the war in Europe and the war in the Pacific: Stephen E. Ambrose, *To America: Personal Reflections of an Historian*, (New York, N.Y.: Simon and Schuster, Inc., 2002), pp. 101-102; and James Bradley with Ron Powers, *Flags of Our Fathers*, (New York, N.Y.: Bantam Dell, 2000), pp. 65-68.

4. Information on Tom Stoops and the Japanese POWs: Banks, n. 3, ch. 1.

5. Re Banks writing Jean Dewey: Banks, n. 3, ch. 1.

6. All quotations and information from Jean C. Dewey-Banks (Dewey) in this and subsequent chapters are from one or more of the following sources: Western Union Telegram, Dewey to Banks, 12 August 1945; interviews, Dewey by Stephen Banks, 3 July 2007 and 23 November 2007; and telephone interviews, Dewey/Stephen Banks, 13 August and 20 August 2007.

7. Re "We are all in this together:" See Stephen E. Ambrose, *To America: Personal Reflections of an Historian* (New York, N.Y.: Simon and Schuster, Inc., 2002), p. 95.

8. For the VC-66 feelings about the NASSAU: Gerald O. Trapp, Lieutenant, A-V(N), USNR, VC-66, Commanding Officer, "UNITED STATES PACIFIC FLEET AIR FORCE COMPOSITE

SQUADRON SIXTY-SIX (VC-66): An Informal Squadron History (June, 1943, to November, 1944)," 1944, pp. 11-12 (used with Navy Department approval); and Piper, n. 6, ch. 5.

11. Rest and Recreation – And Training In Hawaii

1. For VC-66 and NAF Barking Sands, Kauai, Hawaii: Stephens, n. 9, ch. 5; Fox, n. 12, ch. 6; Birdsong, n. 15, ch. 6; Banks, n. 3, ch. 1; Cope, n. 7, ch. 6; and Gerald O. Trapp, Lieutenant, A-V(N), USNR, VC-66, Commanding Officer, "UNITED STATES PACIFIC FLEET AIR FORCE COMPOSITE SQUADRON SIXTY-SIX (VC-66): An Informal Squadron History (June, 1943, to November, 1944)," 1944, pp. 12-13 (used with Navy Department approval).
2. For VC-66 and NAS Kaneohe Bay, Oahu: Stephens, n. 9, ch. 5; and Banks, n. 3, ch. 1.
3. Re the Norden bombsight: Banks, n. 3, ch. 1.

12. Anti-Submarine Warfare

1. For VC-66 reporting to the USS ALTAMAHA (CVE-18) for emergency ASW mission: *USS ALTAMAHA (CVE-18) War Diary*, 30 March 1944; *USS ALTAMAHA (CVE-18) Deck Log*, 30 March 1944; Unknown author, "COMPOSITE SQUADRON SIXTY-SIX (VC-66) June, 1943 – Nov, 1944," six page history, circa 1944, p. 3; Gerald O. Trapp, Lieutenant, A-V(N), USNR, VC-66, Commanding Officer, "UNITED STATES PACIFIC FLEET AIR FORCE COMPOSITE SQUADRON SIXTY-SIX (VC-66): An Informal Squadron History (June, 1943, to November, 1944)," 1944, pp. 12-13 (used with Navy Department approval); "Altamaha," *Dictionary of American Naval Fighting Ships*, Department of the Navy, Naval Historical Center, Washington, D.C. Web Site, <http://www.history.navy.mil/danfs/a7/altamaha-i.htm>, accessed 26 February 2007; William T. Y'Blood, *The Little Giants – U.S. Escort Carriers Against Japan*, (Annapolis, Maryland: Naval Institute Press, 1987), p. 57; Stephens, n. 9, ch. 5; and Banks, n. 3, ch. 1.
2. On the new TBM rocket rails: Stephens, n. 9, ch. 5; and Lou Drendel, *Walk Around TBF/TBM Avenger*, (Carrollton, Texas: Squadron/Signal Publications, Inc., 2001), p. 50.
3. For ALTAMAHA's origin: "Altamaha," *Dictionary of American Naval Fighting Ships*, Department of the Navy, Naval Historical Center, Washington, D.C. Web Site, <http://www.history.navy.mil/danfs/a7/altamaha-i.htm>, accessed 26 February 2007; and William T. Y'Blood, *The Little Giants – U.S. Escort Carriers Against Japan*, (Annapolis, Maryland: Naval Institute Press, 1987), p. 17.
4. For VC-66 activities on the way to the ASW ops area: *USS ALTAMAHA (CVE-18) War Diary*, 30 March – 2 April 1944; *USS ALTAMAHA (CVE-18) Deck Log*, 30 March – 2 April 1944; and Banks, n. 3, ch. 1.
5. Re arrival at the ASW ops area and commencing missions: *USS ALTAMAHA (CVE-18) War Diary*, 3 April 1944; and *USS ALTAMAHA (CVE-18) Deck Log*, 3 April 1944.
6. On the TBM's ASW weapon load: Stephens, n. 9, ch. 5; and Birdsong, n. 15, ch. 6.
7. For the events of 4 April 1944 and the attacks on the Japanese submarines: Banks, n. 3, ch. 1; *USS ALTAMAHA (CVE-18) War Diary*, 4 April 1944; *USS ALTAMAHA (CVE-18) Deck Log*, 4 April 1944; Edwards, n. 3, ch. 5; "Squadron 'X'," *EASTERN AIRCRAFTSMAN*, November 1943, p. 9, col. 5; Gander, n. 6, ch. 6; Fox, n. 12, ch. 6; Paul W. Austin , "COMPOSITE SQUADRON SIXTY-SIX" (hand drawn chart of Pacific Ocean prepared for Austin H. Kiplinger showing where VC-66 operated and annotated with statistics and summaries of the squadron's three combat deployments), 1953; "Altamaha," *Dictionary of American Naval Fighting Ships*, Department of the Navy, Naval Historical Center, Washington, D.C. Web Site, <http://www.history.navy.mil/danfs/a7/altamaha-i.htm>, accessed 26 February 2007; and Stephens, n. 9, ch. 5.
8. All quotations and information from Richard F. Krost (Krost) in this and subsequent chapters are from one or more of the following sources: telephone interview, Krost/Stephen Banks, 27 June 2007; e-mail from Krost to Stephen Banks, 19 August 2007, 1 December 2007, 21 January 2008, 24 January 2008, 29 January 2008, 11 February 2008, and 7 March 2008.
9. For VC-66 missions 5 – 9 April: *USS ALTAMAHA (CVE-18) War Diary*, 5 – 9 April 1944; and *USS ALTAMAHA (CVE-18) Deck Log*, 5 – 9 April 1944.
10. Banks re Russ Jensen's barrier crash: Banks, n. 3, ch. 1.

11. For VC-66 activities and missions 10 – 14 April: *USS ALTAMAHA (CVE-18) War Diary*, 10 – 14 April 1944; and *USS ALTAMAHA (CVE-18) Deck Log*, 10 – 14 April 1944.

12. Banks re Polski and 1000th landing on ALTAMAHA: n. 3, ch. 1.

13. For the Japanese submarine attack of 15 April: *USS ALTAMAHA (CVE-18) War Diary*, 15 April 1944; *USS ALTAMAHA (CVE-18) Deck Log*, 15 April 1944; and "Altamaha," *Dictionary of American Naval Fighting Ships,* Department of the Navy, Naval Historical Center, Washington, D.C. Web Site, <http://www.history.navy.mil/danfs/a7/altamaha-i.htm>, accessed 26 February 2007.

14. All quotations and information from Emidio J. Mardarello (Mardarello) in this and subsequent chapters are from one or more of the following sources: telephone interviews, Mardarello/Stephen Banks, 8 November 2007, 19 November 2007, and 2 February 2008; and letter, Mardarello to Stephen Banks, 21 November 2007.

15. Re Tokyo Rose reporting the sinking of ALTAMAHA: "Tokyo Rose Sinks Them," *Naval Aviation News*, 15 January 1945, p. 23, col. 3; and "'Sunk' Navy Fliers Home On Leave," *Hattiesburg (Mississippi) American*, 1 December 1944.

16. For the Krost, Ruthman, and Riffle crash and rescue of 17 April: *USS ALTAMAHA (CVE-18) War Diary*, 17 April 1944; *USS ALTAMAHA (CVE-18) Deck Log*, 17 April 1944; Krost, n. 8 above; and Clark, n. 16, ch. 5.

17. For Krost, Ruthman, and Riffle's underway transfer back to ALTAMAHA: Krost, n. 8 above; Clark, n. 16, ch. 5; and Stephen Banks' personal recollection of underway transfers.

18. Mardarello on landing on a CVE and close calls: n. 14 above.

19. Keyser re near death flight deck experiences: n. 5, ch. 6.

20. Krost on J.P. Fox's close call: n. 8 above.

21. Fox on his close call on the flight deck: n. 12, ch. 6.

22. Krost's biographical information: n. 8 above.

23. For TBDs at Midway: Gordon W. Prange, Edited by Donald M. Goldstein and Katherine V. Dillon, *Miracle At Midway*, (New York, N.Y.: McGraw-Hill Book Company, 1982), p. 257.

24. Krost on Guy Catterton: n. 8 above.

25. Mardarello re the loose bomb on deck and sleeping aboard ship: n. 14 above.

26. For VC-66 activities 18 – 25 April 1944: *USS ALTAMAHA (CVE-18) War Diary*, 18 – 25 April 1944; and *USS ALTAMAHA (CVE-18) Deck Log*, 18 – 25 April 1944.

27. For recap of the ASW operation: Gerald O. Trapp, Lieutenant, A-V(N), USNR, VC-66, Commanding Officer, "UNITED STATES PACIFIC FLEET AIR FORCE COMPOSITE SQUADRON SIXTY-SIX (VC-66): An Informal Squadron History (June, 1943, to November, 1944)," 1944, p. 14 (used with Navy Department approval); Paul W. Austin , "COMPOSITE SQUADRON SIXTY-SIX" (hand drawn chart of Pacific Ocean prepared for Austin H. Kiplinger showing where VC-66 operated and annotated with statistics and summaries of the squadron's three combat deployments), 1953; and William T. Y'Blood, *The Little Giants – U.S. Escort Carriers Against Japan* (Annapolis, Maryland: Naval Institute Press, 1987), p. 57.

28. ALTAMAHA history after VC-66: "Altamaha," *Dictionary of American Naval Fighting Ships,* Department of the Navy, Naval Historical Center, Washington, D.C. Web Site, <http://www.history.navy.mil/danfs/a7/altamaha-i.htm>, accessed 26 February 2007.

29. Re Rest and Recreation in Hawaii: Banks, n. 3, ch. 1; Stephens, n. 9, ch. 5; Gerald O. Trapp, Lieutenant, A-V(N), USNR, VC-66, Commanding Officer, "UNITED STATES PACIFIC FLEET AIR FORCE COMPOSITE SQUADRON SIXTY-SIX (VC-66): An Informal Squadron History (June, 1943, to November, 1944)," 1944, pp. 14-15 (used with Navy Department approval); and Audrey McAvoy, "Attack Shook Hawaiians Beyond Pearl Harbor," *The Washington Post*, 7 December 2007, p. A17, col. 3-6.

30. On Sailors vs. Marines: Banks, n. 3, ch. 1; and James Bradley with Ron Powers, *Flags of Our Fathers*, (New York, N.Y.: Bantam Dell, 2000), pp. 70-71.

31. Re training and waiting in Hawaii: Banks, n. 3, ch. 1; Gerald O. Trapp, Lieutenant, A-V(N), USNR, VC-66, Commanding Officer, "UNITED STATES PACIFIC FLEET AIR FORCE COMPOSITE SQUADRON SIXTY-SIX (VC-66): An Informal Squadron History (June, 1943, to November, 1944)," 1944, pp. 14-15 (used with Navy Department approval); and "VC-66 Enlisted Gunnery Ground Training," orders, 11 July 1944.

32. For the Polski incidents: e-mail, Joe Mussatto to Stephen Banks, 5 June 2007.

33. For the 21 June 1944 squadron anniversary celebration: Gerald O. Trapp, Lieutenant, A-V(N), USNR, VC-66, Commanding Officer, "UNITED STATES PACIFIC FLEET AIR FORCE COMPOSITE SQUADRON SIXTY-SIX (VC-66): An Informal Squadron History (June, 1943, to November, 1944)," 1944, p. 15 (used with Navy Department approval); and Mardarello, n. 14 above.

34. For President Roosevelt's visit to Hawaii and the alleged Japanese threat of attack: Kenneth I. Friedman, "General Douglas MacArthur," *The Battle of Leyte Gulf* Web Site, <http://www.battle-of-leyte-gulf.com/Leaders/Americans/MacArthur/macarthur.html>, accessed 14 September 2007; William T. Y'Blood, *The Little Giants – U.S. Escort Carriers Against Japan* (Annapolis, Maryland: Naval Institute Press, 1987), p 118; Gerald O. Trapp, Lieutenant, A-V(N), USNR, VC-66, Commanding Officer, "UNITED STATES PACIFIC FLEET AIR FORCE COMPOSITE SQUADRON SIXTY-SIX (VC-66): An Informal Squadron History (June, 1943, to November, 1944)," 1944, p. 16 (used with Navy Department approval); Stephens, n. 9, ch. 5; and Clark, n. 16, ch. 5.

35. Re VC-66's last days on Maui: Gerald O. Trapp, Lieutenant, A-V(N), USNR, VC-66, Commanding Officer, "UNITED STATES PACIFIC FLEET AIR FORCE COMPOSITE SQUADRON SIXTY-SIX (VC-66): An Informal Squadron History (June, 1943, to November, 1944)," 1944, pp. 16-17 (used with Navy Department approval).

36. For Jack Dwight's crash and long swim: Krost, n. 8 above; and Gerald O. Trapp, Lieutenant, A-V(N), USNR, VC-66, Commanding Officer, "UNITED STATES PACIFIC FLEET AIR FORCE COMPOSITE SQUADRON SIXTY-SIX (VC-66): An Informal Squadron History (June, 1943, to November, 1944)," 1944, pp. 14 and 16 (used with Navy Department approval).

37. All quotations and information from John L. "Jack" Dwight (Dwight) in this and subsequent chapters are from one or more of the following sources: letters, Dwight to Stephen Banks, 31 January 2008, 12 February 2008, and 10 March 2008.

38. For Charlie Edwards' ditch and swim: Edwards, n. 3, ch. 5; and Gerald O. Trapp, Lieutenant, A-V(N), USNR, VC-66, Commanding Officer, "UNITED STATES PACIFIC FLEET AIR FORCE COMPOSITE SQUADRON SIXTY-SIX (VC-66): An Informal Squadron History (June, 1943, to November, 1944)," 1944, pp. 14 and 16 (used with Navy Department approval).

39. For Edwards' biographical information: Edwards, n. 3, ch. 5; interviews, Mrs. Marnie Edwards by Stephen Banks, 13 February 2008 and 10 March 2008; "Squadron 'X'," *EASTERN AIRCRAFTSMAN*, November 1943, p. 8, col. 5; and "Edwards 65th Anniversary," *The Washington Post*, 16 March 2008.

13. To The Moluccas Islands, Western New Guinea, And Morotai

1. Re VC-66 reporting to the USS FANSHAW BAY (CVE-70): Banks, n. 3, ch. 1; Stephens, n. 9, ch. 5; *USS FANSHAW BAY (CVE-70) War Diary*, 5 August 1944; *USS FANSHAW BAY (CVE-70) Deck Log*, 5 August 1944; Paul W. Austin , "COMPOSITE SQUADRON SIXTY-SIX" (hand drawn chart of Pacific Ocean prepared for Austin H. Kiplinger showing where VC-66 operated and annotated with statistics and summaries of the squadron's three combat deployments), 1953; Gerald O. Trapp, Lieutenant, A-V(N), USNR, VC-66, Commanding Officer, "UNITED STATES PACIFIC FLEET AIR FORCE COMPOSITE SQUADRON SIXTY-SIX (VC-66): An Informal Squadron History (June, 1943, to November, 1944)," 1944, p. 17 (used with Navy Department approval); and Unknown author, "COMPOSITE SQUADRON SIXTY-SIX (VC-66) June, 1943 – Nov, 1944," six page history, circa 1944, p. 4.

2. For FANSHAW BAY's history: William T. Y'Blood, *The Little Giants – U.S. Escort Carriers Against Japan* (Annapolis, Maryland: Naval Institute Press, 1987), pp. 34-35; and "Fanshaw Bay," *Dictionary of American Naval Fighting Ships,* Department of the Navy, Naval Historical Center, Washington, D.C. Web Site, <http://www.history.navy.mil/danfs/f1/fanshaw_bay.htm>, accessed 26 February 2007.

3. Re Trapp as new VC-66 CO: Gerald O. Trapp, Lieutenant, A-V(N), USNR, VC-66, Commanding Officer, "UNITED STATES PACIFIC FLEET AIR FORCE COMPOSITE SQUADRON SIXTY-SIX (VC-66): An Informal Squadron History (June, 1943, to November, 1944)," 1944, p. 16 (used with Navy Department approval); and Unknown author, "COMPOSITE SQUADRON SIXTY-SIX (VC-66) June, 1943 – Nov, 1944," six page history, circa 1944, p. 4.

4. For VC-66 activities 5 - 8 August 1944: *USS FANSHAW BAY (CVE-70) War Diary*, 5 - 8 August 1944; and *USS FANSHAW BAY (CVE-70) Deck Log*, 5 – 8 August 1944.

5. For getting underway for the Southwest Pacific: *USS FANSHAW BAY (CVE-70) War Diary*, 12 August 1944; *USS FANSHAW BAY (CVE-70) Deck Log*, 12 August 1944; Stephens, n. 9, ch. 5; Banks, n. 3, ch. 1; Paul W. Austin , "COMPOSITE SQUADRON SIXTY-SIX" (hand drawn chart of Pacific Ocean prepared for Austin H. Kiplinger showing where VC-66 operated and annotated with statistics and summaries of the squadron's three combat deployments), 1953; and Gerald O. Trapp, Lieutenant, A-V(N), USNR, VC-66, Commanding Officer, "UNITED STATES PACIFIC FLEET AIR FORCE COMPOSITE SQUADRON SIXTY-SIX (VC-66): An Informal Squadron History (June, 1943, to November, 1944)," 1944, p. 17 (used with Navy Department approval).

6. Re the "Tojo Line:" Gordon L. Rottman, *The Marshall Islands 1944 – Operation Flintlock, the capture of Kwajalein and Eniwetok* (New York, N.Y.: Osprey Publishing Ltd., 2004), p. 21.

7. Background for Morotai Island: William T. Y'Blood, *The Little Giants – U.S. Escort Carriers Against Japan* (Annapolis, Maryland: Naval Institute Press, 1987), pp. 102-103.

8. For MacArthur and the Philippines: Kenneth I. Friedman, "General Douglas MacArthur," *The Battle of Leyte Gulf* Web Site, <http://www.battle-of-leyte-gulf.com/Leaders/Americans/MacArthur/macarthur.html>, accessed 14 September 2007; and William T. Y'Blood, *The Little Giants – U.S. Escort Carriers Against Japan* (Annapolis, Maryland: Naval Institute Press, 1987), p. 102.

9. Re the Bataan Death March: Major Richard M. Gordon, USA (Ret.), "Bataan, Corregidor, and the Death March: In Retrospect," *Battling Bastards of Bataan* Web Site, last updated 28 October 2002, <http://home.pacbell.net/fbaldie/In_Retrospect.html>, accessed 17 September 2007; James Bradley with Ron Powers, *Flags of Our Fathers*, (New York, N.Y.: Bantam Dell, 2000), p. 62; Stephen E. Ambrose, *To America: Personal Reflections of an Historian* (New York, N.Y.: Simon and Schuster, Inc., 2002), p. 112; and Yvonne Shinhoster Lamb, "Melvin H. Rosen: Survived Bataan Death March," *The Washington Post*, 31 August 2007.

10. For VC-66's trip to the Solomons: *USS FANSHAW BAY (CVE-70) War Diary*, 12 - 24 August 1944; *USS FANSHAW BAY (CVE-70) Deck Log*, 12 – 24 August 1944; and Mardarello, n. 14, ch. 12.

11. Banks' advancement in rate: n. 3, ch. 1; and "U.S. Navy Enlisted Pay 1943-1945," *BlueJacket.com* Web Site, <http://www.bluejacket.com/usn_pay-scale_1943-1945_enlisted.html>, accessed 30 August 2007.

12. Re abandon ship drills: Stephen Banks personal recollections; and Banks, n. 3, ch. 1.

13. Re events of 22 August 1944: *USS FANSHAW BAY (CVE-70) War Diary*, 22 August 1944; and *USS FANSHAW BAY (CVE-70) Deck Log*, 22 August 1944.

14. For the "shellback" initiation: Gerald O. Trapp, Lieutenant, A-V(N), USNR, VC-66, Commanding Officer, "UNITED STATES PACIFIC FLEET AIR FORCE COMPOSITE SQUADRON SIXTY-SIX (VC-66): An Informal Squadron History (June, 1943, to November, 1944)," 1944, p. 17 (used with Navy Department approval); Stephens, n. 9, ch. 5; "SUBPOENA & SUMMONS EXTRAORDINARY," The Royal High Court of the Raging Main, circa 22 August 1944; Banks, n. 3, ch. 1; Mardarello, n. 14, ch. 12; and Edwards, n. 3, ch. 5.

15. Re events of 23 August 1944: *USS FANSHAW BAY (CVE-70) War Diary*, 23 August 1944; *USS FANSHAW BAY (CVE-70) Deck Log*, 23 August 1944; and Clark, n. 16, ch. 5.

16. On VC-66 reaching Tulagi: *USS FANSHAW BAY (CVE-70) War Diary*, 24 August 1944; and *USS FANSHAW BAY (CVE-70) Deck Log*, 24 August 1944.

17. For John F. Kennedy and PT-109: "Tulagi," *Wikipedia*, <http://en.wikipedia.org/wiki/Tulagi>, accessed on 16 March 2007.

18. All quotations and information from Albert J. Mayer (Mayer) in this and subsequent chapters are from one or more of the following sources: e-mail, Mayer to Stephen Banks, 29 June 2007, 18 July 2007, 21 January 2008, 22 January 2008, and 5 February 2008.

19. Mayer biographical information: n. 18 above; and "Squadron 'X'," *EASTERN AIRCRAFTSMAN*, November 1943, p. 9, col. 3.

20. For Mayer and the Doolittle Raid: Stephens, n. 9, ch. 5 and n. 18 above.

21. Re sinking of the NORTHAMPTON: n. 18 above.

22. Re events of 25 - 27 August 1944: *USS FANSHAW BAY (CVE-70) War Diary*, 25 - 27 August 1944; and *USS FANSHAW BAY (CVE-70) Deck Log*, 25 - 27 August 1944.

23. Bill Johnson's death: *USS FANSHAW BAY (CVE-70) War Diary*, 28 August 1944; *USS FANSHAW BAY (CVE-70) Deck Log*, 28 August 1944; Banks, n. 3, ch. 1; and Gerald O. Trapp, Lieutenant, A-V(N), USNR, VC-66, Commanding Officer, "UNITED STATES PACIFIC FLEET AIR FORCE COMPOSITE SQUADRON SIXTY-SIX (VC-66): An Informal Squadron History (June, 1943, to November, 1944)," 1944, p. 17 (used with Navy Department approval).

24. For Ponam Island and VC-66: *USS FANSHAW BAY (CVE-70) War Diary*, 29 August 1944; *USS FANSHAW BAY (CVE-70) Deck Log*, 29 August 1944; Gerald O. Trapp, Lieutenant, A-V(N), USNR, VC-66, Commanding Officer, "UNITED STATES PACIFIC FLEET AIR FORCE COMPOSITE SQUADRON SIXTY-SIX (VC-66): An Informal Squadron History (June, 1943, to November, 1944)," 1944, p. 17 (used with Navy Department approval); Ned R. Young, "Regarding Ponam Island Air Field," *Guest Book Archive* Web Site, 1 May 2005, <http://www.royalnavyresearcharchive.org.uk/Old_Gbook_Entries.htm>, accessed 19 April 2007; "Ponam Airstrip," *Pacific Wreck Database* Web Site, <http://www.pacificwrecks.com/provinces/png_ponam.html>, accessed 16 March 2007; and Banks, n. 3, ch. 1.

25. Re the Bob Hope USO show and the "kidnapping" of Patty Thomas: Banks, n. 3, ch. 1; Cope, n. 7, ch. 6; and Gerald O. Trapp, Lieutenant, A-V(N), USNR, VC-66, Commanding Officer, "UNITED STATES PACIFIC FLEET AIR FORCE COMPOSITE SQUADRON SIXTY-SIX (VC-66): An Informal Squadron History (June, 1943, to November, 1944)," 1944, p. 18 (used with Navy Department approval).

26. Re James Michener: "James Michener Biography – Pulitzer Prize Winning Novelist," *Academy of Achievement* Web Site, <http://www.achievement.org/autodoc/page/mic0bio-1>, accessed 13 September 2007.

27. Re events of 4 – 9 September 1944: *USS FANSHAW BAY (CVE-70) War Diary*, 4 – 9 September 1944; *USS FANSHAW BAY (CVE-70) Deck Log*, 4 – 9 September 1944; and Gerald O. Trapp, Lieutenant, A-V(N), USNR, VC-66, Commanding Officer, "UNITED STATES PACIFIC FLEET AIR FORCE COMPOSITE SQUADRON SIXTY-SIX (VC-66): An Informal Squadron History (June, 1943, to November, 1944)," 1944, p. 18 (used with Navy Department approval).

28. Underway for Morotai and events of 10 – 14 September 1944: *USS FANSHAW BAY (CVE-70) War Diary*, 10 – 14 September 1944; *USS FANSHAW BAY (CVE-70) Deck Log*, 10 - 14 September 1944; and Gerald O. Trapp, Lieutenant, A-V(N), USNR, VC-66, Commanding Officer, "UNITED STATES PACIFIC FLEET AIR FORCE COMPOSITE SQUADRON SIXTY-SIX (VC-66): An Informal Squadron History (June, 1943, to November, 1944)," 1944, p. 18 (used with Navy Department approval).

29. For D-Day and the invasion of Morotai: *USS FANSHAW BAY (CVE-70) War Diary*, 15 September 1944; *USS FANSHAW BAY (CVE-70) Deck Log*, 15 September 1944; "Report 6-1 – Morotai," *WWII PT Boats, Bases, Tenders* Web Site, <http://www.ptboats.org/20-07-05-reports-007.html>, accessed 17 November 2006; "Morotai (Moratai) Island," *Pacific Wreck Database* Web Site, <http://www.pacificwrecks.com/provinces/irian_moratai.html>, accessed 16 March 2007; William T. Y'Blood, *The Little Giants – U.S. Escort Carriers Against Japan* (Annapolis, Maryland: Naval Institute Press, 1987), pp. 102-103; Mardarello, n. 14, ch. 12; and Banks, n. 3, ch. 1.

30. Re the invasion of Peleliu: William T. Y'Blood, *The Little Giants – U.S. Escort Carriers Against Japan* (Annapolis, Maryland: Naval Institute Press, 1987), p. 108.

31. Banks re strafing mission: n. 3, ch. 1.

32. For time between missions: Banks, n. 3, ch. 1; and Mardarello, n. 14, ch. 12.

14. VC-66's Finest Hour – Saving Ensign Thompson

1. Rod Rodriquez's death and George Brown's downing of a Zero: *USS FANSHAW BAY (CVE-70) War Diary*, 16 September 1944; *USS FANSHAW BAY (CVE-70) Deck Log*, 16 September 1944; Gerald O. Trapp, Lieutenant, A-V(N), USNR, VC-66, Commanding Officer, "UNITED STATES PACIFIC FLEET AIR FORCE COMPOSITE SQUADRON SIXTY-SIX (VC-66): An Informal Squadron History (June, 1943, to November, 1944)," 1944, p. 18 (used with Navy Department approval); Paul W. Austin , "COMPOSITE SQUADRON SIXTY-SIX" (hand drawn chart of Pacific Ocean prepared for Austin H. Kiplinger showing where VC-66 operated and annotated with statistics

and summaries of the squadron's three combat deployments), 1953; Banks, n. 3, ch. 1; and Stephens, n. 9, ch. 5.

2. On the "friendly fire" incident: *USS FANSHAW BAY (CVE-70) War Diary*, 16 September 1944; *USS FANSHAW BAY (CVE-70) Deck Log*, 16 September 1944; Gerald O. Trapp, Lieutenant, A-V(N), USNR, VC-66, Commanding Officer, "UNITED STATES PACIFIC FLEET AIR FORCE COMPOSITE SQUADRON SIXTY-SIX (VC-66): An Informal Squadron History (June, 1943, to November, 1944)," 1944, p. 19 (used with Navy Department approval); and Gander, n. 6, ch. 6.

3. For the rescue of Ensign Thompson: *USS FANSHAW BAY (CVE-70) War Diary*, 16 September 1944; *USS FANSHAW BAY (CVE-70) Deck Log*, 16 September 1944; Gerald O. Trapp, Lieutenant, A-V(N), USNR, VC-66, Commanding Officer, "UNITED STATES PACIFIC FLEET AIR FORCE COMPOSITE SQUADRON SIXTY-SIX (VC-66): An Informal Squadron History (June, 1943, to November, 1944)," 1944, pp. 18-19 (used with Navy Department approval); "Report 6-2 – Rescue in Wasile Bay," *WWII PT Boats, Bases, Tenders* Web Site, <http://www.ptboats.org/20-07-05-reports-007.html>, accessed 17 November 2006; William T. Y'Blood, *The Little Giants – U.S. Escort Carriers Against Japan* (Annapolis, Maryland: Naval Institute Press, 1987), pp. 103-105; Cope, n. 7, ch. 6; Fox, n. 12, ch. 6; Stephens, n. 9, ch. 5; Banks, n. 3, ch. 1; Birdsong, n. 15, ch. 6; Kennon, n. 12, ch. 4; and Lieutenant William DeLoach Cope AIR MEDAL citation, signed by James Forrestal, Secretary of the Navy, circa 1944.

4. For Japanese regard for their troops and fliers during World War II: James Bradley with Ron Powers, *Flags of Our Fathers*, (New York, N.Y.: Bantam Dell, 2000), p. 67; "Japanese Fighter Planes: Navy's Mitsubishi A6M Zero, Army's Ki-42 Oscar," *American Aces of WWII* Web Site, <http://www.acepilots.com/planes/jap_fighters.html>, accessed 22 February 2007; "A6M Zero," *Wikipedia – The Free Encyclopedia* Web Site, <http://en.wikipedia.org/wiki/A6M_Zero>, accessed 22 February 2007; and "History of World War II", (CD-Rom), (New York, N.Y.: Multieducator, 1997).

5. For Japanese treatment of American fliers at Midway: Gordon W. Prange, Edited by Donald M. Goldstein and Katherine V. Dillon, *Miracle At Midway*, (New York, N.Y.: McGraw-Hill Book Company, 1982), pp. 253-254 and 256-257.

6. On Japanese and Americans fighting to the death: James Bradley with Ron Powers, *Flags of Our Fathers*, (New York, N.Y.: Bantam Dell, 2000), pp. 146-147.

7. For the Kiplinger - Preston meeting: Cope, n. 7, ch. 6.

8. Clark's meeting the TBM radioman after the war: n. 16, ch. 5.

15. The Battle Continues

1. For VC-66 missions 17 – 19 September 1944: *USS FANSHAW BAY (CVE-70) War Diary*, 17 - 19 September 1944; *USS FANSHAW BAY (CVE-70) Deck Log*, 17 - 19 September 1944; and Gerald O. Trapp, Lieutenant, A-V(N), USNR, VC-66, Commanding Officer, "UNITED STATES PACIFIC FLEET AIR FORCE COMPOSITE SQUADRON SIXTY-SIX (VC-66): An Informal Squadron History (June, 1943, to November, 1944)," 1944, p. 19 (used with Navy Department approval).

2. Re bombing the church: Banks, n. 3, ch. 1.

3. On the high intensity of operations: Banks, n. 3, ch. 1; Edwards, n. 3, ch. 5; and Birdsong, n. 15, ch. 6.

4. Birdsong biographical information: n. 15, ch. 6.

5. For Birdsong's inverted attack: Banks, n. 3, ch. 1; and Birdsong, n. 15, ch. 6.

6. Banks' embarrassing moments: n. 3, ch. 1.

7. For the General Quarters alarm and being called to battle stations: Stephen Banks personal recollection.

8. About Halmahera: "Halmahera," *Pacific Wreck Database* Web Site, <http://www.pacificwrecks.com/provinces/irian_halmahera.html>, accessed 16 March 2007.

9. For the events of 20 September 1944: *USS FANSHAW BAY (CVE-70) War Diary*, 20 September 1944; *USS FANSHAW BAY (CVE-70) Deck Log*, 20 September 1944; and Gerald O. Trapp, Lieutenant, A-V(N), USNR, VC-66, Commanding Officer, "UNITED STATES PACIFIC FLEET AIR FORCE COMPOSITE SQUADRON SIXTY-SIX (VC-66): An Informal Squadron History (June, 1943, to November, 1944)," 1944, p. 19 (used with Navy Department approval); Unknown

author, "COMPOSITE SQUADRON SIXTY-SIX (VC-66) June, 1943 – Nov, 1944," six page history, circa 1944, p. 5; and Banks, n. 3, ch. 1.

10. For Holley and Plouffe rescue and time with the Black Cat Squadron: Joe Mussatto e-mail to Stephen Banks, 27 June 2007.

11. For Plouffe's concerns after the accident: telephone interview, Mrs. Roger Plouffe by Stephen Banks, 18 January 2008.

12. For the events of 21 – 23 September 1944: *USS FANSHAW BAY (CVE-70) War Diary*, 21 - 23 September 1944; *USS FANSHAW BAY (CVE-70) Deck Log*, 21 - 23 September 1944; and Gerald O. Trapp, Lieutenant, A-V(N), USNR, VC-66, Commanding Officer, "UNITED STATES PACIFIC FLEET AIR FORCE COMPOSITE SQUADRON SIXTY-SIX (VC-66): An Informal Squadron History (June, 1943, to November, 1944)," 1944, p. 19 (used with Navy Department approval).

13. Re helping shipmates when things were busy: Banks, n. 3, ch. 1; and Mardarello, n. 14, ch. 12.

14. Re James O. Mayo: Banks, n. 3, ch. 1; Mayer, n. 18, ch. 13; Cope, n. 7, ch. 6; Edwards, n. 3, ch. 5; "Kiplinger Foundation honors business grad with $250,000 gift," Mississippi State University Web Site, <http://www.msstate.edu/web/media/detail.php?id=379>, accessed 19 August 2007; and "Mayo," Obituary, *The Washington Post*, 26 August 2007, p. C10, col. 1.

15. For VC-66 events of 23 – 28 September 1944: *USS FANSHAW BAY (CVE-70) War Diary*, 23 - 28 September 1944; *USS FANSHAW BAY (CVE-70) Deck Log*, 23 - 28 September 1944; and Gerald O. Trapp, Lieutenant, A-V(N), USNR, VC-66, Commanding Officer, "UNITED STATES PACIFIC FLEET AIR FORCE COMPOSITE SQUADRON SIXTY-SIX (VC-66): An Informal Squadron History (June, 1943, to November, 1944)," 1944, p. 19 (used with Navy Department approval).

16. Jim Rathbun's death: *USS FANSHAW BAY (CVE-70) War Diary*, 29 September 1944; *USS FANSHAW BAY (CVE-70) Deck Log*, 29 September 1944; Gerald O. Trapp, Lieutenant, A-V(N), USNR, VC-66, Commanding Officer, "UNITED STATES PACIFIC FLEET AIR FORCE COMPOSITE SQUADRON SIXTY-SIX (VC-66): An Informal Squadron History (June, 1943, to November, 1944)," 1944, pp. 19-20 (used with Navy Department approval); Mardarello, n. 14, ch. 12; and Banks, n. 3, ch. 1.

17. All quotations and information from Martin J. "Lucky" Stack (Stack) in this and subsequent chapters are from one or more of the following sources: "Flier Makes Safe Landing Here After Losing Motor," *The Miami Daily News*, 6 July 1945; "Pilot Loses Engine, But Lands Safely," *The Miami Herald*, 6 July 1945; Ed Rombauer, "Just Call Me 'Lucky,'" *WARBIRD FLYER – EAA Warbirds Squadron 2 Newsletter*, July 2005, p. 5, col. 1 and 2; "PERSONAL HISTORY OF MARTIN J. STACK," by Stack, circa 2000; e-mail, Stack to Krost, circa July 2006; e-mail, Stack to Stephen Banks, 11 July 2007 and 9 February 2008; and letter, Stack to Stephen Banks, 25 July 2007.

18. For Stack biographical information: n. 17 above.

19. For VC-66 events and missions of 30 September to 2 October 1944: *USS FANSHAW BAY (CVE-70) War Diary*, 30 September – 2 October 1944; *USS FANSHAW BAY (CVE-70) Deck Log*, 30 September - 2 October 1944; Gerald O. Trapp, Lieutenant, A-V(N), USNR, VC-66, Commanding Officer, "UNITED STATES PACIFIC FLEET AIR FORCE COMPOSITE SQUADRON SIXTY-SIX (VC-66): An Informal Squadron History (June, 1943, to November, 1944)," 1944, p. 20 (used with Navy Department approval); and Banks, n. 3, ch. 1.

20. Re attack by Japanese submarine RO-41 and sinking of the SHELTON and the SEAWOLF: *USS FANSHAW BAY (CVE-70) War Diary*, 3 October 1944; *USS FANSHAW BAY (CVE-70) Deck Log*, 3 October 1944; Gerald O. Trapp, Lieutenant, A-V(N), USNR, VC-66, Commanding Officer, "UNITED STATES PACIFIC FLEET AIR FORCE COMPOSITE SQUADRON SIXTY-SIX (VC-66): An Informal Squadron History (June, 1943, to November, 1944)," 1944, p. 20 (used with Navy Department approval); Unknown author, "COMPOSITE SQUADRON SIXTY-SIX (VC-66) June, 1943 – Nov, 1944," six page history, circa 1944, p. 5; Paul W. Austin , "COMPOSITE SQUADRON SIXTY-SIX" (hand drawn chart of Pacific Ocean prepared for Austin H. Kiplinger showing where VC-66 operated and annotated with statistics and summaries of the squadron's three combat deployments), 1953; William T. Y'Blood, *The Little Giants – U.S. Escort Carriers Against Japan* (Annapolis, Maryland: Naval Institute Press, 1987), pp. 107-108; and Fox, n. 12, ch. 6.

21. On Tokyo Rose's broadcasting the sinking of FANSHAW BAY: "Tokyo Rose Sinks Them," *Naval Aviation News*, 15 January 1945, p. 23, col. 3; Krost, n. 8, ch. 12; Cope, n. 7, ch. 6; and "'Sunk' Navy Fliers Home On Leave," *Hattiesburg (Mississippi) American*, 1 December 1944.

22. For the VC-66 events and missions of 4 – 6 October 1944: *USS FANSHAW BAY (CVE-70) War Diary*, 4 - 6 October 1944; and *USS FANSHAW BAY (CVE-70) Deck Log*, 4 - 6 October 1944.

23. On the success of the Morotai operation: William T. Y'Blood, *The Little Giants – U.S. Escort Carriers Against Japan* (Annapolis, Maryland: Naval Institute Press, 1987), pp. 103 and 106-107.

24. Mayer re his last landing: n. 18, ch. 13.

25. For the VC-66 fly off to Pityilu Island: *USS FANSHAW BAY (CVE-70) War Diary*, 7 October 1944; *USS FANSHAW BAY (CVE-70) Deck Log*, 7 October 1944; Gerald O. Trapp, Lieutenant, A-V(N), USNR, VC-66, Commanding Officer, "UNITED STATES PACIFIC FLEET AIR FORCE COMPOSITE SQUADRON SIXTY-SIX (VC-66): An Informal Squadron History (June, 1943, to November, 1944)," 1944, p. 20 (used with Navy Department approval); Unknown author, "COMPOSITE SQUADRON SIXTY-SIX (VC-66) June, 1943 – Nov, 1944," six page history, circa 1944, p. 5; and "Pityilu Island," *Pacific Wreck Database* Web Site, <http://www.pacificwrecks.com/provinces/png_pityilu.html>, accessed 16 March 2007.

26. For VC-66's time on Pityilu Island 7 – 16 October 1944: Gerald O. Trapp, Lieutenant, A-V(N), USNR, VC-66, Commanding Officer, "UNITED STATES PACIFIC FLEET AIR FORCE COMPOSITE SQUADRON SIXTY-SIX (VC-66): An Informal Squadron History (June, 1943, to November, 1944)," 1944, p. 21 (used with Navy Department approval); VC-66 "Muster Roll of the Crew," October 1944; and Banks, n. 3, ch. 1.

27. Re FANSHAW BAY 7 – 11 October 1944: *USS FANSHAW BAY (CVE-70) War Diary*, 7 – 11 October 1944; and *USS FANSHAW BAY (CVE-70) Deck Log*, 7 – 11 October 1944.

28. On Banks' meeting the VC-68 TBM turret gunner at the World War II Memorial: Stephen Banks' personal recollection.

29. For the condition of the Navy just before the invasion of the Philippines: "Capture of Caroline Islands," *Naval Aviation News*, 1 October 1945, p. 13.

30. Piper on Manus Harbor: n. 6, ch. 5.

31. For the FANSHAW BAY and ST. LO experiences during the battles of Samar and Okinawa: "Fanshaw Bay," *Dictionary of American Naval Fighting Ships*, Department of the Navy, Naval Historical Center, Washington, D.C. Web Site, <http://www.history.navy.mil/danfs/f1/fanshaw_bay.htm>, accessed 26 February 2007; and Robert Jon Cox, "USS FANSHAW BAY (CVE-70)," 10 November 2001, *The Battle Off Samar* Web Site, <http://www.bosamar.com/cve/cve70.html>, accessed 16 November 2006.

32. Dwight re the sinking of the ST. LO: n. 37, ch. 12.

33. For reporting aboard the MAKASSAR STRAIT: Gerald O. Trapp, Lieutenant, A-V(N), USNR, VC-66, Commanding Officer, "UNITED STATES PACIFIC FLEET AIR FORCE COMPOSITE SQUADRON SIXTY-SIX (VC-66): An Informal Squadron History (June, 1943, to November, 1944)," 1944, p. 21 (used with Navy Department approval); Banks, n. 3, ch. 1; Stephens, n. 9, ch. 5; and Keyser, n. 5, ch. 6.

16. Back To The States

1. On getting underway for Pearl Harbor: Stephens, n. 9, ch. 5; Banks, n. 3, ch. 1; and "Makassar Strait," *Dictionary of American Naval Fighting Ships*, Department of the Navy, Naval Historical Center, Washington, D.C. Web Site, <http://www.history.navy.mil/danfs/m2/makassar_strait.htm>, accessed 26 February 2007.

2. For VT-66 accomplishments during combat tour on FANSHAW BAY: Paul W. Austin , "COMPOSITE SQUADRON SIXTY-SIX" (hand drawn chart of Pacific Ocean prepared for Austin H. Kiplinger showing where VC-66 operated and annotated with statistics and summaries of the squadron's three combat deployments), 1953; Gerald O. Trapp, Lieutenant, A-V(N), USNR, VC-66, Commanding Officer, "UNITED STATES PACIFIC FLEET AIR FORCE COMPOSITE SQUADRON SIXTY-SIX (VC-66): An Informal Squadron History (June, 1943, to November, 1944)," 1944, p. 20 (used with Navy Department approval); and Unknown author, "COMPOSITE SQUADRON SIXTY-SIX (VC-66) June, 1943 – Nov, 1944," six page history, circa 1944, p. 5.

3. Re the Presidential Unit Citation: letter dated 27 January 1948, from the Chief of Naval Personnel to Banks authorizing wearing of the Presidential Unit Citation for service with VC-66 while attached to the FANSHAW BAY during 15 September to 12 October 1944; and "Unit Citations and

Commendations," Department of the Navy, Naval Historical Center, Washington, D.C. Web Site, <http://www.history.navy.mil/faqs/stream/faq45-27.htm>, accessed 7 September 2007.

4. Re Rest and Recreation in Hawaii: Banks, n. 3, ch. 1; and Edwards, n. 3, ch. 5.
5. For the GENERAL COLLINS: "General E.T. Collins," *Dictionary of American Naval Fighting Ships,* Department of the Navy, Naval Historical Center, Washington, D.C. Web Site, <http://www.history.navy.mil/danfs/g2/general_e_t_collins.htm>, accessed 26 February 2007; Banks, n. 3, ch. 1, and Stephens, n. 9, ch. 5.
6. For the time at NAS Alameda and the reassignment of most of the squadron: Banks, n. 3, ch. 1; e-mail, Joe Mussatto to Stephen Banks, 5 June 2007; and telephone interview, Russell P. Jensen by Stephen Banks, 17 January 2008.
7. Mardarello after VC-66: n. 14, ch. 12.
8. Gander after VC-66: n. 6, ch. 6.
9. Edwards after VC-66: n. 3, ch. 5.
10. Piper after VC-66: n. 6, ch. 5.
11. For the VC-66 aircrewmen selected for pilot training: Gerald O. Trapp, Lieutenant, A-V(N), USNR, VC-66, Commanding Officer, "UNITED STATES PACIFIC FLEET AIR FORCE COMPOSITE SQUADRON SIXTY-SIX (VC-66): An Informal Squadron History (June, 1943, to November, 1944)," 1944, p. 21 (used with Navy Department approval); Banks, n. 3, ch. 1; and Birdsong, n. 15, ch. 6.
12. For the final goodbyes: Banks, n. 3, ch. 1; Stephens, n. 9, ch. 5; and Mardarello, n. 14, ch. 12.
13. For VC-66 (T-1) squadron accomplishments: Paul W. Austin, "COMPOSITE SQUADRON SIXTY-SIX" (hand drawn chart of Pacific Ocean prepared for Austin H. Kiplinger showing where VC-66 operated and annotated with statistics and summaries of the squadron's three combat deployments), 1953; Gerald O. Trapp, Lieutenant, A-V(N), USNR, VC-66, Commanding Officer, "UNITED STATES PACIFIC FLEET AIR FORCE COMPOSITE SQUADRON SIXTY-SIX (VC-66): An Informal Squadron History (June, 1943, to November, 1944)," 1944, p. 21 (used with Navy Department approval); and Unknown author, "COMPOSITE SQUADRON SIXTY-SIX (VC-66) June, 1943 – Nov, 1944," six page history, circa 1944, p. 6.
14. For Kennedy quote: speech, John F. Kennedy at the U.S. Naval Academy, 1 August 1963.
15. Keyser thoughts: n. 5, ch. 6.

17. Leave And Marriage

1. For the Railway Express shipment: Banks still has a copy of the receipt – dated 10 November 1944.
2. On the flight to Buffalo: Banks, n. 3, ch. 1.
3. On the arrival home and the Banks – Dewey courtship and wedding: Banks, n. 3, ch. 1; and Dewey, n. 6, ch. 10.

18. Starting Over

1. Re reporting to NAS Jacksonville: Banks, n. 3, ch. 1; and Stephens, n. 9, ch. 5.
2. For the Sailor who forgot what his wife looked like: "SHORE STATIONS - NAGS JACKSONVILLE," *Naval Aviation News,* 15 December 1944, p. 27, col. 2 and 3.
3. For the "Fubar" story: "SHORE STATIONS – NAS JACKSONVILLE," *Naval Aviation News,* 1 August 1945, p. 33, col. 1.
4. Re forming combat teams: Stephens, n. 9, ch. 5; Banks, n. 3, ch. 1; and "OPERATIONAL TEAMS UP PILOT AND AIRCREWMEN," *Naval Aviation News,* 15 October 1944, p. 27.
5. On NAS Miami, Opa-Locka: "Florida's World War II Memorial – NAS Miami Opa-Locka Airport," *Florida In WWII* Web Site, <http://www.flheritage.com/wwii/sites.cfm?PR_ID=191>, accessed 21 September 2007.
6. On training at Opa-Locka: Banks, n. 3, ch. 1; and Stephens, n. 9, ch. 5.
7. Re Jean's train trip to Florida and her time in Miami: Dewey, n. 6, ch. 10.
8. For the sleeve shooting incident: Banks, n. 3, ch. 1; Cope, n. 7, ch. 6; and Stephens, n. 9, ch. 5.
9. For Stack's TBM engine falling off: Stack, n. 17, ch. 15.
10. For Stack's biographical information: Stack, n. 17, ch. 15.
11. On the NAS Jacksonville static display: Stephen Banks personal recollection and viewing.

12. Re VT-98: Stephens, n. 9, ch. 5.
13. On ARM3c Paul Newman: James E. Wise, Jr., and Anne Collier Rehill, *Stars In Blue: Movie Actors In America's Sea Services*, (Annapolis, MD.: Naval Institute Press, 1997), *Biographies In Naval History* Web Site, <http://www.history.navy.mil/bios/newman_p.htm>, accessed 31 July 2007.
14. Re John F. Banks: Banks, n. 3, ch. 1; Stephen Banks personal recollections; e-mail, Jan Banks-Doddridge to Stephen Banks, 26 March 2008 and 27 March 2008; and Phil Harris and Patrick Clancey, "Commissioning Roster USS CORONIS (ARL-10)," *Hyper War* Web Site, <http://ibiblio.org/hyperwar/USN/ships/dafs/ARL/arl10-crew.html>, accessed 27 March 2008.
15. For USS CORONIS: "Coronis," *Dictionary of American Naval Fighting Ships,* Department of the Navy, Naval Historical Center, Washington, D.C. Web Site, <http://www.history.navy.mil/danfs/c14/coronis.htm>, accessed 26 March 2008; and Patrick Clancey, "ARL-10 USS CORONIS – Ships of the U.S. Navy, 1940 – 1945," *Hyper War* Web Site, last updated 21 January 1999, <http://ibiblio.org/hyperwar/USN/ships/ARL/ARL-10_Coronis.html>, accessed 27 March 2008.
16. On Okinawa: John Pike, "Battle of Okinawa," *GlobalSecurity.Org* Web Site, <http://www.globalsecurity.org/military/facility/okinawa-battle.htm>, accessed 27 March 2008.
17. Re kamikazes: Bill Gordon, "History of the 'Divine Wind," *Naval History*, April 2008, p. 28.
18. For VT-98 to Thermal, California: Banks, n. 3, ch. 1.
19. For the Japanese training civilians to fight to the death: Ken Burns, *THE WAR*, Episode 7, Public Broadcasting Service, WETA, September 2007.
20. Re Thermal, California: Richard E. Osbourne, "World War II Sites In The United States: A Tour Guide And Directory – Naval Air Facility, Thermal," *The California State Military Museum* Web Site, <http://www.militarymuseum.org/ThermalAAF.html>, accessed 11 October 2007.
21. Banks on being stationed in Thermal: n. 3, ch. 1.

19. To VC-92 And Beyond

1. For VT-98 to Los Alamitos, California: Banks, n. 3, ch. 1.
2. Re Los Alamitos, California: Richard E. Osbourne, "World War II Sites In The United States: A Tour Guide And Directory – NRAB/NAS/NAAS Los Alamitos," *The California State Military Museum* Web Site, <http://www.militarymuseum.org/LosAl.html>, accessed 11 October 2007.
3. Re Banks' liberty near Los Alamitos: Banks, n. 3, ch. 1.
4. For the "Mighty 7th" bond drive: James Bradley with Ron Powers, *Flags of Our Fathers*, (New York, N.Y.: Bantam Dell, 2000), pp. 281-282 and 294.
5. For assignment to VC-92: Banks, n. 3, ch. 1; and Stephens, n. 9, ch. 5.
6. On VC-92: "United States Navy VCs List," *Naval War In Pacific 1941 – 1945* Web Site, last updated 23 February 2001, <http://pacific.valka.cz/airunits/index_frame.htm>, accessed 31 July 2007; "USS Tulagi (CVE-72)," www.*navysite.de* Web Site, <http://navysite.de/cve/cve72.htm>, accessed 31 July 2007; and Don Moore, "North Port Man Flew A Wildcat Off USS Tulagi In WWII," *Charlotte (Port Charlotte, Florida) Sun*, 8 April 2007.
7. For VC-92 to Oxnard: Banks, n. 3, ch. 1.
8. Re an invasion of Japan: Joe A. Mussatto, "History of Composite Squadron VC-66 (T-2) (5 December 1944 to 12 October 1945)," *VC-66 (T-2)* Web Site, <http://www.geocities.com/muzzo2/My_Page.html>, accessed 7 March 2007; and "TOKYO TALKS – TO THE UNITED STATES," *Naval Aviation News*, 1 August 1945, p. 16, col. 1.
9. For Okinawa casualties: "Okinawa History," *U.S. Marines In Japan* Web Site, updated 15 August 2007, <http://www.okinawa.usmc.mil/About%20Okinawa/History%20Page.html>, accessed 23 October 2007.
10. For Jean Banks' decision not to join Banks in California: Dewey, n. 6, ch. 10.
11. Re the last days of the war: "Japs Surrender," *Naval Aviation News*, 1 October 1945, p. 18, col. 1-3.
12. For the end of the war and the last Stephens/Banks flight: Stephens, n. 9, ch. 5.
13. For the King All Navy message: "USS CORONIS (ARL-10) PLAN OF THE DAY – 29 August 1945," Patrick Clancey, *Hyper War* Web Site, last updated 21 January 1999, <http://www.ibiblio.org/hyperwar/USN/ships/img/ARL/arl10-PlanOfDay.jpg>, accessed 27 March 2008.

14. For the Times Square celebration: Alexander Feinberg, "All City 'Lets Go,'" *The New York Times*, 15 August 1945, p. 1, col. 3.
15. Banks re his end of the war reaction: n. 3, ch. 1.
16. Stephens re his end of the war reaction: n. 9, ch. 5.
17. For Banks' marking time at Oxnard and the CASUs: n. 3, ch. 1; and Vern A. Miller, "This Is CASU," *WWW.WARTIMEPRESS.COM* Web Site, <http://www.wartimepress.com/images/Our%20Navy/Articles/This%20is%20CASU.htm>, accessed 11 October 2007.
18. Re receipt of the Combat Aircrew Insignia: letter from CO Carrier Aircraft Service Unit Eight to Banks, 17 September 1945; and Air Crew Insignia Instruction.
19. On orders to San Diego: Banks, n. 3, ch. 1.
20. For VC-66 being decommissioned: Joe A. Mussatto, "History of Composite Squadron VC-66 (T-2) (5 December 1944 to 12 October 1945)," *VC-66 (T-2)* Web Site, <http://www.geocities.com/muzzo2/My_Page.html>, accessed 7 March 2007.
21. On orders to New York and life and theft at the Receiving Station: Banks, n. 3, ch. 1; and 6 November 1945 liberty pass.
22. Back to Sampson: Banks, n. 3, ch. 1.
23. For final pay and enlistment summary: "NOTICE OF SEPARATION FROM THE U.S. NAVAL SERVICE: BANKS, Donald Austin," 8 November 1945.
24. For Forrestal letter: James Forrestal to Banks, 29 November 1945.
25. Stephens after the war: n. 9, ch. 5.
26. Stoops after the war: Banks, n. 3, ch. 1; and letter, Thomas A. Stoops to Banks, 1 May 2002.
27. Edwards after the war: n. 3, ch. 5.
28. Jensen after the war: telephone interview, Russell P. Jensen by Stephen Banks, 17 January 2008; and letter, Jensen to Banks, 21 April 2008.
29. Dwight after the war: n. 37, ch. 12.
30. Gander after the war: n. 6, ch. 6.
31. Mardarello after the war: n. 14, ch. 12.

20. Going Home And Moving On

1. For the homecoming: Banks, n. 3, ch. 1.
2. On life at 100 Roseview: Dewey, n. 6, ch. 10; Banks n. 3, ch. 1; and Stephen Banks personal recollections.
3. Re use of the G.I. Bill: Banks, n. 3, ch. 1; and "A Piece of the American Dream: The G.I. Bill of Rights," *D-Days* – The National D-Day Museum Newsletter, Fall 2004, Volume 5, Number 3, p. 1.
4. For Banks' days at Buffalo State College: n. 3, ch. 1; and Dewey, n. 6, ch. 10.
5. Re changes at the Dewey home: Dewey, n. 6, ch. 10; Banks, n. 3, ch. 1; and Stephen Banks personal recollections.
6. For Banks' career as an art teacher and administrator: n. 3, ch. 1; Dewey, n. 6, ch. 10; and Stephen Banks' personal recollections.
7. For the Mahoney family's military service: Stephen Banks' personal recollections.
8. For other VC-66 (T-1) members' post VC-66 careers: Stephens, n. 9, ch. 5; Birdsong, n. 15, ch. 6; Stack, n. 17, ch. 15; Fox, n. 12, ch. 6; Mayer, n. 18, ch. 13; Kennon, n. 12, ch. 4; telephone interview, Mrs. Larry Carr by Stephen Banks, 9 November 2007; telephone interview, Mrs. Charles R. Jones by Stephen Banks, 17 January 2008; telephone interview, Mrs. Robert B. Muzzy by Stephen Banks, 18 January 2008; letter, Thomas A. Stoops to Banks, 1 May 2002; telephone interview, Dean Summers by Stephen Banks, 21 January 2008; telephone interview, Russell P. Jensen by Stephen Banks, 17 January 2008; letter, Russell P. Jensen to Banks, 21 April 2008; Cope, n. 7, ch. 6; Gander, n. 6, ch. 6; Krost, n. 8, ch. 12; Piper, n. 6, ch. 5; Dwight, n. 37, ch. 12; Mardarello, n. 14, ch. 12; e-mail, G. Berry Catterton to Stephen Banks, 12 November 2007; and Keyser, n. 5, ch. 6.
9. For Catterton's biographical information: e-mail, G. Berry Catterton to Stephen Banks, 12 November 2007.

10. For Carr and the "1000 Aviator Study:" telephone interview, Mrs. Larry Carr by Stephen Banks, 9 November 2007; Charles W. Shilling, CAPT., M.C., USN (Ret.), "History of the Research Division Bureau of Medicine and Surgery, U.S. Department of the Navy," <http://www.nmrc.navy.mil/pdf/Timeline.pdf>, accessed 8 November 2007; and Cope, n. 7, ch. 6.

11. Re VC-66 (T-1) pilots' reunions: Stephens, n. 9, ch. 5; Cope, n. 7, ch. 6; Edwards, n. 3, ch. 5; and Birdsong, n. 15, ch. 6.

12. Banks' final thoughts: n. 3, ch. 1.

BIBLIOGRAPHY

Ambrose, Stephen E. *To America: Personal Reflections of an Historian.* New York, N.Y.: Simon and Schuster, Inc., 2002.

Ambrose, Stephen E. *The Victors: Eisenhower and His Boys: The Men of World War II.* New York, N.Y.: Simon and Schuster, Inc., 1998.

Ambrose, Stephen E. *The Wild Blue: The Men and Boys Who Flew the B-24s Over Germany.* New York, N.Y.: Simon and Schuster, Inc., 2001.

Adams, Cecil. "Was John Wayne A Draft Dodger?" *The Straight Dope* Web Site, 1998, <http://www.straightdope.com/classics/a5_004.html>, accessed 29 December 2007.

Agoratus, Steven. "Clark Gable in the Eighth Air Force." *Centennial Tribute to Clark Gable* Web Site, 1999, <http://www.geocities.com/cactus_st/article/article143.html>, accessed 29 December 2007.

"Aircraft Carriers – CV, CVN." *United States Navy Fact File* Web Site, <http://www.navy.mil/navydata/fact_display.asp?cid=4200&tid=200&ct=4>, accessed 4 April 2007.

"Aircraft, United States." *History of World War II* (CD-ROM), New York, N.Y.: Multieducator, 1997.

Alley, Howard. "The Making of an Aircrewman: The Real Training Begins (1944)." *VC-66 (T-2) Newsletter*, March 2008.

_____. "The Making of an Aircrewman: The Gunnery Range (Part 2)." *VC-66 (T-2) Newsletter*, April 2008.

"A6M Zero." *Wikipedia – The Free Encyclopedia* Web Site, <http://en.wikipedia.org/wiki/A6M_Zero>, accessed 22 February 2007.

"Anchors Aweigh." Plaque at Navy museum, Sampson State Park, Seneca County, New York, 1 October 2007.

Andrews, Harold. "NAVAL AIRCRAFT: F4U CORSAIR." *Naval Aviation News*, May – June 1986, Department of the Navy, Naval Historical Center, Washington, D.C. Web Site, <http://www.history.navy.mil/branches/hist-ac/F4U-4.pdf>, accessed 22 February 2007.

"The Army 27th Infantry Division." *National Park Service American Memorial Park, Saipan, Northern Mariana Islands World War II Virtual Museum* Web Site, <http://www.nps.gov/archive/amme/wwii_museum/preparation_for_war/preparations_for_war.html>, accessed 11 December 2007.

Astor, Gerald. *WINGS OF GOLD: The U.S. Naval Air Campaign In World War II.* New York, N.Y.: Ballantine Books, 2004.

Austin, Paul W. "COMPOSITE SQUADRON SIXTY-SIX." Annotated chart, 1953.

Banks, Donald A. "Wotje and Then Some." *Aviation History*, July 2001.

206

Banks, Stephen A. "Composite Squadron Sixty-Six (VC-66) – A History: June '43 – November '44." May 2007.

Bergerud, Eric M. *FIRE IN THE SKY: The Air War in the South Pacific*. Boulder, Colorado: Westview Press, 2000.

"The Bloody Battle of Tarawa, 1943." *EyeWitnessHistory.com* Web Site, <http://www.eyewitnesstohistory.com/tarawa.htm>, accessed 17 September 2007.

"Boeing Military Aircraft in the 1930s and 1940s." *U.S. Centennial of Flight Commission* Web Site, <http://www.centennialofflight.gov/essay/Aerospace/boeing-1930s_1940s/Aero19.htm>, accessed 31 August 2007.

Bradley, James with Ron Powers. *Flags of Our Fathers*. New York, N.Y.: Bantam Dell, 2000.

Buell, Hal (ed.) with Cesare Salmaggi and Alfredo Pallavisini. *WORLD WAR II: A Complete Photographic History*. New York, N.Y.: Black Dog & Leventhal Publishers, Inc., 2002.

Burns, Ken. *THE WAR*. Public Broadcasting Service, WETA, September 2007.

"Capture of Caroline Islands." *Naval Aviation News*, 1 October 1945.

Chacon, Jose Andres "Andy." "United States Navy." *West-Point.Org – The West Point Connection* Web Site, <http://www.west-point.org/users/usma1951/18250/us%20navy.htm>, accessed 31 August 2007.

"Civilian Pilot Training Program – U.S. Air Force Fact Sheet." *National Museum of the USAF* Web Site, <http://www.nationalmuseum.af.mil/factsheets/factsheet.asp?id=8475>, accessed 4 September 2007.

Clancey, Patrick. "ARL-10 USS CORONIS – Ships of the U.S. Navy, 1940 – 1945." *Hyper War* Web Site, last updated 21 January 1999, <http://ibiblio.org/hyperwar/USN/ships/ARL/ARL10_Coronis.html>, accessed 27 March 2008.

Cope, William DeLoach. "THE HALMAHERA RESCUE." *VC-66 (T-2) Newsletter*, undated.

Cox, Robert Jon. "USS FANSHAW BAY (CVE-70)." 10 November 2001, *The Battle Off Samar* Web Site, <http://www.bosamar.com/cve/cve70.html>, accessed 16 November 2006.

_____. "We Do Remember." *Memorial Monuments of Task Unit 77.4.3*, Web Site , 1997, <http://www.bosamar.com/monts/mont63.html>, accessed 14 March 2008.

Crosby, Francis. *The Complete Guide to Fighters and Bombers of the World*. London, England: Anness Publishing Ltd., 2006.

Dictionary of American Naval Fighting Ships. Department of the Navy, Naval Historical Center, Washington, D.C. Web Site, <http://www.history.navy.mil/danfs/index.html>, accessed 26 February 2007.

Dorr, Robert F. "'Jeep' carrier Gambier Bay fought gallantly to the end." *Navy Times*, 13 January 2003.

_____. "Radioman-Gunner Flew Despite Silent Missions." *Navy Times*, 1 May 2006.

_____. "TBF/TBM Avenger Was Navy's Greatest Torpedo Bomber." *Navy Times*, 8 January 2001.

Dorr, Robert F. and Fred L. Borch. "Air Medal Recognizes Heroism, Merit In Flight." *Navy Times*, 22 October 2007.

Drendel, Lou. *Walk Around TBF/TBM Avenger*. Carrollton, Texas: Squadron/Signal Publications, Inc., 2001.

"Edwards 65th Anniversary." *The Washington Post*, 16 March 2008.

Ellsworth, Harold F. *History of VC-82* Web Site, <http://home.comcast.net/~bmmelvin/warhero/wwiipac.htm>, accessed 8 March 2007.

"Escort Aircraft Carriers." *DANFS Online* Web Site, <http://www.hazegray.org/danfs/carriers/cve.htm>, accessed 16 November 2006.

Feinberg, Alexander. "All City 'Lets Go.'" *The New York Times*, 15 August 1945.

".50 Caliber Machine Gun." Exhibit, National Air and Space Museum, Washington, D.C., December 2006.

"Flier Makes Safe Landing Here After Losing Motor." *The Miami Daily News*, 6 July 1945.

"Florida's World War II Memorial – NAS Miami Opa-Locka Airport." *Florida In WWII* Web Site, <http://www.flheritage.com/wwii/sites.cfm?PR_ID=191>, accessed 21 September 2007.

"Flying Radioman." *Naval Aviation News*, 15 February 1944.

Forrestal, James, Secretary of the Navy. Letter to Donald A. Banks, 29 November 1945.

Fox, John P. "REPORT OF RESCUE MISSION SEPTEMBER 16, 1944." 16 September 1944.

"FREE GUNNERY TRAINING," "FIRST SCHOOL USED GUNS FROM PLANES WRECKED IN JAP ATTACK," "GUNNER MUST MASTER SIGHTS IF HE WANTS TO BECOME MARKSMEN," "SHIP AND PLANE RECOGNITION IS STRESSED IN GUNNER'S TRAINING," "STUDENT FIRES 6,500 ROUNDS IN MACHINE GUNS DURING TRAINING," and "STUDENT USES TRAINING DEVICES ALONG WITH ACTUAL RANGE FIRING." *Naval Aviation News*, 1 November 1944.

Friedman, Kenneth I. "General Douglas MacArthur." *The Battle of Leyte Gulf* Web Site, <http://www.battle-of-leyte-gulf.com/Leaders/Americans/MacArthur/macarthur.html>, accessed 14 September 2007.

"Gallantry Disclosed." *The Buffalo Evening News*, 22 March 1945.

"General Motors FM-2 'Wildcat' Fighters." Department of the Navy, Naval Historical Center, Washington, D.C. Web Site, <http://www.history.navy.mil/photos/ac-usn22/f-types/fm2.htm>, accessed 22 February 2007.

"The Gilberts and Marshalls Campaign." *Naval Aviation News*, 1 October 1945.

Gillies, Judith S. "A Presidential Portrait." *The Washington Post (TV Week)*, 4 May 2008.

"GOOD GUNNERY PROTECTS AVENGERS AGAINST ENEMY FIGHTER ATTACKS." *Naval Aviation News,* 15 July 1944.

Gordon, Bill. "History of the 'Divine Wind." *Naval History*, April 2008.

Gordon, Richard M., Major, USA (Ret.). "Bataan, Corregidor, and the Death March: In Retrospect." *Battling Bastards of Bataan* Web Site, last updated 28 October 2002, <http://home.pacbell.net/fbaldie/In_Retrospect.html>, accessed 17 September 2007.

"Gordon 'Tex' Beneke." *The Big Band Broadcast* Web Site, <http://www.bigbands.org/benekebio.htm>, accessed 30 August 2007.

"Grumman F4F-4 (FM-1) Wildcat." Exhibit, National Museum of the Marine Corps, Quantico, Virginia, December 2006.

"Grumman F4F-4 (FM-1)." Exhibit, National Air and Space Museum, Washington, D.C., December 2006.

"Grumman TBF Avenger." *Pacific Aviation* Web Site, <http://www.microworks.net/pacific/aviation/tbf_avenger.htm>, accessed 26 October 2007.

"Grumman TBF/TBM Avenger." Exhibit, National Museum of the Marine Corps, Quantico, Virginia, December 2006.

"Halmahera." *Pacific Wreck Database* Web Site, <http://www.pacificwrecks.com/provinces/irian_halmahera.html>, accessed 16 March 2007.

Hanson, Victor David. *A War Like No Other – How the Athenians and Spartans Fought the Peloponnesian War*. New York, N.Y.: Random House, Inc., 2005.

Harris, Phil, and Patrick Clancey. "Commissioning Roster USS CORONIS (ARL-10)." *Hyper War* Web Site, <http://ibiblio.org/hyperwar/USN/ships/dafs/ARL/arl10-crew.html>, accessed 27 March 2008.

Heiferman, Ronald. *U.S. NAVY IN WORLD WAR II*. Secaucus, N.J.: Chartwell Books, Inc., 1978.

"History of World War II." (CD-Rom), New York, N.Y.: Multieducator, 1997.

"Hold-Off Barrier Crashes." *Naval Aviation News*, 1 October 1945.

Ignoff, Alice. Letter re taking photos of servicemen, 18 March 1944.

"In Memoriam: Robert Stack." *Industry News* Web Site, <http://scoop.diamondgalleries.com/public/default.asp?t=1&m=1&c=34&s=259&ai=43284&ssd=5/17/2003&arch=y>, accessed 31 August 2007.

"Introduction to Life Aboard an Aircraft Carrier." Four pages from unidentifiable Navy Manual, circa 1943.

"IX-64 WOLVERINE." *GlobalSecurity.org* Web Site, <http://www.globalsecurity.org/military/systems/ship/ix-64.htm>, accessed 14 August 2007.

"James Michener Biography – Pulitzer Prize Winning Novelist." *Academy of Achievement* Web Site, <http://www.achievement.org/autodoc/page/mic0bio-1>, accessed 13 September 2007.

"Japanese Fighter Planes: Navy's Mitsubishi A6M Zero, Army's Ki-42 Oscar." *American Aces of WWII* Web Site, <http://www.acepilots.com/planes/jap_fighters.html>, accessed 22 February 2007.

"Japs Surrender." *Naval Aviation News*, 1 October 1945.

"Joan Holmes Crews Recalls Life and Times as WAVE – The Rare Breed – Recognizing Area Veterans of World War II." *Palacios (Texas) Beacon Online* Web Site, <http://www.palaciosbeacon.com/home/features-crews.shtml>, accessed 30 August 2007.

"Kiplinger Foundation honors business grad with $250,000 gift." Mississippi State University Web Site, <http://www.msstate.edu/web/media/detail.php?id=379>, accessed 19 August 2007.

Lacitis, Erik. "This Is One Of The Places That Won The War." *The Seattle Times* Web Site, 25 September 2006, <http://www.highbeam.com/doc/1G1-151865447.html>, accessed 31 August 2007.

Lamb, Yvonne Shinhoster. "Melvin H. Rosen: Survived Bataan Death March." *The Washington Post*, 31 August 2007.

Lawson, Robert and Barrett Tillman. *Carrier Air War In Original WWII Color: U.S. Navy Air Combat 1939-1946*. Osceola, Wisconsin: MBI Publishing, Co., 1996.

"Lieutenant Junior Grade George Bush, USNR." Department of the Navy, Naval Historical Center, Washington, D.C. Web Site, <http://www.history.navy.mil/faqs/faq10-1.htm>, accessed 6 September 2007.

"The Marshall Islands." Exhibit, National Museum of the Marine Corps, Quantico, Virginia, November 2006.

"MARSHALLS." *Naval Aviation News*, 1 March 1944.

"Mayo." Obituary, *The Washington Post*, 26 August 2007.

McAvoy, Audrey. "Attack Shook Hawaiians Beyond Pearl Harbor." *The Washington Post*, 7 December 2007.

Miller, Vern A. "This Is CASU." *WWW.WARTIMEPRESS.COM* Web Site, <http://www.wartimepress.com/images/Our%20Navy/Articles/This%20is%20CASU.htm>, accessed 11 October 2007.

"Mission and Description." Department of the Navy, Naval Historical Center, Washington, D.C. Web Site, <http://www.history.navy.mil/branches/hist-ac/snj-6.pdf>, accessed 22 February 2007.

Moore, Don. "North Port Man Flew A Wildcat Off USS Tulagi In WWII." *Charlotte (Port Charlotte, Florida) Sun*, 8 April 2007.

Moore, Harold G., Lt. Gen. USA (Ret.) and Joseph L. Galloway. *We Were Soldiers Once and Young*. New York, N.Y.: Random House, 1992.

Moore, Sam. "The History of the USS Nassau (CVE-16) – 'The Princess' aka 'The Nasty Maru.'" March 2002, *USS NASSAU* Web Site, <http://www.ussnassaucve16.com/History/ussnassauhistory.htm>, accessed 15 November 2006.

"Morotai (Moratai) Island." *Pacific Wreck Database* Web Site, <http://www.pacificwrecks.com/provinces/irian_moratai.html>, accessed 16 March 2007.

Mussatto, Joe. "THE 18 PASSENGER TBM." *VC-66 (T-2) Newsletter*, April 2008.

_____. "History of Composite Squadron VC-66 (T-2) (5 December 1944 to 12 October 1945)." *VC-66 (T-2)* Web Site, <http://www.geocities.com/muzzo2/My_Page.html>, accessed 7 March 2007.

_____. "Holley's Rescue." E-mail to Stephen Banks, 27 June 2007.

_____. "TOP GUNS OF 1943." *VC-66 (T-2) Newsletter*, November 2007.

_____. "VC-66 (T-1) pilots to VC-66 (T-2)." E-mail to Stephen Banks, 5 June 2007.

"NAVAL AIRCRAFT: AVENGER." *Naval Aviation News*, Department of the Navy, Naval Historical Center, Washington, D.C. Web Site, <http://www.history.navy.mil/branches/hist-ac/TBF-1.pdf>, accessed on 16 February 2007.

"NAVAL AIRCRAFT: WILDCAT." *Naval Aviation News*, December 1971, Department of the Navy, Naval Historical Center, Washington, D.C. Web Site, <http://www.history.navy.mil/nan/backissues/1970s/1971/dec71.pdf>, accessed 22 February 2007.

"Norman, Oklahoma." *U.S. Naval Activities World War II By State* Web Site, <http://ibiblio.org/hyperwar/USN/ref/USN-Act/OK.html>, accessed 30 August 2007.

"Norman Supplies Steady Flow of Mechs," "RUGGED PHYSICAL PROGRAM FITS NORMAN TRAINEES FOR COMBAT," and "AM'S SIMULATE REAL SQUADRON OPERATIONS AT NORMAN SCHOOL." *Naval Aviation News*, 15 November 1944.

"Okinawa History." *U.S. Marines In Japan* Web Site, updated 15 August 2007, <http://www.okinawa.usmc.mil/About%20Okinawa/History%20Page.html>, accessed 23 October 2007.

"OPERATIONAL TEAMS UP PILOT AND AIRCREWMEN." *Naval Aviation News*, 15 October 1944.

Osbourne, Richard E. "World War II Sites In The United States: A Tour Guide And Directory – Naval Air Facility, Thermal." *The California State Military Museum* Web Site, <http://www.militarymuseum.org/ThermalAAF.html>, accessed 11 October 2007.

_____. "World War II Sites In The United States: A Tour Guide And Directory – NRAB/NAS/NAAS Los Alamitos." *The California State Military Museum* Web Site, <http://www.militarymuseum.org/LosAl.html>, accessed 11 October 2007.

Pearl Harbor Memorial Fund, Web Site, <http://www.pearlharbormemorial.com/site/pp.asp?c=fqLQJ2NNG&b=137919>, accessed 29 June 2007.

"A Piece of the American Dream: The G.I. Bill of Rights." *D-Day* – The National D-Day Museum Newsletter, Fall 2004.

Pike, John. "Battle of Okinawa." *GlobalSecurity.Org* Web Site, <http://www.globalsecurity.org/military/facility/okinawa-battle.htm>, accessed 27 March 2008.

"Pilot Loses Engine, But Lands Safely." *The Miami Herald*, 6 July 1945.

"Pilot Weapons Training – Gunnery: U.S. Navy NATC No. 2667, Gunnery Manual, 1944: Free Gunnery." 10 July 1944, *WW2 AIRFRONTS* Web Site, <http://ww2airfronts.org/Flight%20School/transition/weaponsschool/natc-2667-44/pages/natc-2667-44-2.html>, accessed 19 October 2007.

"Pityilu Island." *Pacific Wreck Database* Web Site, <http://www.pacificwrecks.com/provinces/png_pityilu.html>, accessed 16 March 2007.

"Ponam Airstrip." *Pacific Wreck Database* Web Site, <http://www.pacificwrecks.com/provinces/png_ponam.html>, accessed 16 March 2007.

"Port of Shelton." *Port of Shelton* Web Site, <http://www.portofshelton.com/about_port.html>, accessed 13 March 2007.

Prange, Gordon W., Edited by Donald M. Goldstein and Katherine V. Dillon. *Miracle At Midway*. New York, N.Y.: McGraw-Hill Book Company, 1982.

Reader's Digest Illustrated Story Of World War II. Pleasantville, N.Y.: The Reader's Digest Association, Inc., 1969.

"Report 6-1 – Morotai." *WWII PT Boats, Bases, Tenders* Web Site, <http://www.ptboats.org/20-07-05-reports-007.html>, accessed 17 November 2006.

"Report 6-2 – Rescue in Wasile Bay." *WWII PT Boats, Bases, Tenders* Web Site, <http://www.ptboats.org/20-07-05-reports-007.html>, accessed 17 November 2006.

Rombauer, Ed. "Just Call Me 'Lucky.'" *WARBIRD FLYER – EAA Warbirds Squadron 2 Newsletter*, July 2005.

Roosevelt, Franklin D. *Declaration of War Address to Congress*, 8 December 1941.

Rottman, Gordon L. *The Marshall Islands 1944 – Operation Flintlock, the capture of Kwajalein and Eniwetok*. New York, N.Y.: Osprey Publishing Ltd., 2004.

Rumerman, Judy. "Boeing Military Aircraft in the 1930s and 1940s." *U.S. Centennial of Flight* Web Site, <http://www.centennialofflight.gov/essay/Aerospace/boeing-1930s_1940s/Aero19.htm>, accessed 31 August 2007.

Sabin, William A. *The Gregg Reference Manual*. New York, N.Y.: McGraw-Hill/Irwin, 2005.

"Sampson Naval Training Base." *New York State Military Museum and Veterans Research Center, NYS Division of Military and Naval Affairs* Web Site, <http://www.dmna.state.ny.us/forts/fortsQ_S/sampsonNavalTrainingBase.htm>, accessed 27 July 2006.

"Sand Point Naval Air Station: 1920 – 1970." *Historylink.org – The Online Encyclopedia of Washington State History* Web Site, <http://www.historylink.org/essays/output.cfm?file_id=2249>, accessed 31 August 2007.

Shettle, M.L., Jr. "Naval Auxiliary Air Station, Brown Field." *Historic California Posts*, The California State Military Museum, California State Military Department Web Site, <http://www.militarymuseum.org/NAASBrownField.html>, accessed 13 March 2007.

_____. "Naval Auxiliary Air Station, Holtville." *Historic California Posts*, The California State Military Museum, California State Military Department Web Site, <http://www.militarymuseum.org/NAASHoltville.html>, accessed 13 March 2007.

Shilling, Charles W., CAPT., M.C., USN (Ret.). "History of the Research Division, Bureau of Medicine and Surgery, U.S. Department of the Navy." <http://www.nmrc.navy.mil/pdf/Timeline.pdf>, accessed 8 November 2007.

"SHIP AND PLANE RECOGNITION IS STRESSED IN GUNNER'S TRAINING." *Naval Aviation News*, 1 November 1944.

"Ship's Cook Third Class Doris "Dorie" Miller, USN." Naval Historical Center, Washington, D.C. Web Site, <http://www.history.navy.mil/faqs/faq57-4.htm>, accessed 5 September 2007.

"SHORE STATIONS - NAGS JACKSONVILLE." *Naval Aviation News*, 15 December 1944.

"SHORE STATIONS – NAS JACKSONVILLE." *Naval Aviation News*, 1 August 1945.

"SNJ Trainer." *Air Group 32* Web Site, <http://www.vf31.com/aircraft/snj.html>, accessed 22 February 2007.

Spennemann, Dirk H.R. "The Japanese seaplane base at Wotje Island, Wotje Atoll." *Marshalls – digital Micronesia* Web Site, <http://marshall.csu.edu.au/Marshalls/html/WWII/Wotje.html>, accessed 16 April 2007.

_____. "Taroa, Maloelap Atoll – A brief virtual tour through a Japanese airbase in the Marshall Islands." *Marshalls – digital Micronesia* Web Site, <http://marshall.csu.edu.au/Marshalls/html/japanese/Taroa/Taroa.html>, accessed 16 April 2007.

"Squadron 'X'." *EASTERN AIRCRAFTSMAN*, November 1943.

Stoops, Thomas A. Letter to Donald A. Banks, 1 May 2002.

"SUBPOENA & SUMMONS EXTRAORDINARY." The Royal High Court of the Raging Main, circa 22 August 1944.

"'Sunk' Navy Fliers Home On Leave." *Hattiesburg (Mississippi) American*, 1 December 1944.

"TBF TEAMWORK." *Naval Aviation News*, 15 July 1944.

"TBM Avenger." Exhibit, Naval Air Station, Jacksonville, Florida, 11 January 2007.

Thomas, Gerald. "A Tribute To Avenger Air Crewman." *Air Group 4 "Casablanca to Tokyo"* Web Site, <http://www.airgroup4.com/crewmen.htm>, accessed 1 December 2006.

"THOROUGH TRAINING READIES PILOTS AND AIRCREWMEN FOR THE FLEET" and "IN OPERATIONAL TRAINING PILOTS LEARN FLEET TEAMWORK TACTICS." *Naval Aviation News*, 15 July 1944.

Tillman, Barrett. *TBF/TBM AVENGER UNITS OF WORLD WAR 2*. Botley, Oxford, England: Osprey Publishing, 1999.

"Tokyo Rose Sinks Them." *Naval Aviation News*, 15 January 1945.

"TOKYO TALKS – TO THE UNITED STATES." *Naval Aviation News*, 1 August 1945.

Trapp, Gerald O. "UNITED STATES PACIFIC FLEET AIR FORCE COMPOSITE SQUADRON SIXTY-SIX (VC-66): An Informal Squadron History (June, 1943, to November, 1944)." 1944 (used with permission of the Department of the Navy).

"Tulagi." *Wikipedia – The Free Encyclopedia* Web Site, <http://en.wikipedia.org/wiki/Tulagi>, accessed 16 March 2007.

"Unit Citations and Commendations." Department of the Navy, Naval Historical Center, Washington, D.C. Web Site, <http://www.history.navy.mil/faqs/stream/faq45-27.htm>, accessed 7 September 2007.

"United States Navy VCs List." *Naval War In Pacific 1941 – 1945* Web Site, last updated 23 February 2001, <http://pacific.valka.cz/airunits/index_frame.htm>, accessed 31 July 2007.

Unknown author. "COMPOSITE SQUADRON SIXTY-SIX (VC-66) June, 1943 – Nov, 1944." Six page history, circa 1944.

"U.S. Naval Chronology Of WWII, 1944." *NavSource Naval History* Web Site, <http://www.navsource.org/Naval/1944.htm>, accessed 16 November 2006.

"U.S. Navy Enlisted Pay 1943-1945." *BlueJacket.com* Web Site, <http://www.bluejacket.com/usn_pay-scale_1943-1945_enlisted.html>, accessed 30 August 2007.

USS ALTAMAHA (CVE-18) Deck Log. 30-31 March 1944 and 1-25 April 1944.

USS ALTAMAHA (CVE-18) War Diary. 30-31 March 1944 and 1-25 April 1944.

"USS Arizona National Memorial – People." *U.S. National Park Service* Web Site, <http://www.nps.gov/usar/historyculture/people.htm>, accessed 29 June 2007.

"USS Fanshaw Bay (CVE-70)." *www.navysite.de* Web Site, <http://navysite.de/cve/cve70.htm>, accessed 8 March 2007.

USS FANSHAW BAY (CVE-70) Deck Log. 5-31 August 1944, 1-30 September 1944, and 1-7 October 1944.

USS FANSHAW BAY (CVE-70) War Diary. 5-31 August 1944, 1-30 September 1944, and 1-7 October 1944.

USS NASSAU (CVE-16) Deck Log. 4-31 January 1944, 1-29 February 1944, and 1-5 March 1944.

USS NASSAU (CVE-16) War Diary. 4-31 January 1944; 1-29 February 1944, and 1-5 March 1944.

"USS Tulagi (CVE-72)." www.*navysite.de* Web Site, <http://navysite.de/cve/cve72.htm>, accessed 31 July 2007.

Veigele, William J. "WWII Navy Boot Camps." *Navy Knowledge Online – Astral Publishing Co.* Web Site, <http://www.astralpublishing.com/wwii-navy-boot-camps.html>, accessed 29 August 2007.

"WAVES Aviation Metalsmiths." Department of the Navy, Naval Historical Center, Washington, D.C. Web Site, <http://www.history.navy.mil/photos/prs-tpic/females/wvw2-am7.htm>, accessed 30 August 2007.

Wilma, David. "Sand Point Naval Air Station: 1920 – 1970." *Historylink.Org – The Online Encyclopedia of Washington State History* Web Site, <http://www.historylink.org/essays/output.cfm?file_id=2249>, accessed 31 August 2007.

"Wings Over WNY." *The Digital Collection Of The Niagara Aerospace Museum* Web Site, <http://aerospace.bfn.org/DL/museum.htm>, accessed 28 June 2007.

Wise, James E., Jr., and Anne Collier Rehill. *Stars In Blue: Movie Actors In America's Sea Services.* (Annapolis, MD.: Naval Institute Press, 1997), *Biographies In Naval History*, Web Site, <http://www.history.navy.mil/bios/newman_p.htm>, accessed 31 July 2007.

"World War II Era WAVES – Overview and Special Image Selection." Department of the Navy, Naval Historical Center, Washington, D.C. Web Site, <http://www.history.navy.mil/photos/prs-tpic/females/wave-ww2.htm>, accessed 30 August 2007.

"World War II Naval Aircraft Squadron Designations." *BLUEJACKET.COM* Web Site, <http://www.bluejacket.com/usn-usmc_avi_ww2_squadron_desig.htm>, accessed 8 March 2007.

"WORLD WARS BOOM NAVAL PILOT TRAINING TO MEET FLEET NEEDS," "AVIATION CADETS GET STIFF PHYSICAL COURSE," "PRIMARY SCHOOLS GIVE STUDENTS FIRST FLYING," "INTERMEDIATE TRAINING EXPANDS TO 20 WEEKS," and "OPERATIONAL TEAMS UP PILOT AND AIRCREWMEN." *Naval Aviation News*, 15 October 1944.

"WWII U.S. Navy Enlisted Base Pay." *Valor at Sea* Web Site, <http://www.valoratsea.com/paygrade.htm>, accessed 4 September 2007.

Y'Blood, William T. *The Little Giants – U.S. Escort Carriers Against Japan.* Annapolis, Maryland: Naval Institute Press, 1987.

Young, Ned R. "Regarding Ponam Island Air Field." *Guest Book Archive* Web Site, 1 May 2005, <http://www.royalnavyresearcharchive.org.uk/Old_Gbook_Entries.htm>, accessed 19 April 2007.

INDEX

(**NOTE:** The numbers in this index refer to **Chapter** numbers)

ABOUT THE AUTHOR

The author (on the left) and Banks in front of the TBM displayed at Naval Air Station, Jacksonville, Florida, 11 January 2007 (Photo: courtesy S.A. Banks)

STEPHEN A. BANKS was born in Lackawanna, New York. After high school, he attended Miami University in Ohio on an NROTC scholarship. He graduated in 1968 with a B.S. in History and Government Education and was commissioned as an Ensign, U.S. Navy. He served aboard the destroyers USS SPROSTON (DD-577) (gunnery officer) and USS CARPENTER (DD-825) (ASW officer). With CARPENTER, he made deployments to the Western Pacific and the Gulf of Tonkin during the Vietnam War. He attended the University at Buffalo Law School via the Navy's Excess Leave to Study Law Program. After graduation and admission to the bar, he transferred to the Navy Judge Advocate General's Corps. In 1988, he retired from active duty and joined the Navy's Office of General Counsel as a civilian environmental litigation attorney. He retired from Navy OGC in 2006. In addition to *Looking Backward*, he is the author of *A History of Composite Squadron Sixty-Six (VC-66) 21 June 1943 – 3 November 1944*, and the creator of a VC-66 (T-1) Web site <http://mysite.verizon.net/vzeuo4yx/index.html>. He spends his time now reading, researching, and writing about military history.